Federal Taxation: cases and notes

Federal Taxation: cases and notes

J. Peter Williamson

Professor of Business Administration

The Amos Tuck School of Business Administration

Dartmouth College

Scott, Foresman and Company

Letter from the president of Citizens Utilities Company to shareholders reprinted
by permission.

Notice of special meeting of shareholders together with text of proposed Amendment to the Certificate of Incorporation of Citizens Utilities Company reprinted by
permission.

Letter to stockholders of the Litton Industries, Inc., dated February 10, 1966, reprinted by permission.

Table of Contents

Preface

Taxation in the United States is an enormous subject. A single book or course cannot begin to give even a general idea of the whole field, let alone develop any real expertise. Yet a businessman cannot afford to remain ignorant; disregarding taxes and their effects can lead a business into bankruptcy about as easily as the opposite extreme — letting tax considerations dominate every decision.

The purpose of *Federal Taxation* is to give the businessman some understanding of the importance of federal income taxes (and, to some extent, of estate taxes), to give him an appreciation of the value of tax planning and the possibilities for legitimate tax avoidance, to help him see tax problems as they develop and make intelligent use of professional tax advice, and to give him some familiarity with controversial aspects of our tax system and the public policy issues behind new and proposed legislation. In summary, to borrow an expression from Dan Throop Smith, this book is designed to help keep a businessman "from making a damn fool of himself."

The topics covered here have been chosen for a variety of reasons. Some, like capital gains and losses, are of fundamental importance because they affect virtually every taxpayer. Others, like depreciation, are far-ranging in importance and also present examples of current controversy and change. Still others, like the tax factors involved in the sale of a corporation, indicate the variety of choices available in a business transaction and the very different tax consequences that can flow from the various ways of accomplishing what might seem to be the same objective. There is nothing absolute about this selection of topics. Many topics not included could just as well be substituted, but the ones covered here seem to offer a reasonable possibility for accomplishing the objectives described above.

Federal Taxation consists of cases, several court decisions, a few revenue rulings and revenue procedures issued by the Internal Revenue Service, and text. The purpose of the text is to provide a guide to the Internal Revenue Code and the Regulations. The tax law of the United States is statutory law, and there is no substitute for the Internal Revenue Code as a source of substantive tax rules. The Code is a very lengthy and complicated document. The text is not intended to provide a substitute for the Code, but to serve as a guide to someone unfamiliar with the Code. The text also raises some questions and provides some historical background and some explanation as to why the Code has developed as it has.

As suggested above, this book is intended to be used along with the Internal Revenue Code and the Regulations. Anyone who will be dealing with federal taxes might as well get used to reading the Code and the Regulations. This is never easy, but with a little experience the reader should begin to see some patterns of both logic and phraseology, and before he reaches the end of this book, he should be able to anticipate much of what he will find in the Code itself.

For further information, either of two fairly short volumes will prove useful: *Federal Tax Reform*, by Dan Throop Smith (McGraw-Hill Book Company, Inc., 1961), and *The Federal Tax System: Facts and Problems 1964*, assembled by the Committee Staff for the Joint Economic Committee of the United States Congress in 1964 (U.S. Government Printing Office). Both of these books deal clearly and concisely with aspects of federal taxation that are important and controversial. Both complement this book by emphasizing the public policy aspect of tax legislation, the recognition and balancing of conflicting interests in the more or less continuous process of amending the Internal Revenue Code.

Although it seems unlikely that the highly complicated field of federal income and estate taxes will ever be compressed into a single adequate volume, the importance of change should become evident from reading both this book and either of the books referred to above. The reader may, in fact, become somewhat discouraged at the apparently ephemeral nature of what he is learning. There is certainly little point in memorizing detailed tax rules. For the most part, however, only the details change frequently. The basic principles underlying the Internal Revenue Code modify slowly and in generally predictable ways. And a sensible approach to the solution of tax problems, or business problems involving tax elements, will survive even these slow changes. It is for the development of this approach that *Federal Taxation* is designed.

Chapter one

Sources of federal tax law

Introduction

There are three principal sources of federal tax law—the Constitution, the Congress, and the courts. A fourth source, the Internal Revenue Service, is an administrative agency with limited lawmaking powers.

Superimposed on this simple framework is a vast array of published tax material—some of it "official," published by the United States government; most, however, is put out by private publishers.[1] Unfortunately, it is easy to be confused by this mass of material and to become lost in what appears to be a maze of tax information. The purpose of this chapter is to reduce the confusion by listing and describing the sources of tax law—in order of authoritativeness—with hints on the proper way to use the available materials in researching a tax problem. In this book, the emphasis will be almost entirely on federal income taxation, but the sources described below apply as well to a wide variety of other federal taxes.

The Constitution

The Congress must have constitutional authorization for its tax laws, just as it does for any laws that it passes. The power of Congress to levy taxes, and the limitations upon that power, are found at several points in the Constitution:

Article 1, section 2, clause 3
. . . direct taxes shall be apportioned among the several states which may be included within this Union, according to their respective

---

[1]Some of these publications are listed in the last section of this chapter.

numbers, which shall be determined by adding to the whole number of free persons, including those bound to service for a term of years, and excluding Indians not taxed, three fifths of all other persons.

Article 1, section 7, clause 1
All bills for raising revenue shall originate in the House of Representatives; but the Senate may propose or concur with amendments as on other bills.

Article 1, section 8, clause 1
The Congress shall have power to lay and collect taxes, duties, imposts and excises, to pay the debts and provide for the common defence and general welfare of the United States; but all duties, imposts and excises shall be uniform throughout the United States.

Article 1, section 9, clauses 4 and 5
No capitation, or other direct, tax shall be laid, unless in proportion to the census or enumeration herein before directed to be taken.
No tax or duty shall be laid on articles exported from any state.

Article 1, section 10, clauses 2 and 3
No state shall, without the consent of the Congress, lay any imposts or duties on imports or exports, except what may be absolutely necessary for executing its inspection laws: and the net produce of all duties and imposts, laid by any state on imports or exports, shall be for the use of the Treasury of the United States; and all such laws shall be subject to the revision and control of the Congress.
No state shall, without the consent of Congress, lay any duty of tonnage. . . .

The fifth amendment
No person shall . . . be deprived of life, liberty, or property, without due process of law; nor shall private property be taken for public use, without just compensation.

The sixteenth amendment (which establishes the constitutional basis for the federal income tax as we know it today):
The Congress shall have power to lay and collect taxes on incomes, from whatever source derived, without apportionment among the several States, and without regard to any census or enumeration.

Federal tax laws, from the start, have been challenged under one or another of these provisions.[2] Today constitutional challenge is rare because the tax law now in use has been in essentially the same form for

---

[2]For example, in a 1920 decision the United States Supreme Court upheld a taxpayer's contention that stock dividends did not come within the meaning of "income" in the Sixteenth Amendment and could not constitutionally be taxed as such. *Eisner* v. *Macomber*, 252 U.S. 189 (1920).

many years. The constitutional problems have largely been ironed out, and it is only with respect to new methods of taxation, or unique applications of old methods, that a constitutional question is likely to be raised.[3]

The Congress: statutes and treaties

Federal tax law has always been based on acts of Congress — from the first statute imposing taxes on whiskey and carriages in revolutionary times to the comprehensive tax statutes in force today. The statute with which this book is concerned is the Internal Revenue Code of 1954 (hereafter referred to as the Tax Code or Code). It may be found as Title 26 in the United States Code. The Tax Code, or parts of it, is also published by numerous tax services, either alone, with the Regulations, or with explanatory material. Regardless of publication, the Tax Code is the same. Of course, amendments are frequent; therefore, you must be sure you are using a current edition.

Why is the Tax Code designated the Internal Revenue Code of *1954*? In 1954 the federal tax provisions were substantially amended and reorganized. This was the first major revision since 1939, the year all federal taxes were first brought together into a single statute: the Internal Revenue Code of 1939.[4] The 1954 statute has been amended frequently, but its general form has not changed. We therefore still refer to the current Code as the "1954 Code."

In addition to the Code, tax legislation includes several tax treaties with other countries, designed primarily to limit or prevent double taxation.[5] Section 894 of the Code provides that income will be exempt from taxation to the extent required by any treaty obligation of the United States. Tax treaties are becoming increasingly important as business becomes more international; a later chapter will discuss in some detail the tax consequences of doing business abroad.

Legislative history

Because the English language is often ambiguous, any reference to the provisions of the Code may raise more tax problems than it solves. If ambiguities do arise, the tax researcher can turn to the legislative history of the Code section with which he is concerned in order to ascertain the Congressional purpose behind the provision. That interpretation of an

---

[3]For example, the Controlled Foreign Corporation provisions of the Revenue Act of 1962 came under fire on constitutional grounds. It was claimed that the provisions that were designed to tax shareholders on undistributed earnings of a corporation would exceed the mandate of the Sixteenth Amendment as interpreted in the *Eisner* case. See *Hearings before the Senate Committee on Finance on H.R. 10650,* Part 8, 87th Cong. 2d sess., 3452, 3588 (1962).

[4]The 1954 Code was the work of the Eisenhower Administration, and a number of tax practitioners, who had become accustomed to the form of the 1939 Code, grumbled that the chief innovation in 1954 was the substitution of Republican for Democratic section numbers. (Most editions of the 1954 Code contain cross references to the corresponding sections in the 1939 Code.)

[5]There are currently tax treaties in effect between the U.S. and about twenty-eight foreign countries, and new ones are constantly being negotiated.

ambiguous section which best achieves the apparent Congressional purpose will be the most persuasive interpretation if a dispute arises.

What constitutes legislative history? This is the recorded development of a tax measure from its inception, usually in the House of Representatives, through various committees to the Senate, and, finally, into law. Often the President will initiate a tax measure by sending his recommendations to the House Ways and Means Committee; it is also possible for that committee to initiate a Bill itself. The Ways and Means Committee will frequently hold public hearings on the Bill; it will approve the Bill or a modification of it, and send the Bill, together with a Report, to the House. The Report is a useful document because it sets out the committee's reasons for approving the Bill and explains, usually with examples, what the new provisions mean.

If the Bill passes the House and reaches the Senate, it normally will be referred to the Senate Finance Committee. This committee may hold hearings and will send its version of the Bill, with a Report, to the Senate for a vote. The Bill as it is approved by the Senate may differ from the House-approved version, and a Joint Conference Committee may be required to work out a compromise and submit its Report.[6]

Reports on tax legislation are also prepared by the Joint Committee on Internal Revenue Taxation. This is a joint House and Senate committee whose function it is "to investigate the operation and effects of the Federal system of internal revenue taxes. . . ."[7] Records of the legislative hearings, statements on the floor of Congress, and preliminary drafts of Bills are also available and useful in the interpretive process.

A note of caution is in order at this point. The Federal Tax Regulations, which we will discuss below, can be described as the "official" interpretation of the Tax Code. It has just been indicated that legislative materials also help interpret the tax law where it is ambiguous. This double source of interpretative material should not be misleading. The statute is still the primary source of tax law, and in issuing his official interpretation of the Code in the form of Regulations, the Secretary of the Treasury must follow the statute. If a taxpayer is adversely affected by a Regulation, he may successfully challenge the Regulation if he can show that it is contrary to the legislative history of the relevant Code section. It is for this reason that we treat the legislative materials making up the history of a tax measure as a more authoritative source of tax law than the Regulations.

Court decisions

After statutes and treaties the most authoritative source of tax law is decided tax cases, where the legislation is interpreted and applied. The United States Supreme Court, the Courts of Appeals, Court of Claims, Dis-

---

[6]All of these reports are printed and should be available in any depository library. Since 1939, the reports have also been reprinted in the Internal Revenue Service's semi-annual cumulative bulletins, discussed below.

[7]Code Section 8022(1)(a).

trict Courts, and Tax Court all hear tax cases.[8] (The diagram below illustrates the relationship of these courts to each other and to the Internal Revenue Service.) These decisions are printed in the appropriate reporters for those courts as well as in the privately published tax services (see p. 9). The cases appearing in the private tax services, periodically bound into volumes, are in two sets—The American Federal Tax Reports (A.F.T.R.) and the United States Tax Cases (U.S.T.C.). Some opinions of the Tax Court are designated as memorandum decisions and are not officially published in the Tax Court Reporter. These may be found in the tax services (see p. 9).

A court decision represents the outcome of a particular dispute between a taxpayer and the Commissioner of Internal Revenue. This decision can be a source of tax law because if the court, in reaching the decision, has to interpret the meaning of a provision in the Tax Code, or decide how the provision is to be applied, then it is almost certain that this court, and others under it, will follow the same interpretation in the future. This interpretation has become part of the tax law, and any taxpayer could be affected by it.

The Treasury Department

The machinery for the administration of the Internal Revenue laws is found within the Treasury Department. The Internal Revenue Service (hereafter referred to as *the Service*) is headed by the Commissioner of Internal Revenue and administers these laws. Each state has at least one district, with a District Director of Internal Revenue who is in charge of all revenue operations in his district. The District Directors' offices are organized into eight Internal Revenue Regions, each under the control of a Regional Commissioner of Internal Revenue. It is within this administrative framework that the day-to-day administration of the tax laws takes place. (See diagram on p. 6.)

The Regulations. The formal Regulations issued under the authority of Section 7805(a) of the Tax Code are the most important publications of the Treasury Department. Just as the Code is officially published in the United States Code as Title 26, the Regulations are published in the official Code of Federal Regulations under Title 26. The private, unofficial services also publish the Regulations and explanations of them.

Amendments to the Regulations are issued in the form of Treasury Decisions. These appear in the *Internal Revenue Bulletin,* a weekly publication issued by the Service, and in the semi-annual cumulative bulletins.

Though they are easily located, the power of the Regulations is often difficult to comprehend. It has already been mentioned that the

---

[8]Tax litigation may commence in one of the Federal District Courts, in the Court of Claims, or in the Tax Court. Appeals are then taken to the Court of Appeals and, in some cases, eventually to the Supreme Court. A good description of the mechanics of tax litigation in the courts and before the Internal Revenue Service will be found in Edgar J. Goodrich, Lipman Redman, and James W. Quiggle *Procedure Before the Internal Revenue Service* (Philadelphia: Joint Committee on Continuing Legal Education, 1965), 245 pages.

INCOME TAX APPEAL PROCEDURE
Internal Revenue Service

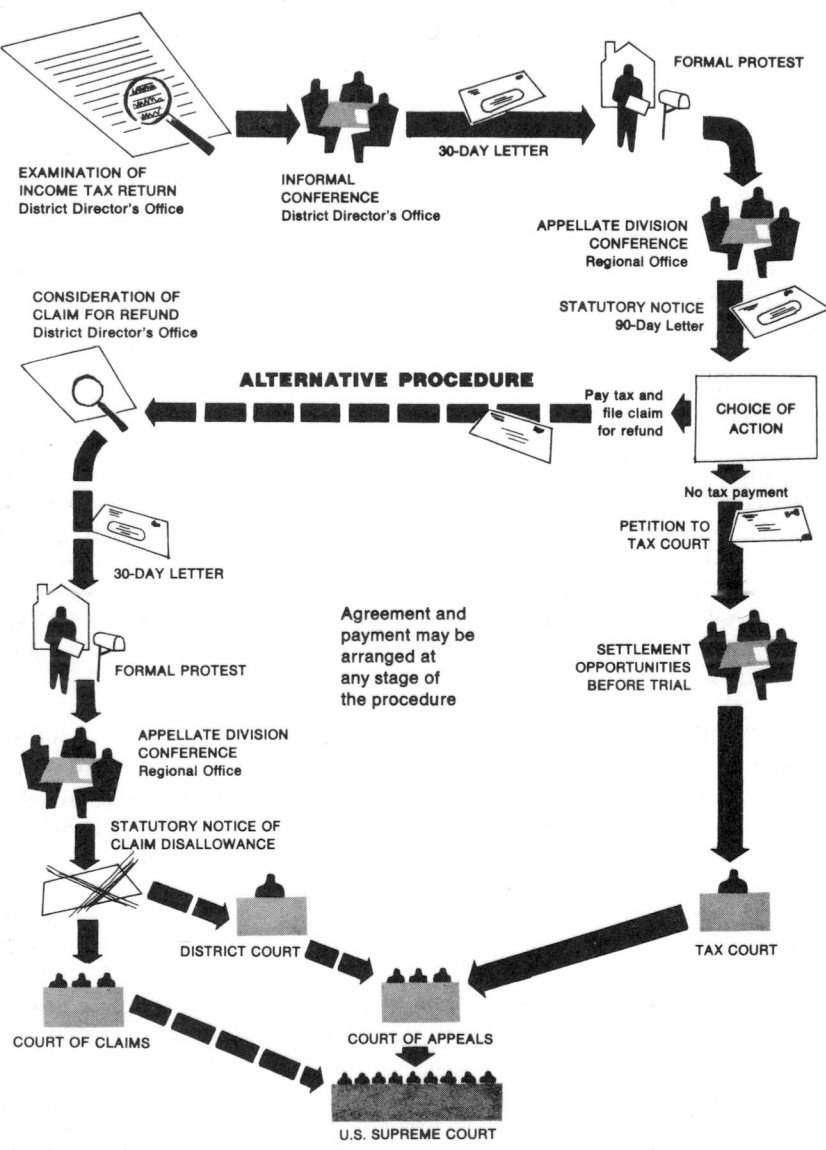

EXAMINATION OF
INCOME TAX RETURN
District Director's Office

INFORMAL
CONFERENCE
District Director's Office

30-DAY LETTER

FORMAL PROTEST

APPELLATE DIVISION
CONFERENCE
Regional Office

STATUTORY NOTICE
90-Day Letter

CONSIDERATION OF
CLAIM FOR REFUND
District Director's Office

ALTERNATIVE PROCEDURE

Pay tax and
file claim
for refund

CHOICE OF
ACTION

No tax payment

PETITION TO
TAX COURT

30-DAY LETTER

Agreement and
payment may be
arranged at
any stage of
the procedure

SETTLEMENT
OPPORTUNITIES
BEFORE TRIAL

FORMAL PROTEST

APPELLATE DIVISION
CONFERENCE
Regional Office

STATUTORY NOTICE OF
CLAIM DISALLOWANCE

DISTRICT COURT

TAX COURT

COURT OF CLAIMS

COURT OF APPEALS

U.S. SUPREME COURT

Document No. 5204 (Rev. 4-61)
U. S. GOVERNMENT PRINTING OFFICE 1961 0-591507

Regulations are subordinate to the statute and may be attacked on the ground that they go beyond statutory authority. If, on the other hand, legislative history can be marshaled to support a Regulation, then the Regulation may suffice to make taxable a transaction that would not appear taxable on the face of the statute alone.[9] Although a taxpayer may ultimately challenge a Regulation in the courts, it should be noted that as far as the Commissioner is concerned, the Regulation has the force of law. That is, a taxpayer cannot hope for a determination contrary to a Regulation until he gets beyond the administrative level and into the courts.

A Regulation that is issued shortly after a statutory provision becomes effective, and is adhered to consistently over a period of time, will be of great weight in any judicial controversy. As these elements vary, the effectiveness of the Regulation varies as well—a point that is well illustrated in cases where the Commissioner tries to change a Regulation, especially where a retroactive application of the change is sought.[10]

Revenue Rulings. A Revenue Ruling is another publication of the Service which also appears in the weekly bulletins and in the cumulative bulletins. In essence, a Ruling is the published version of the Service's response to a question from a taxpayer on a particular set of facts. A taxpayer may wish to know what tax result to expect from a proposed transaction in order to decide whether or not to go ahead with the transaction. Or, having completed a transaction, the taxpayer may want to know the tax consequences so that he may prepare his return properly. If the transaction is completed and if it presents a question that is covered specifically by statute, Regulation, or any prior decision or ruling, then the District Director (of the district in which the taxpayer files his return) can answer the taxpayer's question in what is called a *determination letter.* In the case of a proposed transaction or one involving a novel question, the National Office will handle the taxpayer's request and may issue a ruling. Some of these responses, with the names disguised and with some polishing to insure wider interest, are published in the Internal Revenue bulletins and cumulative bulletins as Revenue Rulings.

The Rulings are quite important to all taxpayers, not merely to the individuals to whom they were originally addressed, because the Service relies heavily on them in dealing with similar cases. Strictly speaking, however, a Ruling applies only to the specific set of facts which prompted its issuance.[11] Thus, if the transaction that actually takes place after a Ruling is secured differs from those facts stated by the taxpayer in his Ruling request, the agent checking the return is free to disregard the Ruling.

---

[9]For examples, see *U.S.* v. *Kirby Lumber Co.,* 284 U.S. 1 (1931) and *Commissioner* v. *Acker,* 361 U.S. 87 (1959).

[10]The Supreme Court has held that the retroactive application of a reversal of a long-standing Regulation is improper. *Helvering* v. *Reynolds Tobacco Co.,* 306 U.S. 110 (1939).

[11]The introduction to each volume of the *Cumulative Bulletin* states: "Since each published ruling represents the conclusion of the Service as to the application of the law to the entire state of facts involved, you . . . are cautioned against reaching the same conclusions in other cases unless the facts and circumstances are substantially the same."

However, a taxpayer in a situation analogous to one set forth in a Ruling can still use it as a fair indication of how the Service will treat his case. Furthermore, if a Ruling is issued and published, both the taxpayer to whom it is issued and those who rely on the published version will probably be protected against an intervening change of statutory law or Regulations, at least until the Ruling is changed. This is due to a Service policy not to revoke or modify a Ruling retroactively. This is only Service policy, however; a ruling is not legally final and conclusive. It may be revoked retroactively.

"Acquiescence" and "nonacquiescence." There is another kind of decision made by the Service that appears in the Internal Revenue bulletins and cumulative bulletins and might cause some confusion. This is the Service's *acquiescence* or *nonacquiescence*. Suppose that the Service takes a position as to the proper interpretation of a provision of the Code. Suppose further that litigation arises over this interpretation and the Service loses. What does the Service do if it is still convinced that its interpretation is correct? It announces that it will not follow the case in subsequent matters of a similar kind. It will continue to litigate the issue until it is convinced that the courts are right or until the law is amended by Congress. A Service decision to follow or not to follow a particular case is known as an *acquiescence* or *nonacquiescence*, as the case may be.

The courts still determine the outcome of litigation between the Service and the taxpayer. If the court decides in favor of the taxpayer, a nonacquiescence cannot change the result for that taxpayer. Furthermore, a court decision favorable to a taxpayer is good precedent for subsequent taxpayer litigation despite the nonacquiescence. In dealings with the Service, however, a nonacquiescence will be controlling. That is, another taxpayer will be treated by the Service as though the court decision had been in favor of the Service rather than the first taxpayer. This causes strange things to happen when a taxpayer is faced with a favorable court decision with respect to which a nonacquiescence has been issued. In this situation, the taxpayer may be forced to argue to the Service that the favorable case is not applicable, so that he will not come within the pall of the nonacquiescence.

Principal sources of law

The following is a tabular view of principal sources of tax law in order of authoritativeness, with references to publications.

The U.S. Constitution (can be found in the *United States Code*)
ARTICLE 1, SECTION 2, CLAUSE 3.
ART. 1, SEC. 6, CLAUSE 1.
ART. 1, SEC. 9, CLAUSES 4 and 5.
ART. 1, SEC. 10, CLAUSES 2 and 3.
The Fifth Amendment.
The Sixteenth Amendment (basis of the present Federal Income Tax)

The statutes and treaties

Internal Revenue Code of 1954, *United States Code, Title 26.*

The Code is also available from private publishers, including Commerce Clearing House, Inc., and Prentice-Hall, Inc.

Tax treaties

These are published by the government but are easiest to find in the commercial tax services, including those of the two publishers referred to above.

Case law

United States Supreme Court. Decisions are published in the *U.S. Reports* (official); *Supreme Court Reporter* (West Publishing Company); and *Lawyers Edition of the U.S. Supreme Court Reports* (Annotated: Lawyers Cooperative Publishing Company); and in the commercial tax services, for example: Commerce Clearing House, Inc., *U.S. Tax Cases.*

Courts of Appeals. Decisions are published in the *Federal Reporter* (West Publishing Company) and in the commercial services.

District Courts. Decisions are published in the *Federal Supplement* (West Publishing Company) and in the commercial services.

Court of Claims. Decisions are published in the *Federal Supplement,* in the *Court of Claims Reports* (official), and in the commercial services.

Tax court. Regular decisions can be found in *Tax Court of the United States Reports* (official) and in the *Federal Supplement,* as well as in the commercial services — for example, *Tax Court Reporter* (Commerce Clearing House, Inc.). Tax Court Memorandum decisions can be found in the commercial services — for example, *Tax Court Memorandum Decisions* (Commerce Clearing House, Inc.).

Internal Revenue Service

Regulations. These are published in Title 26 C.F.R. (Code of Federal Regulations) and in the commercial services.

Treasury Decisions. These are published in the Internal Revenue bulletins and cumulative bulletins and in the commercial services.

Revenue Rulings. These are published in the Internal Revenue bulletins and cumulative bulletins and in the commercial services.

Chapter two

Income taxation of a business: the choice between corporation and partnership

Almost all large businesses, and a great many small businesses, are organized as corporations. But in the case of the small business, it is generally worth considering the use of partnership, rather than corporate, form. A major factor in the choice will be the impact of income taxes.

Generally speaking, a corporation is taxed as a single entity, on its taxable income, with the shareholders paying tax only on the dividends they receive. A partnership, on the other hand, is not taxed at all as an entity: the partners are taxed on their shares of the partnership income.

Section 11 of the Tax Code imposes the corporate income tax. The rate is 22 per cent on taxable income up to $25,000 and 48 per cent on the balance. Section 701 establishes that a partnership is not a taxable entity; but section 703 makes clear that a partnership *can* have taxable income. Each partner is taxed personally on his share of this taxable income as described in section 702. (Section 704 indicates how the shares are to be determined.)

Should a corporation incur a loss, the taxes of the shareholders are not affected, but the loss can be carried back three years and forward five years, under section 172, to offset corporate income in any of these years. Partners, however, can make use of partnership losses to reduce their own taxes.

Can you find specific provision for this in section 702?

Can you explain why section 703 (a) (2) (E) is necessary to produce an equitable result in the event of partnership losses?

Section 704(d) puts a limit on a partner's use of partnership losses to reduce his taxes; section 705 explains what is meant by *adjusted basis* of a partner's interest in a partnership. We will consider adjusted basis in more detail in the next chapter. At this point, simply note that sections 704(d) and 705 prevent a partner from reporting for tax purposes a loss greater than what he had invested in the partnership.

Can you see any need for this sort of provision?

There is no general rule that will indicate which of the corporate or partnership forms will be least costly in terms of taxes. In any particular case you can only calculate estimated taxes for each form and compare the results.

A complication is introduced by sections 1371-1378 of the Tax Code, which permit the shareholders of certain corporations, commonly referred to as *Subchapter S Corporations*, to elect to have the corporation treated as a partnership for tax purposes. And until it was repealed in 1966, section 1361 permitted partners to elect to have their partnerships taxed as corporations. No elections under this section have been permitted since April 14, 1966; and January 1, 1969, was set as the expiration date for all elections made before the 1966 date. (The Subchapter S election, however, is still available.)

The following case concerns the choice between partnership and corporate form.

Pennington and Fraser (A)

Two men, Charles Pennington and Stewart Fraser, propose to establish a jointly owned business, either a corporation or a partnership. The enterprise will require $45,000 initial capital of which Pennington will provide $30,000 and Fraser will provide $15,000.

The men have agreed that each will be entitled to a salary from the business, beginning in the second year of operation, and that the remaining profits, after the salaries have been paid, will be shared 2/3 to Pennington and 1/3 to Fraser. If there are losses these too will be shared 2/3 and 1/3.

Following is a projection of the income the two men expect the business to generate during its first three years, with the salaries agreed upon:

Projected Income

Year	1st	2nd	3rd
Gross Revenue	$160,000	$200,000	$300,000
Less Expenses (not including owners' salaries)	172,000	184,000	227,000
Owners' Salaries			
Pennington		6,000	6,000
Fraser		10,000	10,000
Net Income after Salaries	-12,000	0	57,000

The men have agreed that if the business is incorporated, it will pay dividends of $8000 to Pennington and $4000 to Fraser in the third year, but no dividends before then. If the business is operated as a partnership, the partners will be entitled to withdraw amounts in the third year in addition to their salaries. The amount which Pennington may withdraw will be twice the amount which Fraser may withdraw, and the total withdrawals are to leave the business with the same retained income it would have if it were operated as a corporation. In other words, first calculate the income tax and the dividends the corporation would have to pay each year and then how much of its income it will still retain at the end of the third year. This is the amount that the partnership must retain at the end of its third year, and any funds that the partnership has above this amount may be withdrawn by the partners. This arrangement simply assures that whichever form of business is chosen—corporation or partnership—the enterprise will have the same amount of assets at the end of its third year.

> Calculate the federal income taxes Pennington, Fraser, and the business will have to pay in each of the three years on their income from the business, first on the assumption that the business is incorporated and then assuming it operates as a partnership. Pennington already has about $100,000 taxable income from other business sources and is a bachelor; Fraser and his wife have about $10,000.

> For both the corporate and the partnership forms calculate how much cash, net of income taxes, each man will have received from the business by the end of the third year and how much of its earnings the business will have retained. Considering only income taxes, which is better, the corporate or partnership form?

> If the corporate form is chosen, could Pennington and Fraser elect "Subchapter S" treatment?

> What will social security taxes be for the three years for both the corporate and partnership forms?

Chapter three

Capital gains and losses

Most people are aware that certain kinds of capital gains are taxed at lower rates than ordinary income is, but few people are familiar with exactly how this result is reached in the Tax Code, and even fewer have any idea *why* capital gains are given special treatment. There are many who would argue that capital gains are not income and should not be taxed at all. This is the reasoning that lies behind the absence of capital gains taxation in Canada—and in England until recent years. The tax laws of both Canada and England tax "income," and the courts of both countries concluded long ago that capital gains simply are not income and are therefore tax-free. Although the British statutes have been changed to tax some capital gains, the Canadian statutes have never been altered to extend taxation beyond income.

> *Is there any possibility of arguing successfully in the U.S. courts that capital gains are not income and therefore not subject to income taxation? Check the Tax Code for explicit definition of capital gains as income.*

Whatever your feelings about whether or not capital gains are truly income, the principal argument for taxing capital gains along with income is that capital gains represent, like income, an increase in wealth. There are two arguments against taxing long-term capital gains in the same way that ordinary income is taxed. One is essentially an equity argument: a long-term gain may have been building up for many years, and it is unfair, with our progressive tax rates, to tax this entire gain in the single year in which it is realized. For example, if you bought some shares of stock for $1000 and held them for twenty years while they rose to a value of $50,000 and then sold them, it might seem unfair that $49,000 of income is taxed all in one year when, in fact, it took twenty years for the shares to rise that much in value. Of course, there are ways of dealing with this "bunching" problem that do not involve special rates of tax for long-term capital gains and, in fact, the Code was amended in 1964 to permit income averaging.

A second argument in favor of relatively low taxation of long-term capital gains is purely an economic one. In an economy that demands large-scale investment, it may simply be economically desirable to provide tax incentives for investment. The Internal Revenue Code is full of incentives to encourage economic and social activities that Congress thinks should be encouraged.

> *Find the section in the Code that defines capital gains. Note that it leads immediately to the need for a definition of capital assets. And when you find the section defining capital assets, it may strike you as a rather extraordinary one. It seems to exclude from the definition of capital assets virtually all the business assets that one would normally think of, in non-tax terms, as capital assets. What assets might a business have that could be considered capital assets?*

Prior to 1938, the definition of *capital asset* included what we would normally think of as capital assets—buildings and equipment. This led to difficulties in the Depression of the 1930's. At that time, as today, capital losses were deductible only to the extent of capital gains realized (although an individual, as opposed to a corporation, is permitted to deduct an extra $1000 of his capital losses against ordinary income). During the 1930's, buildings and equipment generally were worth considerably less than the amounts to which these assets had been depreciated, and consequently when they were sold they were sold at a loss. Since there were few capital gains during the 1930's, the losses produced by sales of depreciable property were generally not deductible at all for tax purposes. This naturally inhibited the sale of depreciable assets, and it was felt that as a matter of national economic policy it was desirable to encourage businesses to sell assets for which they no longer had a use. The obvious method of encouraging such sales seemed to be to turn the losses from sales of depreciable assets into ordinary losses which would then be deductible for at least any business that was showing a profit. And the simplest method to bring about this change in loss treatment was to define depreciable assets as no longer capital assets. This was done with the result that the sale of a depreciable asset used in a business produced ordinary, rather than capital, gain or loss.

This arrangement backfired, however, during World War II, when shortages generally drove market values of depreciable equipment to figures *above* depreciated book value so that the sale of a depreciable asset was likely to produce an ordinary gain. With excess-profits taxes, the corporate tax rate reached as high as 88 per cent, and naturally few businesses were eager to dispose of surplus equipment. Again, because tax structure seemed to be working against the national interest, Congress felt that the rule had to be changed. The most obvious change might have been to revert to the pre-1938 definition of a capital asset and simply restore depreciable assets to this category. However, Congress decided to retain the rule introduced during the 1930's for sales resulting in a loss but to go back to the pre-1938 rule for sales resulting in a gain. This plan became section 1231 of the Tax Code which, in general, treats gains on the sale of depreciable assets used in a business as capital gains and losses as ordinary losses.

Notice that section 1231 picks up virtually all the assets that we would generally think of as capital assets and that have been excluded from the Tax Code definition of capital assets. Section 1231 also adds a few other assets that we might not think of as capital assets. It is easy to see the handiwork of various lobbies in section 1231(b).

Section 631 presents similar examples. Read the last sentence in section 631(a). What industry lobbied to have this sentence included?

Section 1231 is an interesting example of a phenomenon quite common in the Code. You may have begun with a belief that capital gains can result only from the sale of capital assets. But section 1231 indicates that Congress is quite capable of granting capital gains treatment in situations where no capital assets are involved. Notice that section 1231 does not create any capital assets; it simply says that even noncapital assets of a certain kind may produce capital gain. (We will run into more instances where receipts that are clearly not from the sale of a capital asset are given capital gain treatment.)

Find the sections in the Code explaining how capital gains and losses are treated for tax purposes. Notice that corporations and noncorporate taxpayers are separated and that the rules relating to both gains and losses, including the carry-over of losses, differ for these two kinds of taxpayer.

Long- and short-term capital gains are not treated alike. It is common knowledge that long-term capital gains are taxed to individuals at 25 per cent of the gain. But this is not quite correct: 25 per cent is the *maximum* rate; in general the rate applicable to long-term capital gains is half the rate applicable to ordinary income.

Trace the mechanics—that is, the sequence of calculations—that lead to this result. Begin with the question: Are long-term capital gains included in gross income? And then note the effect of sections 1202 and 1201(b).

Compare the pre-1964 rule for loss carry-overs for noncorporate taxpayers with the present rule. (For this you need a copy of the Tax

Code setting out the 1964 amendment to section 1212.) Can you see any timing strategy suggested by section 1212(a)? For example, suppose a corporation has realized a $1000 long-term capital loss this year. It has no other capital gains or losses but is considering a sale that would produce a $1000 long-term capital gain. What are the merits of postponing this sale until next year?

Section 582(c), applying to bond portfolios of banks, is analogous to section 1231(a). Banks normally have large portfolios of bonds, and section 582(c) presents some interesting problems in deciding when to sell bonds. It is customary for a bank to designate a year as a "loss year" or a "gain year," as a guide to policy in selling bonds. What do you think is the significance of this designation? Why is section 582(c) necessary; wouldn't section 1231(a) bring about the same result?

Measure of gain or loss—amount realized

Section 1001 presents the general rule that gain is the excess of the amount realized on the disposition of an asset over the asset's adjusted basis. Adjusted basis is, roughly speaking, book value determined on the basis of tax accounting rather than conventional accounting unhampered by tax limitations. We will discuss basis and adjusted basis a little later on, but first we will deal with amount realized.

If property is sold for cash, the amount realized is simply the amount of cash paid. Suppose payment is made partly in cash and partly by check and is received in a high-income year but the check is not cashed until a low-income year. You might ease your tax burden by waiting to cash the check, if cashing constituted the taxable event. Unfortunately, you cannot defer income in this way, because checks are treated as cash when received. Within some limits, however, it *is* possible to defer part of a purchase price and put off full realization. Section 453 of the Code applies to installments paid.

Suppose property with a basis (cost) of $8000 is sold for $10,000; $2000 paid the first year, $4000 the second year, and $4000 the third year. If the seller selects to use section 453, what will his gain be in each of the three years?

What would happen in this case without section 453? Suppose the purchaser pays $3500 in the year of sale, giving his note payable in two years for the balance. Does the seller have $2000 of income that first year ($3500 cash plus the note for $6500, less $8000 basis)? The answer is a qualified yes. The note will be treated as value received but only to the extent of its fair-market value. If the buyer is solvent, the note's fair-market value will probably be close to its face value discounted at a normal interest rate, and that amount will constitute value received. Suppose the note has a fair-market value of 80 per cent of its face value. The seller realizes the fair-market value of the note in the year in which he receives it. If he later collects in full on this note, the remaining 20 per cent of the face value is then taxed. Is it treated as ordinary income or capital gain? This depends. If the buyer is an individual then ordinary income will result, but if the buyer is a corporation the seller may get capital gains treatment under section 1232 of the Code. He gets no capital gains treatment without section 1232 because he is *collecting* the note, not selling or exchanging it, and the capital gains definition requires that there be a sale or exchange.

If the buyer is an individual and section 1232 therefore does not apply, it may be still possible to produce capital gain by selling the obligation just before maturity rather than collecting it. There are cases, too, where if the buyer's obligation is nonnegotiable, the seller realizes taxable gain only when he has received value in excess of his basis. What this amounts to is placing no value on the promise to pay until the payment is actually made; that is, the installment-payment situation is authorized under section 453 even though the conditions of that section are not met. It is hard to be sure, however, when this rule will be applied.

Where the buyer's promise to pay has no fair-market value, no tax will be incurred by the seller until he has realized his basis.[1] the taxpayer, however, has the burden of proving that the promise has no fair-market value, and although the value of an obligation may be low, it almost always has some value. The cases that have been decided on this point suggest that when the taxpayer wins, it is usually not because the buyer's obligations have no value, but because the transaction has not really been closed until the final payment is made. For example, in *Burnet* v. *Logan*,[2] the taxpayer sold stock partly for cash and partly for a promise by the buyer to pay the taxpayer 60¢ per ton for all ore removed from a certain mine. The taxpayer claimed that she had no taxable income from the sale until she had recovered her basis (original cost of the stock) in the stock that she sold. The court agreed with her, not because the promise had no value, but because the deal was not closed. The taxpayer could not know whether she would have any gain at all until she had recovered her basis.

Measurement of gain or loss — basis and adjusted basis

Once we have determined the amount realized upon the sale or exchange of property, we are faced with the problem of determining basis and adjusted basis, in order to determine the taxable gain so that the taxpayer can recover his investment tax-free. Section 1012 sets forth the general rule that the basis of property is the cost of the property. Cost is defined as the amount paid for the property in cash or other property. Sections 1014 and 1015 deal with the special cases where property is acquired from a decedent or by gift. In the former case the basis is the fair-market value of the property used in computing the decedent's estate taxes, which is usually the fair-market value of the property at his death. You can see that if the basis of the property in the hands of the decedent was less than this fair-market value, then the basis has been "stepped-up"

---

[1]Regulations, section 1.453–6(a) (2).

[2]283 U.S. 404, (1931).

due to his death without anyone paying a tax on the step-up, although, of course, the estate paid a tax on the full fair-market value. This tax-free step-up at time of death is currently subject to a good deal of criticism as a serious loophole in the taxation of capital gains.

Notice that where property is acquired by gift, there is no tax-free step-up. The recipient of the gift will be taxed on appreciation in the hands of the donor when he sells the property (except to the extent that basis has been increased by gift tax paid).

So far we have considered basis. Section 1016 deals with *adjusted* basis. Section 1016 (a) (1) allows a taxpayer to adjust his basis to reflect any expenditure or receipt which is properly chargeable to capital account. This means, for example, that the cost of improvements made to the property can be added to the basis. Section 1016 (a) (2) requires that basis be adjusted to reflect amortization, depreciation, and depletion to the extent that these have reduced the taxpayer's taxes in the past.

Recapture of depreciation

Prior to 1962, the interaction between the depreciation deduction[3] and capital-gains taxation left a loophole in the tax laws which allowed taxpayers to turn ordinary income into capital gain. By taking accelerated depreciation or by underestimating the useful life of a particular asset, a taxpayer could claim substantial depreciation in the early years of ownership, which, if allowed, would provide a valuable deduction against ordinary income. After depreciating the asset for a while, the taxpayer could sell it, realizing more on the sale than his adjusted basis for the asset. Because the gain on the sale would generally be capital gain, the taxpayer would, in effect, have turned ordinary income into capital gain.

This situation was created in large part in 1954 when accelerated depreciation was introduced into the Code. The Treasury was reluctant to liberalize depreciable lives following the changes of 1954 until this loophole could be plugged. It was, therefore, only in 1962, when the Treasury was confident that section 1245 would be introduced to the Code, that the new Depreciation Guidelines were introduced.

Section 1245 provides that the sale of "section 1245 property" will give rise to ordinary income to the extent that post-1961 depreciation is recovered. Generally speaking, section 1245 property is depreciable property used in a trade or business, although buildings are specifically excluded. It was not until 1964 that the loophole was plugged for buildings in section 1250, and even this section is much more liberal to taxpayers than is section 1245.[4]

Suppose a taxpayer purchases equipment in 1960 for $10,000 and takes depreciation deductions of $2000 in 1960, $1600 in 1961, $1280 in 1962, $1020 in 1963, $820 in 1964, and then sells the equip-

---

[3]Depreciation will be dealt with in more detail in Chapter Eight.

[4]Section 1250 will be dealt with in more detail in Chapter Eleven.

ment in 1965 for $6500. Assuming section 1245 applies, what will be the capital gain and what will be ordinary income?

Basis and tax-free exchanges

Before leaving the subject of basis, you should notice that the Code permits certain kinds of property exchanges to be made without recognition of gain or loss, and in these cases special provisions have to be made for carrying-over and adjusting basis. These exchanges are dealt with in sections 1031 – 1038 of the Code.

The best known of these special exchanges is the "like-kind" exchange provision of section 1031. Under this section, no gain or loss is recognized if property held for productive use in a trade or business or for investment is exchanged solely for property of a like-kind, also held for productive use in a trade or business or for investment. Certain property does not qualify for a tax-free exchange under this section – stock in trade, stock, bonds, and other securities, for example. As might be expected, it is not always easy to tell what is "property of like-kind." The Regulations give some indication of the tests that are applied.

Section 1031 also applies where cash or other property – "unlike" property – is included in the exchange. In this case, some gain may be recognized, up to the amount of the unlike property (designated *boot*) but no more. For example, if the owner of apartment house A, having a tax basis of $100,000 and a fair-market value of $200,000, exchanges the building for apartment house B, having a fair-market value of $175,000 and other property with a value of $25,000, he will realize a gain of $100,000, but the section limits the recognition to the $25,000 boot. This is called a partially tax-free exchange.

We must also be concerned with what happens to the *basis* of property exchanged under section 1031. Section 1031(d) provides that if property is acquired pursuant to a section 1031(a) like-kind exchange, or under various other sections authorizing tax-free exchanges, then the basis of the property acquired shall be the same as the basis of the property given up. If money or unlike property is involved in the exchange, then the basis will be adjusted.

Suppose the taxpayer trades an apartment building having an adjusted basis of $10,000 for a store building worth $12,000 plus $800 worth of shares of stock in a corporation and cash payment of $200. The taxpayer realizes a gain of $3000, but only $1000 is recognized under section 1031 (the sum of the cash and value of the stock received). What is the basis of the property received in the exchange?

You should be able to see now that the total result of the tax-free exchange rule and the basis adjustment that goes with it is not avoidance but simply postponement of tax. The person who exchanges an old for a new piece of property does not have to pay a tax on this exchange; but when he comes to sell or exchange his new property, in a transaction that does not come within the tax-free exchange rules, he will have to pay taxes determined on the basis of the old property.

A section similar to section 1031, but of little importance to business, is section 1034 which postpones the recognition of gain when an individual sells his residence and purchases a new home within a year. Section 1033 is more important to business, dealing with cases of involuntary conversion, such as destruction of property by fire, where similar property is acquired soon enough afterwards.

Revenue Ruling 62 – 141[5]

Advice has been requested as to the proper treatment for Federal income tax purposes of the proceeds from sales by the producers of television films (including "live" shows taped for reproduction). A similar question has been raised as to motion picture films that are sold by the producers after initial theater showings.

Producers of films for television exhibition often lease their product rather than sell it initially. In some instances, after the films had been rented for various periods, ranging from several months to several years, they are then sold by the producers to television distributors or exhibitors.

Section 1231(a) of the Internal Revenue Code of 1954 provides, in effect, for capital-gains treatment in specified circumstances for gains from the sale or exchange of property used in the trade or business.

Section 1231(b)(1) of the Code provides, in part, as follows:

> (1) General rule – The term "property used in the trade or business" means property used in the trade or business, of a character which is subject to the allowance for depreciation provided in section 167, held for more than 6 months . . . which is not . . .
> (B) property held by the taxpayer primarily for sale to customers in the ordinary course of his trade or business . . . .

The Internal Revenue Service has previously concluded that television films are subject to depreciation under section 167 of the Code. See Rev. Rul. 60–358, C.B. 1960–2, 68.

Therefore, the question arises whether the films in question are ex-

---

[5]*Cumulative Bulletin,* 1962 – 2, 182.

cepted from the definition of "property used in the trade or business" by section 1231(b)(1)(B) of the Code, although they have been leased prior to sale and are subject to the allowance for depreciation provided in section 167 of the Code. If the television films are held by producers for sale to customers in the ordinary course of the trade or business within the meaning of section 1231(b)(1)(B) of the Code, gains and losses from the sales of such films by them will be treated as ordinary gains and losses.

In *Rollingwood Corp.* v. *Commissioner,* 190 Fed. (2d) 263 (1951), the taxpayer had arranged for the construction of houses for war workers under the condition imposed by the United States Government that each of the houses would be rented by the taxpayer with an option to the tenant to purchase. The houses were rented for an average time of 22 months and all but four of the houses were sold. The United States Court of Appeals for the Ninth Circuit affirmed the decision of the Tax Court of the United States that the houses were property held primarily for sale to customers in the ordinary course of the taxpayer's trade or business and that the proceeds from their sales should be taxed as ordinary income. The court stated as follows:

> "Although the requirements of the statute are to some extent over-lapping, the emphasis in this case is whether the houses were held primarily for sale or primarily for rent. Petitioners contend that the word *primarily* means 'principal' or 'chief,' while the Commissioner contends it means 'essential' or 'substantial.' For reasons herein-after stated we think the latter view is more consonant with the legislative policy.
>
> Suppose the taxpayer in the instant case intended to rent the houses for as long as he was required to do so under existing regulations and then to sell them. Or suppose his intention was to pursue whichever of these activities proved to be the most profitable, that is, if the *rental market* were good he would continue to rent but if the *sales market* were high he would sell. In either of these suppositions we think it is fair to say that one of the essential purposes (in acquiring or holding the houses) is the purpose of sale. Under such circumstances, if the taxpayer does dispose of the houses by sale, is it within the legislative *purpose* to allow him to treat the proceeds of these sales as a capital gain? We think not."

Other cases in which courts have held that the word "primarily" in the statute is to be interpreted as meaning "essential" or "substantial" rather than "principal" or "chief" and accordingly have denied capital gains treatment for the proceeds of sale from property that the taxpayers had rented are *S.E.C. Corp.* v. *United States* 140 Fed. Supp. 717 (1956), affirmed *per curiam* 241 Fed. (2d) 416 (1957), certiorari denied 354 U.S. 209 (1957), involving electric water and food coolers, and *Greene-Haldeman* v. *Commissioner* 282 Fed. (2d) 884 (1960), rehearing denied December 9, 1960, which concerned the sale of rental cars by dealers. In the latter decision the court pointed out that—

". . . In *Corn Products Refining Co.* v. *Commissioner*, 1955, [350 U.S. 46], at page 52 . . . the Court indicated that a narrow construction should be given to provisions of the Code which authorize capital gain treatment. If we were to accept the taxpayer's contention we would of necessity be expanding the types of transactions which are entitled to capital gain treatment."

In view of the fact that television film producers are aware of the market that exists for sales of television films after initial leasing periods, it is reasonable to assume that generally, from the time of their production, a producer's intention is either to sell, to rent, or to rent and then sell, whichever method proves most profitable in its business. Under the rationale of the cases referred to above, the fact that the films were leased prior to sale would not prevent their being held "primarily" for the purpose of sale, within the meaning of section 1231(b)(1)(B) of the Code.

Moreover, even if the producer originally has no intention to sell, he may develop a substantial intent to sell by the time of sale. In *Joseph A. Harrah* v. *Commissioner,* 30 T.C. 1236 (1958), a corporation had constructed a saw mill, which it originally used for experimental purposes, but later leased, subject to an option in the lessee to buy. In holding that the corporation's gain upon sale of the mill pursuant to the option constituted ordinary income, the court commented, at page 1241, that under the applicable decisions

". . . While the underlying purpose of the original acquisition of property is to be given consideration, it is clear that such purpose may change over a given period of time. Where this has been the case, the original purpose necessarily must give way to the purpose for which the property is held at the time of its sale . . . ."

Therefore, regardless of the purpose for which television films were originally held, if at the time of sale they are then being held with a substantial purpose of selling to customers in the ordinary course of trade or business, gain or loss realized upon the sale will be within the exception to capital gains treatment provided by section 1231(b)(1)(B) of the Code.

Some television film producers have made few or no past sales of films. These situations differ from most of the cases cited above, in which the sellers had made numerous sales of properties previously leased. On the other hand, unlike many such cases, the producers have in each instance produced the property in question. In an analogous situation involving a sale by a playwright of the movie rights to his first play, a majority of the court in an opinion by Judge Learned Hand in *Clifford Goldsmith et al.* v. *Commissioner* 143 Fed. (2d) 466, 467 (1944), certiorari denied, 323 U.S. 774 (1944), in upholding ordinary-income treatment of the sales proceeds, concluded that the taxpayer's business was both the production of that play and exploiting it for profit and that as a consequence the movie rights constituted property held for sale to customers in the ordinary course of his trade or business. See also *Joseph A. Fields* v. *Commissioner* 189 Fed. (2d) 950 (1951). Similarly, the business of television film producers also embraces exploiting of the films through whatever methods are within their reasonable contemplation at the time of production or at a later time.

In accordance with the above, it is held that television films sold by the producers ordinarily will be considered to be property held primarily for sale to customers in the ordinary course of the trade or business, within the meaning of section 1231(b)(1)(B) of the Code. Therefore, gains or losses resulting from such sales will be treated as ordinary gains or losses.

The considerations set forth above are also applicable to sales of motion picture films by producers. Following World War II, the motion picture industry became aware that substantial profits might be realized through television exhibition of its old films and of films it would produce in the future. Beginning August 1, 1948, collective bargaining agreements in the industry incorporated provisions allowing unions to cancel the agreements if feature motion picture films made on or after that date were released to television. It is reasonable to assume that no later than that date the industry recognized the distinct possibility that its films might be sold for exhibition on television after being leased for theater showings and that producers generally contemplated sales to television following such showings as a likely means of exploiting their product. In other instances, including some cases where the films were produced prior to August 1, 1948, the producers may not have had a substantial purpose of sale at the time of production but, as the value of motion picture films for television increased, may later have developed such a purpose.

The Service will therefore determine in each case, on the basis of the relevant facts and circumstances, whether motion picture films sold by the producers were at the time of sale held by them primarily for sale to customers in the ordinary course of their trade or business, within the meaning of section 1231(b)(1)(B) of the Code. Accordingly, it is further held that motion picture films completed on or after August 1, 1948, and thereafter sold by the producers ordinarily will be considered as property held by the taxpayer primarily for sale to customers in the ordinary course of his trade or business.

In Revenue Ruling 55-706, C.B. 1955-2, 300, it was determined that where a motion picture producer sold in one unusual and isolated transaction a quantity of its own films which it had previously rented, the gain realized from the sale was taxable as a long-term capital gain under section 1231 of the Code. There, the films sold had all been originally produced and released during the period from 1931 to 1946, prior to general recognition that sales of films to television might be an important future source of income to the motion picture industry and, at the time of production, the films were not held for sale to customers in the ordinary course of the taxpayer's trade or business.

Pursuant to the authority contained in section 7805(b) of the Code, this ruling will not be applied to the sale of motion picture films produced for initial theater showings either before or after August 1, 1948, and sold prior to August 27, 1962, the date of the publication of this ruling, provided that the sale is an isolated and unusual one.

Revenue Ruling 55-706, C.B. 1955-2, 300, is accordingly superseded as it applies to sales made on or after August 27, 1962.

ABC Motor Freight

ABC Motor Freight was engaged almost exclusively in transportation for the United States Defense Department when it was threatened with a strike. Caught between a union that was ready to close it down and the Defense Department that was demanding continued operations, the company refused to yield to the union's demands and decided to take its chances with the government.

A strike on August 4 completely shut down the company's operations, and the following day the President of the United States by executive order took possession and control of "all the company's property used or useful in connection with its operations."

On July 10 of the following year, an agreement was reached between the union and the company, and the U.S. government returned the property it had seized. The company began a suit against the United States for compensation. In awarding compensation, the court concluded that the correct amount would be the rental that ABC could have obtained had it chosen to rent the equipment that was seized by the government, for the period of seizure. The equipment included fifty-five tractor-trailer combinations, fourteen spare tractors, twenty-three pick-up delivery trucks, and five passenger-service vehicles. The court found that when equipment of this sort was leased, the rent was based on mileage, with a minimum of 5000 miles per month. For each vehicle the compensation was figured then at 5000 miles times the number of months the vehicle had been seized times the appropriate mileage rental for that class of equipment.

> *Do you think the compensation could be treated by the company as long-term capital gain rather than ordinary income? All of the vehicles involved had been held by the company for more than six months at the time of seizure by the government.*

Malat *v.* Riddell[6]

PER CURIAM: Petitioner was a participant in a joint venture which acquired a 45-acre parcel of land, the intended use for which is somewhat in dispute. Petitioner contends that the venturers' intention was to develop and operate an apartment project on the land; the Commissioner's position is that there was a "dual purpose" of developing the property for rental purposes or selling, whichever proved to be the more profitable. In any event, difficulties in obtaining the necessary financing were encountered, and the interior lots of the tract were subdivided and sold. The profit from those sales was reported and taxed as ordinary income.

The joint venturers continued to explore the possibility of commercially developing the remaining exterior parcels. Additional frustrations in the form of zoning restrictions were encountered. These difficulties persuaded petitioner and another of the joint venturers of the desirability of terminating the venture; accordingly, they sold out their interests in the remaining property. Petitioner contends that he is entitled to treat the profits from this last sale as capital gains; the Commissioner takes the position that this was "property held by the taxpayer primarily for sale to customers in the ordinary course of his trade or business,"[7] and thus subject to taxation as ordinary income.

The District Court made the following finding:

> The members of [the joint venture], as of the date the 44.901 acres were acquired, intended either to sell the property or develop it for rental, depending upon which course appeared to be most profitable. The venturers realized that they had made a good purchase price-wise and, if they were unable to obtain acceptable construction financing rezoning . . . which would be prerequisite to commerical development, they would sell the property in bulk so they wouldn't get hurt. The purpose of either selling or developing the property continued during the period in which [the joint venture] held the property.

---

[6]383 U.S. 569 (United States Supreme Court, 1966).

[7]Internal Revenue Code of 1954, section 1221(I), 26 U.S.C. section 1221(1): "For purposes of this subtitle, the term 'capital asset' means property held by the taxpayer (whether or not connected with his trade or business), but does not include—

"(1) . . . property held by the taxpayer primarily for sale to customers in the ordinary course of his trade or business."

The District Court ruled that petitioner had failed to establish that the property was not held *primarily* for sale to customers in the ordinary course of business, and thus rejected petitioner's claim to capital gain treatment for the profits derived from the property's resale. The Court of Appeals affirmed, 347 F. 2d 23. We granted certiorari (382 U.S. 900) to resolve a conflict among the Courts of Appeals[8] with regard to the meaning of the term "primarily" as it is used in section 1221(1) of the Internal Revenue Code of 1954.

The statute denies capital gain treatment to profits reaped from the sale of "property held by the taxpayer *primarily* for the sale to customers in the ordinary course of his trade or business." (Emphasis added.) The Commissioner urges upon us a construction of "primarily" as meaning that a purpose may be "primary" if it is a "substantial" one.

As we have often said, "the words of statutes — including revenue acts — should be interpreted where possible in their ordinary everyday senses." *Crane* v. *Commissioner*, 331 U.S. 1, 6. And see *Hanover Bank* v. *Commissioner*, 369 U.S. 672, 687-688; *Commissioner* v. *Korell*, 339 U.S. 619, 627-628. Departure from a literal reading of statutory language may, on occasion, be indicated by relevant internal evidence of the statute itself and necessary in order to effect the legislative purpose. See, *e.g. Board of Governors* v. *Agnew*, 329 U.S. 441, 446-448. But this is not such an occasion. The purpose of the statutory provision with which we deal is to differentiate between the "profits and losses arising from the everyday operation of a business" on the one hand (*Corn Products Co.* v. *Commissioner*, 350 U.S. 46, 52) and "the realization of appreciation in value accrued over a substantial period of time" on the other. (*Commissioner* v. *Gillette Motor Co.*, 364 U.S. 130, 134). A literal reading of the statute is consistent with this legislative purpose. We hold that, as used in section 1221(1), "primarily" means "of first importance" or "principally."

Since the courts below applied an incorrect legal standard, we do not consider whether the result would be supportable on the facts of this case had the correct one been applied. We believe, moreover, that the appropriate disposition is to remand the case to the District Court for fresh factfindings, addressed to the statute as we have now construed it.

Vacated and remanded.

Mr. Justice Black would affirm the judgments of the District Court and the Court of Appeals.

Mr. Justice White took no part in the decision of this case.

---

[8]Compare *Rollingwood Corp.* v. *Commissioner*, 190 F. 2d 263, 266 (C.A. 9th Cir.); *American Can Co.* v. *Commissioner*, 317 F. 2d 604, 605 (C.A. 2d Cir.), with *United States* v. *Bennett*, 186 F. 2d 407, 410-411 (C.A. 5th Cir.); *Municipal Bond Corp.* v. *Commissioner*, 341 F. 2d 683, 688-689 (C.A. 8th Cir.). Cf. *Recordak Corp.* v. *United States*, 325 F. 2d 460, 463-464 (Ct. Cl.).

Chapter four

Tax factors in the purchase and sale of a proprietorship

Federal income tax law plays an important role in any purchase and sale transaction, whether of an entire business or of a portion of its assets. Both buyer and seller are affected in many significant ways. The tax rules applicable to purchases and sales are extremely diverse, ranging from basic rules of general applicability to complicated special rules that apply only to certain sales or business reorganizations. In chapters four through seven, we will examine the most important of these rules.

Each of these chapters considers one of the three major forms of business organizations—sole proprietorship, partnership, and corporation. This is a convenient approach because it begins with the proprietorship, the simplest form of business organization, where a sale of the business is little more than a sale of individual business assets; moves through the partnership, where for tax purposes characteristics of the proprietorship and the corporation are both evident; and ends with the corporation which, as a legal entity, is treated quite differently in its purchase and sale from the proprietorship.

The asset sold

When we speak of a proprietorship, we are using a shorthand expression for the many assets that may go into making up a business. The tax law reflects the general legal principle that a proprietorship is not a legal entity. That is, the business assets of a proprietorship are simply assets of the owner of the business, so that even when the entire business making up the proprietorship is sold, the tax consequences are based upon the simple concept of an individual selling a collection of personally owned assets. The sale of a proprietorship, then, is really the sale of ordinary business assets. Our conclusions, to a large extent, apply not only to the sale of an individual's assets but also to the sale of business assets of any organization including a corporation (although the corporate case also involves other special rules).

The concept of a proprietorship as a bundle of assets is not an unchallenged one. In fact, in the case of *Williams* v. *McGowan*[1] Judge Frank, dissenting from the majority opinion, believed that the sale of a proprietorship as a going business was like the sale of a single capital asset and said that "to carve up this transaction into distinct sales — of cash, receivables, fixtures, trucks, merchandise, and goodwill — is to do violence to the realities." The majority of the court, however, held that the sale of a proprietorship must be treated as a series of sales of the individual parts of the business; and that is the law today.

Allocation

Since the seller of a proprietorship cannot treat his transaction as the sale of a single asset, he will want to know how the sale of each of his business assets will be treated — whether it will produce gain or loss and what kinds of gains or losses will result. The buyer, in turn, who, for tax purposes, is making a series of purchases of individual assets, will be concerned about the subsequent tax treatment of each of these assets. That is, he will be concerned about which are depreciable, which may be amortized, and, in general, to what extent he will be able to recover his investment through tax deductions.

The foregoing should suggest that one of the major problems in the purchase and sale of a business is the allocation to the various assets purchased of the price to be paid. The seller, of course, will prefer an allocation that as far as possible turns gains into long-term capital gains and losses into ordinary losses, or at least short-term capital losses. That is, his tax burden will be minimized if he can make the most of the opportunities offered by the long-term capital gains tax, section 1231, and various other special sections of the Code. The buyer, on the other hand, will wish to have as fast a recovery of his investment, for tax purposes, as possible. This means he will be looking for a relatively large allocation of the price paid to the kinds of assets that will generate a fast recovery. For example, inventory which is sold quickly will produce tax benefits quickly. Depreciable assets will produce tax benefits through depreciation a little more slowly, and nondepreciable assets, such as land, will confer tax advantages on the purchaser of the business only when he sells those assets, perhaps far in the future.

It should be obvious at this point that what is an ideal allocation for the purchaser may be far from ideal for the seller. Allocation is further complicated by the fact that even if the parties can agree, their decision is not necessarily final. The Internal Revenue Service may challenge it, and

---

[1] 152 F. 2d 570 (U.S. Court of Appeals, 2nd Circuit, 1945).

unless the parties can justify the allocation they have made, they may be forced to accept another.

In the discussion of capital gains and losses in Chapter three, we considered the definition of a capital asset and the importance of section 1231. Most of the assets of a proprietorship will be either section 1231 assets or assets that are neither capital assets nor section 1231 assets. Section 1231 has the attractive feature of offering capital gains and ordinary losses. But there are a good many conditions and limitations in section 1231; perhaps the most important is that all of the section 1231 gains must be netted against all of the section 1231 losses for the year. This means that a business cannot sell one depreciable asset at a gain and have this gain taxed at long-term capital gain rates and during the same year sell other section 1231 property at a loss and deduct this loss from its ordinary income.

We can now become somewhat more specific about the allocation aims of the seller and the purchaser of a proprietorship. If there is to be overall gain to the seller, any allocation of price to capital assets that have been held for six months will benefit him because this will result in long-term capital gains. On the other hand, the purchaser will want as much of the price as possible attributed to noncapital assets, such as inventory, so that when he resells them and realizes ordinary income, his gain, for tax purposes, will be as small as possible. The seller will want to allocate as small a portion of the purchase price as possible to these noncapital assets in order to hold down his ordinary income, or even produce some loss on these items which, of course, will be noncapital loss.

The one common ground for both buyer and seller is found in section 1231. Depreciable assets classified under section 1231 will produce capital gain or ordinary loss for the seller, while at the same time they will give the buyer depreciation deductions. It is true that the buyer might prefer faster deductions obtained through allocation of the purchase price to inventory, but allocation of the price to depreciable assets is at least better than allocation to capital assets. The netting provisions of section 1231 (which we discussed previously) may reduce the value, to the seller, of allocations to section 1231 assets, of course, and may point to careful timing of a sale in order to minimize the effects of netting gains and losses.

Substantiation of allocation

The rules

If the buyer and seller make no allocation of price to the various assets involved, the Commissioner of Internal Revenue or the courts may make an allocation for them. In *Copperhead Coal Co., Inc.* v. *Commissioner*[2] a mining operation run as a partnership sold out to a corporation

---

[2] 272 F. 2d 45 (U.S. Court of Appeals, 6th Circuit, 1959).

for $1 million. The contract of sale listed each item of equipment and the agreed sale price for each. The entire $1 million was allocated to the equipment, and each item was entered on the corporate books and depreciated on the basis of the price allocated in the contract of sale. Since all the property was depreciable section 1231 property, the allocation suited both the buyer and the seller. Nothing was allocated to "goodwill," which is generally treated as a capital asset and is not depreciable. The Commissioner concluded that some part of the purchase price should have been allocated to goodwill. The court found that the equipment was worth considerably less than $1 million and that the balance could only represent goodwill. Failure to allocate anything to this item did not prevent subsequent allocation by the court, which said, "The fact that goodwill was not discussed by the parties and the corporation in their negotiations or in the contract of purchase is not controlling as to the government."

From the rule above, you can easily deduce another: the allocation of the purchase price made by the parties will not be binding on the Internal Revenue Service. In *Particelli* v. *Commissioner*,[3] a winery and its stock of wine were sold. The buyer did not want the winery but could not get the wine under existing Office of Price Administration regulations in any other way. The seller, however, allocated most of the purchase price to the winery, which produced for him capital gain, and allocated the balance to the wine, which as inventory was not a capital asset and produced ordinary income. As the case stood, it appeared that a good part of the price which was allegedly paid for the winery was actually paid for the wine. Accordingly, the court reallocated the price, placing most of the value on the wine. This, of course, meant far more ordinary income for the seller than he had anticipated. The court found that although "the total purchase price was arrived at through arms-length negotiations, the allocation of the selling price to the two pieces of property involved was not."

Allocation in practice

In general, where the allocation of the price to the assets is the result of genuine arms-length bargaining between the parties, a challenge by the Internal Revenue Service is not likely. As you have already seen, there often are conflicts between the purchaser and seller over the subject of allocation, and this should guarantee that the final allocation will be, to some extent, a reasonable arms-length allocation. However, there are certain kinds of allocation on which the parties are likely to agree, and unless these allocations can be supported by demonstrable values, a challenge from the Internal Revenue Service is quite likely. It may be a good idea to have actual expert appraisals made in anticipation of arguments with the Internal Revenue Service. In any case, both the buyer and seller should be prepared to defend their allocations.

One allocation that is likely to cause trouble is the allocation to good-

---

[3]212 F. 2d 498 (U.S. Court of Appeals, 9th Circuit, 1954).

will. As we noted above, goodwill is treated as a capital asset, which means that for the seller it will give rise to capital gain. It is not depreciable, and hence the buyer will have little reason to want any of the purchase price allocated to it. Goodwill is closely allied to a covenant not to compete, a promise by the seller that he will not go into business again in competition with the proprietorship he has just sold. In fact, the usual way of guaranteeing that the purchaser of a proprietorship actually receives what goodwill the proprietorship has generated is for the seller to agree to a covenant not to compete. Such an agreement, however, produces very different tax consequences from those which occur from the ordinary sale of goodwill. The covenant not to compete is generally viewed as a kind of negative service contract or surrender of income, and any part of the purchase price of a business allocated to the covenant will be ordinary income in the seller's hands. The covenant is, however, a depreciable asset for the buyer. In a choice between allocating purchase price to goodwill and to a covenant not to compete, then, the preferences of the buyer and seller will conflict. And, as mentioned above, even if the buyer and seller reach an agreement, the Internal Revenue Service may not be satisfied.

In *Schulz* v. *Commissioner*[4] a partnership had been dissolved and the continuing partners had purchased the retiring partner's interest. The price paid over and above the asset value of the retiring partner's interest was allocated to a covenant not to compete with the continuing business on the part of the retiring partner. This worked to the advantage of the continuing partners since the covenant was a depreciable asset in the partnership. The Commissioner challenged the allocation, arguing that the price paid above the asset value was, in fact, attributable to goodwill. In finding in favor of the Commissioner (and denying a depreciation deduction to the partnership), the court looked at the history of the sale and was influenced by a number of factors: (1) the continuing partners knew that their old partner did not want to compete with them anyway; (2) the continuing partners knew that their old partner lacked the skill and contacts necessary to compete; (3) the covenant was only for a short period of time during which business conditions made competition unlikely; (4) the covenant was of insignificant scope; (5) the former partner was unaware that the covenant would mean ordinary income to him and that it was, therefore, less attractive than goodwill; (6) the covenant was not discussed until late in the bargaining process. On the basis of these facts, the covenant was held to have no meaningful substance and was disregarded.

As in the case of the corporation-partnership choice, there are no rules of thumb that will tell you how to allocate a purchase price. You can test the results of different allocations, from both the buyer's and seller's points of view, and consider how the total price might be renegotiated on the basis of changes in allocation. A purchaser, for example, if he can have an allocation that is attractive to him, should be willing to pay more than he would with an unattractive allocation.

---

[4]294 F. 2d 52 (U.S. Court of Appeals, 9th Circuit, 1961).

The Double M Belt Company (A)

Morris Mace, a sixty-three-year old widower with no children, owns a small unincorporated ladies' belt business known as The Double M Belt Company. He both manufactures and markets the belts.

Mace's father died several months ago, leaving a trust for Mace that will pay him approximately $40,000 a year beginning next year. (This year his only source of income is the business.) Taking into account this new source of wealth, his age, and health, Mace began to consider a long-awaited retirement and to look for someone to buy his business. The business has done well for its size in the past and indications are that the ladies' belt business will be strong in years to come, so Mace has not had much trouble in finding a prospective buyer. The buyer is a young, ambitious man named Peter Carson, and the two have already agreed on a price for the business. Carson will pay $125,000 in cash and will assume all the outstanding liabilities of the business, which amount to $327,400. Carson will receive all the assets of the business except the cash, including the "Double M" name. Carson, through his attorney, has insisted that Mace execute a five-year covenant not to compete with the sales end of the business in the New York area where the merchandising takes place. This end of the business has built a reputation for excellent service and fair prices under Mace's control in the past.

The price negotiations took place during the fall of the year. It is now November, and Mace has announced that he wants to wrap things up and get to Florida before the bad weather sets in. Some pertinent background facts about the business are:

(1) Last September, a warehouse was destroyed by fire. Its tax basis was $40,000 but it was underinsured, and only $20,000 in insurance was recovered. In October, Mace purchased another warehouse for $10,000 which he expected to depreciate over fifteen years.

(2) Two years ago Mace bought a patent covering one step of the belt-making operation from his father, who was an amateur inventor.

(3) The real estate owned by Mace, and used in the business, was purchased ten years ago when the surrounding area was still largely suburban. It is now part of a thriving industrial area.

(4) For the first ten months of this year, the business has earned $15,000 before taxes. (This figure does not take into account the fire loss, and no salary for Mace has been deducted.) Before tax,

income for November and December is expected to run about $1800 per month. Average earnings for the preceding five years have been $10,000 per year after taxes (again without allowing for a salary to Mace).

A balance sheet for the company as of October 31, this year, follows:

The Double M Belt Company
Balance Sheet, October 31*

Assets		Liabilities	
Cash	$ 33,400	Accounts payable	$113,700
Accounts receivable	144,500	Accrued expenses	37,300
(less allowance for bad		Income tax payable	2,100
debts)	(8,900)	Notes payable	100,000
Inventory	139,400	Other (taxes, interest)	14,300
Prepaid expenses	6,300		
		Current liabilities	$267,400
Current assets	$314,700		
		Mortgage (4%)	60,000
Real estate (land)	$ 60,000	Proprietorship	35,000
Warehouse	10,000	Investment	
Furniture and fixtures	16,900	Retained earnings	104,000
(less depreciation)	(1,800)		
Lasts and patterns	43,700	Long-term debt and capital	199,000
(less depreciation)	(4,600)		
Automobiles	5,600		
(less depreciation)	(5,600)		
Patent	12,000		
(less depreciation)	(2,000)		
Goodwill	17,500		
Fixed assets	151,700		
Total assets	$466,400	Total liabilities and capital	$466,400

*Assume that the net values on the balance sheet are the adjusted bases of the assets, for tax purposes.

Allocate the $452,400 value received by Mace for his business among the assets sold, from both the seller's and the buyer's point of view.

Calculate gain or loss for the seller under this allocation.

Is there any advice Mace could use with respect to the timing of the sale?

Chapter five

Tax factors in the purchase and sale
of a partnership

We have already referred to the fact that the tax status of a partnership lies somewhere between that of a proprietorship and that of a corporation; we have seen that the sale of a proprietorship involves the sale of the individual assets that make up the proprietorship, and we will see that the sale of a corporation can be achieved with the sale of a single asset which is generally a capital asset—the stock in the corporation. The partner's interest in a partnership, however, is treated *almost* as a single capital asset. Not quite all of the amount realized on the sale of that interest will be receipt from the sale of a capital asset, if the partnership has unrealized accounts receivable that have not been taken into income or inventory items which have appreciated substantially in value.

The tax treatment of partners and partnerships is very complicated, largely because here the Code seeks to strike a compromise between the tax treatment of the proprietorship and the tax treatment of the corporation. Although there is relatively small interest in partnerships among business-men today, for the sake of constructing a complete picture of the proprie-torship-partnership-corporation spectrum, we will review the general tax consequences of the purchase and sale of a partnership interest.

In the chapter on capital gains and losses, we considered the question of basis and adjusted basis of an asset. In the case of the capital asset that is a partner's interest in a partnership, there are some special rules for determining basis. Section 721 states that no gain or loss is recognized to the partnership or to the partners when they contribute their property to the partnership in exchange for a partnership interest. Since no gain or loss is recognized, you should anticipate some sort of basis carry-over to the new owner of the asset. And, you might also expect that a partner's interest in the partnership will carry the same basis as that of the assets which he contributed in exchange for that interest. These are precisely the results brought about by sections 723 and 722. And you should already have looked at section 705, which governs the determination of the current basis of a partner's interest and prescribes the adjustments to the initial section 722 basis.

We have already considered, in connection with an earlier case, the income tax treatment of partnership taxable income. Suppose three men, X, Y, and Z, set up a partnership in 1963 with each partner contributing $10,000 in value. Z contributes property worth $10,000 but with an adjusted basis to him of only $8,000; the others contribute $10,000 each in cash. Profits are shared equally, and the partnership taxable income is:

1965		$15,000
1966		12,000
1967		−6,000
January	1968	3,000
February	1968	900
March	1968	−300

The partnership makes no distributions to the partners, and on April 1, 1968, Z sells his interest in the partnership. What is his adjusted basis on that date for purposes of determining gain on the sale?

We noted above that the partnership interest is treated almost as a capital asset. Sections 741 and 751 produce this result. Why is section 751 included in the Code?

It should occur to you that the rules in section 751 are going to create some problems for the person who buys a partnership interest from a partner. The receivables and the inventory of the partnership are going fairly soon to produce taxable income for the partnership which will be taxed in part to the new partner. But they have already been taxed in part, under section 751, to the partner who sold out. Double taxation, that is, taxation at ordinary income rates to two different taxpayers, is avoided by the basis adjustment described in section 743 (b). Sections 754 and 755 also relate to this point.

So far what we have been considering is a situation where a partner sells his interest perhaps to other partners or to an outsider. Rather different results come from a liquidation where the partnership itself buys a partner out by liquidating his interest. Two sections deal with partnership liquidations: section 731 and section 736. The former applies where both property and money are distributed by the partnership on liquidation; the latter applies to liquidations solely in cash. Section 731 should remind you of the allocation problem in the sale of a proprietorship.

We discussed the problem of goodwill in connection with the sale of a proprietorship. You will see that section 736(b) deals explicitly with partnership goodwill. In Revenue Ruling 60-301, the Internal Revenue Service recognized that goodwill can exist in a business that does not depend *solely* for its success upon the personal characteristics of the owner even though the firm name is not assigned; but it also reaffirmed an earlier position to the effect that where the business depends *solely* on the personal characteristics of its owner then no part of the sale price may be allocated to goodwill unless the sale includes the exclusive rights to the firm's name.

THE DOUBLE M BELT COMPANY (B)

Just as Morris Mace was about to settle the details of a sale of his business to Peter Carson (see Double M Belt Company (A), in Chapter Four) Carson proposed a different arrangement.

"What I have in mind is this," he said. "We form a partnership. You contribute all the assets of your business, except the cash, and I contribute $125,000 in cash. The result will be a much stronger business than what you now own. Then you retire and the partnership pays you $15,000 a year for twenty years. In exchange for this, you give up your interest in the partnership. In other words, instead of taking $125,000 cash now you get $300,000 spread over 20 years."

"Why do we have to go through the partnership routine?" asked Mace. "Why don't you just pay for my business in installments?"

"My tax adviser thinks I can deduct the annual payments, for tax purposes, if we use a partnership," replied Carson.

As tax adviser to Mace, what do you suggest?

What do you think of the advice Carson has been given?

Chapter six

Corporate distributions

The starting point for a discussion of corporate distributions is Tax Code section 301. Section 301 (c) describes the treatment of a receipt by a shareholder, and section 301 (d) deals with the basis of property received if the distribution is not entirely in cash. Section 301(c) takes us to section 316 for a definition of *dividends*. Section 316 tells us essentially that it is not up to the corporation to decide, for tax purposes, whether or not a distribution is a dividend. Keep in mind the difference between the financial definition of *dividend* and the Tax Code definition. This difference enables some corporations to pay "tax-free dividends." Whether the distribution is considered a dividend, for tax purposes, depends upon whether the corporation has what are called "earnings and profits." There is no concise definition of earnings and profits in the Code. Essentially, they consist of taxable income, with various modifications to record distributions that were not deductible for tax purposes, such as dividends, and to record some receipts that did not go into gross income. Section 312 deals with special rules for adjusting earnings and profits.

Notice that a distribution is considered to be from earnings and profits if it is covered either by the earnings and profits of the current year or by earnings and profits since February 28, 1913, when the first income tax was enacted. This means that even though a corporation has an overall earnings-and-profits deficit, a distribution made during a year when there are earnings and profits for that year will be treated as a dividend at least up to the amount of the earnings and profits for the year.

If a corporation has a very large accumulated earnings-and-profits deficit but is currently earning money and expects to continue to have earnings and profits in future years, is there any strategy that might be adopted to make the best tax use of the accumulated deficit?

In general, a corporation does not realize income when it distributes property to its shareholders. That is, even though the fair market value of the property distributed is much greater than the adjusted basis of the property to the corporation, there is no recognition of gain. Sections 1245 and 1250 provide exceptions to this rule, however (see Regulations section 1.1245-1 (c)[1]). Section 311 provides another exception. In connection with section 311 you might also look at section 341, which deals with collapsible corporations. Sections 311, 312, and 341 are designed simply to plug loopholes that would make it possible to convert ordinary business income into capital gain.

Stock dividends

One of the most important tax decisions of the United States Supreme Court was *Eisner* v. *Macomber*,[2] which held that a stock dividend did not constitute income within the meaning of the Sixteenth Amendment to the Constitution and, hence, could not be taxed under an income tax. The particular case was concerned with a dividend in common stock, but the Court did not explicitly limit its decision to this sort of situation. Whether, for example, a dividend in *preferred* stock distributed on common stock could be income was left somewhat in doubt. In 1920, the Supreme Court decided *Koshland* v. *Helvering*,[3] which established that a dividend in preferred distributed on common may be treated as income for tax purposes if there is preferred stock already outstanding. If there is no preferred stock already outstanding, then the holders of the common stock will end up with exactly the same proportional claim against the same company as they had before the distribution, and the *Eisner* v. *Macomber* doctrine would say there was no income.

This latter rule was the basis for a tax gimmick, useful until 1954, called the "preferred stock bail-out." The corporation, which would have to have no preferred stock already outstanding, would distribute a preferred stock dividend to its common stock shareholders. This distribution would be tax free. The shareholders would then sell their preferred stock, frequently to an insurance company, realizing capital gains on the sale. The corporation would then redeem the preferred stock. The end result was that the corporation had distributed money which, in a roundabout way, reached the shareholders at capital gains rather than ordinary income tax rates.

In 1954, section 306 was enacted to eliminate the preferred stock bail-out. Section 305 continues the tax-free rule for dividends distributed

---

[1]We discussed section 1245 in Chapter three.

[2]252 U.S. 189 (U.S. Supreme Court, 1920).

[3]298 U.S. 441 (U.S. Supreme Court, 1936).

in common stock on common stock. But while section 306 establishes the same tax-free rule at the time a preferred dividend is distributed, it attaches certain characteristics to the dividend stock (called "section 306 stock") which produces ordinary income instead of capital gains at the time of its sale or redemption. There are some exceptions to this consequence for situations that seemed to Congress to be legitimate.

Distributions in redemption of stock

Section 301 (c) tells us that a corporate distribution is a dividend to the extent the corporation has earnings and profits. Once the earnings and profits are used up, however, the distribution is taxed as a return of capital to the shareholder. This return of capital is not going to cause us much trouble, since in general the shareholder will simply get his money back and pay a capital gains tax on any gains. What is more to the point here is the possibility of avoiding the dividend treatment of the distribution even though the corporation does have earnings and profits, on the grounds that the distribution is a return of capital and that such payments simply should not be taxed as dividends.

Section 302 provides the relief we are looking for in certain cases. This section, in effect, converts the *distribution* into an *exchange* (which will be treated as producing capital gain or loss) in certain cases. Section 302 raises some difficult questions. For example, there is no answer in the Code or the Regulations to the question: When is a redemption not essentially equivalent to a dividend? The Internal Revenue Service has said that redemption by a corporation of all its preferred stock for bona fide business reasons will be treated as a capital transaction and not a dividend. And cases involving the genuine contraction of a business and a subsequent redemption of stock are often classified as redemptions not equivalent to a dividend. Even if you cannot be sure that a distribution is not substantially equivalent to a dividend, it is possible to meet some of the specific circumstances in section 302(b) (2). In these special cases it is not necessary to show that the redemption is not essentially equivalent to a dividend.

The distributions described in section 302 are, of course, not liquidating distributions, at least from a corporation's point of view. Section 302 does apply to distributions that terminate the interest of a particular shareholder in the corporation, so from his point of view the distribution might be considered a liquidating distribution. But although there may have been a contraction in its scope of operations which led to the distribution classified under section 302, in general the corporation will continue its existence.

Section 331 deals more explicitly with liquidation of a corporation. It provides that amounts distributed in complete liquidation of a corporation are treated as payments in exchange for the stock and that amounts distributed in partial liquidation are treated as a part or full payment in exchange for the stock. Section 346 tells us what a partial liquidation is.

Section 346 may appear to you very similar to section 302, in that both sections contemplate distributions which do not result in a complete liquidation of the corporation. But notice that section 302 imposes its limitations in terms of the effect of the distribution on the shareholder, while section 346 imposes its limitations in terms of the effect on the corporation. It may well be that a particular distribution would fit the description in both sections 302 and 346, but there are distributions that come under section 346 and do not qualify under section 302. Notice that section 346 takes care of a distribution that is only one step in a complete liquidation. Essentially, it covers a complete liquidation taking place over a period of time, and section 346 simply treats each step in the same manner as the entire liquidation will be treated in sections we have not yet discussed.

> *Do you see any reason for preferring the distribution under section 346 to a distribution under section 302, if a choice is available? Notice, for example, that section 311 applies to section 302, but not to section 346 (to which section 336 applies).*

Section 301(d) deals with the basis of property received in a distribution in the general case to which section 301 applies. Section 302 does not have its own basis rules, and the basis rules of section 301 will apply. Section 334 deals with basis in a liquidating distribution and will therefore apply to section 346 distributions. For the effects of distributions under sections 302 and 346 on the corporation itself we turn to section 331, which we have already discussed and to section 336.

> *Section 336 relieves the corporation of taxes on a distribution of assets in a liquidation, as section 311 does in the case of dividend distributions. But does it eliminate sections 1245 and 1250 tax liabilities?*

> *Suppose a corporation with earnings and profits of $300,000 owns real estate worth $1 million which has an adjusted basis of only $100,000. A proposal is made to borrow $500,000, giving a mortgage on the real estate which gives the lender recourse only against the property, not against the corporation. The corporation will then distribute the real estate, subject to the mortgage, to its shareholders in a section 302 redemption. The basis of the stock to be redeemed is $200,000, so the shareholders will realize a $300,000 capital gain; but earnings and profits of the corporation will be wiped out and then the borrowed $500,000 can be distributed to the remaining shareholders tax-free as a return of capital. The result will be to pass the $1 million to the shareholders half tax-free and half at capital gains rates, wipe out earnings and profits, and avoid completely capital gains tax at the corporate level on the real estate. Will the proposal work? Would it be better to distribute the property as a dividend rather than in redemption of stock?*

Complete liquidations

We have already referred to section 331 which simply says that distributions in complete liquidation are treated as payments in exchange for stock. That is, in the usual case they produce capital gains or losses. And we have seen sections 334 and 336 describe the basis of property received in the hands of the shareholders and the tax treatment of the corporation as a result of liquidation. Some problems arise, however, concerning exactly what constitutes a complete liquidation. Although there is no definition in section 331 or in the Regulations, there is one in section 332. It seems probable that this definition will generally be held to explain what is meant in section 331 by complete liquidation.

A serious problem involved with complete liquidation is the so-called "reincorporation problem." Consider this example. Corporation A with one shareholder X decides to liquidate. The sole assets are $100,000 cash and a machine with a fair market value of $100,000 and a tax basis of $50,000. Earnings and profits are $100,000. A distributes the machine and cash to X in redemption of all of X's stock, which has a tax basis of $100,000. X realizes a capital gain of $100,000, the amount by which the cash and fair market value of the machine exceeds the basis of the stock he has given up. In X's hands the machine receives a stepped-up basis of $100,000, its fair market value. Now X forms a new corporation and contributes the machine to the new corporation in exchange for all its stock. The basis of the machine in the new corporation is $100,000. The result is that the old corporation, which had only $50,000 of depreciation left on the machine, has disappeared along with its earnings and profits, and the new corporation has $100,000 potential depreciation on the machine and as yet no earnings and profits, all at the expense of only a capital gains tax. The Treasury's answer to this device you will find in the Regulations, which say essentially that such a liquidation and reincorporation will be treated as a reorganization. We will be discussing Reorganizations later; the important point here is that in reorganization there is no step-up in basis. That is, the machine would have the same basis in the new corporation as it had in the old one, and the cash retained by X might be taxed as a dividend.

Other special liquidations

Section 332 applies to the special case of the liquidation of a subsidiary with a distribution of its assets to its parent. In cases covered by section 332 there is not even a capital gains tax to pay. Recognition of gain or loss is really just postponed, however, because the basis of each asset distributed to the parent does not change. This is specified in section 334 (b)(1). (Section 334(b)(2) contains a special rule we will discuss in the notes on the purchase and sale of a corporation.) It is possible, of course, that the subsidiary is not completely owned by the parent, and a liquidating distribution to a minority shareholder will be subject to section 331, not section 332. The latter applies to the position of the liquidating distribution that goes to the parent.

Section 333 is a very specialized provision of the Code affecting certain complete liquidations which take place wholly within a single calendar month. The principal value of the section is its postponement of recognition of the portion of a shareholder's gain on liquidation which would otherwise be recognized under section 331 and which is attributable to appreciation in the value of certain corporate assets unrealized by the corporation at the time of distribution. Section 333 will be extremely useful if the owners of a corporation wish to liquidate it but intend to carry on the business with the corporate assets—for example, as a partnership or a proprietorship—or if the corporation has few earnings and profits but a large amount of appreciated property.

Hoffman v. United States[4]

Solomon, Judge: Plaintiffs, Lee and Judy Hoffman, seek to recover $9,345.61 in federal income taxes paid in their 1958 through 1961 joint returns. The case was submitted on stipulated facts.

The issue is whether the Hoffmans' payments to a bonding company are deductible as losses in a transaction entered into for profit under section 165(c)(2), Internal Revenue Code of 1954, or whether these payments are either nonbusiness bad debts deductible under section 166 (d), or losses from the sale or exchange of capital assets under section 165 (f).

In 1958, Lee Hoffman organized Lee Hoffman Inc., to operate the contracting business which he had operated as an individual. He was president, director, and the sole stockholder. He received a salary for his services as president.

In 1958, General Insurance Company of America (the Bonding Company) agreed to furnish performance and payment bonds for the corporation's construction jobs and the Hoffmans individually agreed to indemnify the Bonding Company for any loss.

In 1959 and 1960, the corporation obtained construction contracts from Oak Lodge Sanitary Districts No. 1 and No. 2, and delivered two payment and performance bonds to the Sanitary Districts.

The corporation suffered financial losses. On April 11, 1961, to obtain additional funds, the corporation contracted not only with the Hoffmans individually, but also with the Bonding Company and The First National Bank of Oregon. The bank agreed to loan money to the corporation if the

---

[4]226 F. Supp. 884 (United States District Court, District of Oregon, 1967).

Bonding Company requested the loan and if the Hoffmans individually indemnified the bank and Bonding Company for all sums advanced. Ten days later the Hoffmans sold real property and turned over the entire proceeds, $20,400.83, on account of the funds advanced.

On November 20, 1961, the Bonding Company paid the bank in full, and it terminated the agreement with the bank. On the following day, the Bonding Company agreed to advance the corporation the funds needed to complete its construction contracts, and the Hoffmans individually agreed to indemnify the Bonding Company for any losses resulting from the advances.

Prior to November 30, 1962, the Hoffmans paid the Bonding Company $3,740.00. On November 30, 1962, the Hoffmans transferred $56,283.40 in cash, stocks and realty to the Bonding Company for a release from all liability, which amounted to in excess of $900,000.

In 1965, the Hoffmans filed a claim for a tax refund with Internal Revenue. They contended that they were entitled to deductions in their 1958-1961 tax returns under section 165 (c) (2) for the amounts paid the Bonding Company in 1961 and 1962. Internal Revenue rejected the claim.

Here, the Hoffmans raise the same issues they raised before Internal Revenue. The government contends Internal Revenue's decision is supported by either section 166(d) or section (f).

The issue under section 165 (c) (2) of whether a transaction is one entered into for profit is determined by the motive of the taxpayer and not by hard and fast rules. *United States* v. *Keeler,* 9 Cir. 1962, 308 F. 2d 424, *cert. denied* 373 U.S. 932 (1963). Lee Hoffman, sole stockholder and a salaried employee of the corporation, could expect substantial profits if the corporation was successful. The corporation could not conduct business without performance and payment bonds. The Hoffmans agreed to indemnify the Bonding Company only because they hoped to realize these profits.

I find that the transactions here were entered into for profit. See: *J. J. Shea* v. *Commissioner,* 36 T.C. 577 (1961), *aff'd per curiam* 5 Cir. 1964, 327 F. 2d 1002; *Rietzke* v. *Commissioner,* 40 T.C. 443 (1963); and *Horner* v. *Commissioner,* 35 T.C. 231 (1961).

The government relying on *Putnam* v. *Commissioner,* 352 U.S. 82 (1956), contends that regardless of the Hoffmans' motive, their loss is deductible only as a nonbusiness bad debt under section 166 (d).

In *Putnam,* the taxpayer was an incorporator and stockholder of a corporation. He guaranteed the corporation's notes and when it defaulted he paid $9,000 to the bank. He was unable to collect from the corporation, which had no assets. The Court held that Putnam was a guarantor and that he was only entitled to a worthless debt deduction because his liability to the bank was secondary. When Putnam paid the bank under a guaranty agreement, he became subrogated to the bank's rights against the corporation.

Putnam is not in point. Unlike Putnam, the Hoffmans were indemnitors. An indemnitor has a primary obligation to the creditor and he is not subrogated to the creditors' rights. See: *Howell* v. *Commissioner,* 8 Cir. 1934, 69 F. 2d 447.

In *Shea, supra,* and *Rietzke, supra, Putnam* was distinguished and guarantors of corporate debts were permitted to deduct their losses under section 165(c)(2). In each of these cases the taxpayer paid less than the full amount due under the guaranty agreement and he was relieved of liability. Since the taxpayer did not pay the full amount, the Court in both cases held that the taxpayer had not paid the corporation's debt and that the taxpayer's loss could not be treated as a worthless debt because he had no cause of action against the corporation.

The Hoffmans had a primary obligation to the Bonding Company. They did not reserve a right of subrogation against the corporation and after they paid the Bonding Company, they had no cause of action against the corporation. Their loss cannot be treated as a worthless debt because the corporation owed them no debt.

The Government contends that even if section 165(d) is not applicable, the Hoffmans are limited to a capital loss deduction under section 165(f) under *Keeler, supra.* Internal Revenue did not rely on section 165(f) when it made its original determination, and I find that the section is not applicable.

Section 165(f) only refers to losses "from sales or exchanges of capital assets." *Commissioner* v. *Condit,* 10 Cir. 1964, 333 F. 2d 585. Here there was no "sale or exchange."

I find that the Hoffmans incurred a loss in a transaction entered into for profit though not connected with their trade or business. They are therefore entitled to recover $9,345.61 plus interest and costs.

This opinion will serve as findings of fact and conclusions of law pursuant to Rule 52(a), Federal Rules of Civil Procedure.

Pennington and Fraser (B)

Following a comparison of the tax consequences of using the partnership and corporation forms (see Pennington and Fraser (A), Chapter Two), and considering limited liability, transferability of ownership, and other distinguishing features, Pennington and Fraser have decided to incorporate their venture.

Both men are concerned about selecting an appropriate capital structure. They intend that two thirds of the voting common stock will be held by Pennington and one third by Fraser, but they are not sure what other securities should be used. In addition, they have now decided that $60,000, rather than $45,000, will be needed to begin operations.

Pennington has agreed to put up the extra $15,000 without any change in the two thirds versus one third ownership of common stock. He is not even much concerned about receiving stock or securities for this amount—he is willing to pay more for his stock than Fraser, because Fraser will be doing most of the work; but if there should be an early liquidation, Pennington would like to recover his extra contribution before he and Fraser share the remainder of the assets two thirds and one third.

Partly because he has a substantial income and considerable investments, Pennington has given further thought to what might happen if the enterprise has a short and disastrous life. He would like to take advantage of any tax benefits that are available to an investor in the event of a loss on his investment. An investment-banker friend has suggested that he consider a "section 1244" corporation.

Fraser takes a more optimistic point of view in his planning. He has two children and would like to find ways of enabling them to share in the expected growth of the corporation. What he has in mind is finding some means of transferring to them the benefits of growth without his having to pay estate or gift taxes on the transfer. He also sees the possibility of the corporation generating profits that are not needed in its business, and he would like to see some provision for the owners to recover their investment from the company by a means less heavily taxed than dividends. Repayment of debt might be the answer, he feels, and the use of unneeded profits to pay off debt might be a way around the penalties of section 531.

Fraser's accountant has told him that preferred stock is hopelessly old-fashioned, that modern corporations use only debt and common stock. Fraser can see some sense in this statement, but he is not sure that it is entirely good advice.

What capital structure would you recommend?

Citizens Utilities Company

Citizens Utilities, incorporated in Delaware in 1935, provides a remarkably diversified line of utility services in ten states. At the end of 1965, the Company was supplying electricity in three states, telephone service in three, water in seven, gas in two, and ice and cold-storage facilities in one. The percentage of total revenue of about $16.7 million received from each service in 1965 was: electricity 34.2 per cent, telephone 26.6 per cent, water 23.4 per cent, gas 14.4 per cent, ice and cold storage 1.4 per cent.

In 1945, the company was taken over by an aggressive new management, headed by Mr. Richard L. Rosenthal. This management's philosophy is perhaps best expressed in quotations from the company's annual reports. In the 1955 report Mr. Rosenthal said:

> We are continuing to look at a number of acquisition possibilities but always in conformance with the fundamental philosophy previously conveyed to you: We have no desire to get bigger merely for the sake of size; we shall grow, but only as growth contributes to the goal of making Citizens Utilities Company better. Our test in this last connection continues to be increased *earnings per common share.*

In the 1962 annual report, Mr. Rosenthal said:

> We at Citizens do not subscribe to the "stateman" philosophy, which has become so endemic in professional management and academic circles. Adherents of this philosophy define management's role (and responsibility!) as the balancing of the interests of consumer, employee, general public and shareholder. To my knowledge, no labor union head even pretends that his role is anything but advocacy of what he believes to be the interests of his union's members. No organization representing consumers is concerned about the position or benefits of investors or employees as such. The executives of each such group firmly advocate, single-mindedly, the interest by which they are employed—and leave to government the responsibility for balancing consumer, employee, public and shareholder interests. . . .
>
> We are utterly committed to the viewpoint that we represent, advocate, and are responsible to the interest by whom we are employed: the owners of this business. Because we see our role and responsibilities as delineated above, we could not, in fact, be otherwise motivated.
>
> Although increases in investment facilities, revenues, number of customers, employees, and even in aggregate net income itself are all signposts of growth, they are meaningless to shareholders, and do not constitute progress, unless translated into the tangible results of per share earnings improvement, without undue weakening of a company's equity capital position.
>
> Thus, over the years, there has evolved the Citizens' theme:

"Growth in Service *founded on* Progress in Earnings." This is a fundamental orientation which has benefited consumers, employees and governments, too—as the data in this Report demonstrate. It was fashioned from the realistic awareness that in an incentive society, capital flows only to those enterprises which achieve for capital—that is, secure the requisite, compensatory return on investment. Adequate service to consumers in growth areas of an expanding economy depends on capital investment of very large magnitude. In turn, success in attracting such aggregates of capital—and such success is possible *only* with adequate earnings—permits the expansion of service to consumers, provides opportunity and security for employees and, of course, produces ever-increasing tax revenues for all levels of government. Thus, on realistic reflection, it is clear that it is this very emphasis on progress for our owners which has made it possible for us to continue to achieve for all.

The company's earnings record prior to the change in management and for 1956 to 1965 is shown in Table 1.

Table 1: **Citizens Utilities Company**
Record of earnings 1956–1965
(Years ending December 31)

Year	Operating revenue	Depreciation	Interest	Taxes	Net income after taxes
1945	$ 2,418,600	$ 277,204	$ 279,129	$ 406,338	$ 179,022
1956	6,512,772	656,861	384,413	1,231,686	1,126,298
1957	7,123,561	737,355	444,561	1,360,182	1,276,424
1958	8,063,788	924,177	446,964	1,750,539	1,402,535
1959	8,764,951	1,064,146	494,289	2,070,506	1,593,833
1960	9,980,161	1,225,765	648,097	2,241,313	1,873,668
1961	11,078,052	1,389,765	772,582	2,439,210	2,096,504
1962	12,350,546	1,495,027	978,470	2,588,500	2,320,715
1963	13,197,950	1,624,945	1,019,310	2,521,041	2,559,092
1964	14,685,141	1,750,871	943,677	2,770,783	3,426,415
1965	16,669,732	2,041,862	1,024,257	3,117,555	4,039,326

In 1955, the Company proposed to its stockholders a change in capital structure, designed to give increased importance to the company's use of stock dividends. Since 1947 the company had distributed a 3 per cent stock dividend each year (that is, three shares in dividends for every hundred shares owned) as well as paying a cash dividend. During these years the company had only one class of common stock outstanding, and hence stockholders had no choice as to the form in which they received their dividends. The changes proposed in 1955 offered considerably greater flexibility. The text of the proposal follows:

CITIZENS UTILITIES COMPANY

December 31, 1955

NOTICE OF SPECIAL MEETING OF SHAREHOLDERS

To the Shareholders of

CITIZENS UTILITIES COMPANY:

NOTICE IS HEREBY GIVEN that a special meeting of shareholders of CITIZENS UTILITIES COMPANY will be held on Friday, January 27, 1956, at 2:00 P.M. (E.S.T.) in the Music Room of the Roger Smith Hotel, 55 River Street, Stamford, Connecticut, for the following purposes, namely:

(1) To consider and take action upon a proposal approved by the Board of Directors of the Company that the Company's Certificate of Incorporation, as heretofore amended be further amended by striking out in its entirety, all of Article FOURTH of said Certificate of Incorporation and substituting in lieu thereof the text appearing in Exhibit A annexed hereto;

(2) To transact any and all other business that may properly come before the meeting.

Shareholders of record at the close of business on December 8, 1955 will be entitled to vote at the meeting. If you do not expect to be present personally at the meeting, the Board of Directors of the Company requests that you please date and sign the attached Proxy and return it. Postage has been paid and you need affix no postage.

By Order of the Board of Directors,

R. A. Dickerson, *Secretary*

Exhibit A: Text of proposed amendment to the certificate of incorporation of Citizens Utilities Company

"FOURTH: (a) The total number of shares of stock which this corporation shall have authority to issue is Three Million Two Hundred Fifty Thousand (3,250,000) shares of which Two Hundred Fifty Thousand (250,000) shares shall be shares of Preferred Stock without par value, One Million Five Hundred Thousand (1,500,000) shares shall be shares of Common Stock Series A of the par value of Thirty-Three and One-Third (33-1/3¢) Cents each amounting in the aggregate to Five Hundred Thousand ($500,000) Dollars, and One Million Five Hundred Thousand (1,500,000) shares shall be shares of Common Stock Series B of the par value of Thirty-Three and One-Third (33-1/3¢) Cents each amounting in the aggregate to Five Hundred Thousand ($500,000) Dollars.

(b) The Preferred Stock may be issued from time to time in one or more series, and in such amounts as may be determined by the Board of Directors. The designations, powers, preferences and relative, participating, optional, conversion and other special rights, and the qualifications, limitations and restrictions thereof, of the Preferred Stock of each series, shall be such as may be stated and expressed by the Board of Directors (authority so to do being hereby expressly granted) to the full extent now or hereafter permitted by the laws of Delaware, except as otherwise provided in the Certificate of Incorporation, or any amendment thereto or any Certificate setting forth the resolutions fixing the terms of any series, and stated and expressed in a resolution or resolutions providing for the issue of Preferred Stock of such series.

(c) The designations, powers, preferences and relative, participating, optional, conversion and other special rights, and the qualifications, limitations and restrictions thereof, of the Common Stock Series A and the Common Stock Series B shall be as follows:

(1) Whenever full dividends have been paid or declared and funds set apart for the payment of dividends on each series of Preferred Stock which may hereafter be issued and outstanding, for the current dividend period and for all past dividend periods in respect of which dividends are cumulative and remain unpaid, and a cash dividend upon the Common Stock Series B shall at any time and from time to time be declared and paid, there shall at that time or any time thereafter but within the time limits hereinafter in this paragraph set forth, be declared and paid a stock dividend or dividends on the Common Stock Series A payable in shares of Common Stock Series A, the fair value as of the respective dates of declaration (as hereinafter defined) of such stock dividend or dividends paid or payable on each share of Common Stock Series A during any calendar year to be equivalent to the cash dividend or dividends paid or payable on each share of Common Stock Series B during such calendar year pursuant to this paragraph. For the purpose of the foregoing sentence the determination of the fair value of the Common Stock Series A shall be made as of the respective dates of declaration of such dividend or dividends by the Board of Directors of the corporation in its sole discretion and such determination shall be final and conclusive. Without limiting the generality of the foregoing, the Board of Directors may, in making such determination of fair value, consider the bid and asked price of the Common Stock Series A on the business day next preceding the date of the

declaration of such dividend (or if not available for such date on the next preceding date on which such quotation is available) as quoted by the National Quotation Bureau, Inc. or an organization performing functions similar thereto and such other factors as the Board of Directors may deem to be relevant, including without limitation, that the value of such stock after the record date may be reduced by the declaration of the dividend and any factors which would affect the market value of such stock dividend shares. The Board of Directors of the corporation may in its sole discretion declare a dividend or dividends on the Common Stock Series A on dates different from the dates on which a cash dividend or dividends are declared on the Common Stock Series B and may fix separate record dates and/or separate payment dates different from the record dates or payment dates of the cash dividend or dividends declared on the Common Stock Series B, provided however, that the record date and payment date of any dividend on the Common Stock Series A shall be within one year from the date of declaration thereof, and provided further that the fair value as of the respective dates of declaration (as herein defined) of all stock dividends paid on each share of Common Stock Series A during any calendar year pursuant to this paragraph shall be equivalent to the total cash dividends paid only on each share of Common Stock Series B during such calendar year pursuant to this paragraph. This paragraph shall be applicable only where a dividend is declared on the Common Stock Series B payable only in cash and the Board of Directors does not at the same time declare a dividend in an equal amount only in cash on the Common Stock Series A, which the Board of Directors shall have the right to do. The provisions of this paragraph are not intended to cover, or apply to, any case where a dividend is declared on the Common Stock Series B payable in stock or any other property in which event the same dividend shall be declared at the same time on the Common Stock Series A as provided in paragraph (4) of the subdivision (c) of this Article FOURTH. The corporation shall not issue fractional shares in satisfaction of any stock dividend but in lieu of fractional shares it shall issue scrip certificates (exchangeable, together with other scrip certificates aggregating one or more full shares, for stock certificates representing such full share or shares of stock), for any fraction of a share of stock, the terms and form of which are to be approved by the Board of Directors of the corporation. Until the exchange thereof for certificates for full share of stock, the holders of such scrip certificates shall not be entitled to receive dividends or to vote or to any other rights and /or privileges as stockholders of the corporation. The Board of Directors of the corporation shall, in any instance, have the full power and authority to prescribe other methods by which settlement for fractional shares shall be made, in lieu of delivering such scrip certificates for fractional shares, and may, without limiting the generality of the foregoing, make a cash settlement in respect thereof in such amount as shall be determined by the Board of Directors or provide for the combination of such fractions into a number of whole shares of stock equal to the aggregate of the fractional shares which the holders of the shares of Common Stock of the corporation would otherwise be entitled to receive and the delivery thereof to the corporation or its designee as agent for said stockholders to sell the said whole shares of stock and to pay the net proceeds of the sale to those stockholders who would otherwise have been entitled to fractional shares pro rata in accordance with their respective fractional share interests and upon such other terms as may be provided by the Board of Directors of the corporation.

(2) The Common Stock Series A, at the option of the respective holders thereof, shall be exchangeable for Common Stock Series B of the corporation, at any time subsequent to the expiration of the seventy five day exchange period provided for in subparagraph (e) hereof, and from time to time, subject to the provision hereinafter set forth in the ratio of one (1) share of Common Stock Series B for one (1) share of Common Stock Series A (whether or not any dividend shall have been declared on the Common Stock Series A and remain unpaid but this shall not prevent a stockholder who shall exchange his shares after a record date from receiving any dividend payable to Series A stockholders of record on that date), upon surrender to the corporation or to its transfer agent of the certificates of Common Stock Series A, so to be exchanged, duly endorsed in blank for transfer; provided however that if any such shares of Common Stock Series A are surrendered for exchange on or between the date on which a cash dividend is declared on the Common Stock Series B and the date fixed by the Board of Directors of the corporation for determining the holders of the Common Stock Series B entitled to receive such cash dividend, the said shares of Common Stock Series A shall be exchanged for shares of Common Stock Series B on and as of the business day next following the record date for determining the holders of the Common Stock Series B entitled to receive such cash dividend and until such exchange is so made any such stockholder shall be treated for all purposes as the holder of the shares of Common Stock Series A so surrendered for exchange. So long as any of the Common Stock Series A remains outstanding, there shall be reserved such number of shares of Common Stock Series B for exchange as shall be required pursuant to the provisions herein contained.

(3) The Board of Directors of the corporation shall have the right, in its sole discretion, to require all of the holders of the Common Stock Series A to exchange all of their Common Stock Series A for Common Stock Series B of the corporation in the ratio of one (1) share of Common Stock Series B for one (1) share of Common Stock Series A (whether or not any dividend shall have been declared on the Common Stock Series A and remain upaid but this shall not

prevent a stockholder who shall exchange his shares after a record date from receiving any dividend payable to Series A stockholders of record on that date). Notice of the requirement for such exchange shall be given by the corporation at least thirty days prior to the date fixed for such exchange to the holders of record of all the outstanding Common Stock Series A and an affidavit of mailing of such notice by an employee of the corporation or any employee of the transfer agent shall be conclusive evidence of the mailing of such notice. If notice of such exchange shall have been duly given as herein provided, and any holder of Common Stock Series A shall not have surrendered all his certificates of Common Stock Series A to the corporation or its transfer agent for exchange, duly endorsed in blank for transfer, then from and after the exchange date so specified in the notice, any and all rights and privileges of such holders of Common Stock Series A, as holders of Common Stock Series A, shall cease and terminate, except the right to receive shares of Common Stock Series B in exchange for his shares of Common Stock Series A as hereinabove provided, and from and after the exchange date so specified in the notice all Common Stock Series A outstanding shall be and become Common Stock Series B with the effect that each holder of the outstanding shares of Common Stock Series A shall thereupon be and become the holder of one share of Common Stock Series B for every share of Common Stock Series A then held by him.

(4) In all other respects the designations, powers, preferences and relative, participating, optional, conversion and other special rights, and the qualifications, limitations and restrictions thereof, of the Common Stock Series A and the Common Stock Series B shall be the same, and without limiting the generality of the foregoing, in the event any dividends payable in any class of stock of the corporation, or in any property, are declared upon the shares of Common Stock Series B of the corporation (which the corporation by action of its Board of Directors shall have the full power and authority to do) the same dividend shall be declared upon the Common Stock Series A of the corporation and in the event any dividends payable in any class of stock of the corporation, or in any property, (except stock dividends which are paid to equalize cash dividends as hereinabove set forth) are declared upon the shares of Common Stock Series A of the corporation, (which the corporation by action of its Board of Directors shall have the full power and authority to do) the same dividend shall be declared upon the Common Stock Series B of the corporation and in the event a cash dividend shall be declared on the shares of Common Stock Series A of the corporation (which the corporation by action of its Board of Directors shall have the full power and authority to do, whenever full dividends have been paid or declared and funds set apart for the payment of dividends on each series of Preferred Stock which may hereafter be issued and out-

standing, for the current dividend period and for all past dividend periods in respect of which dividends are cumulative and remain unpaid) an equal cash dividend shall be declared on the shares of Common Stock Series B of the corporation.

(d) Unless otherwise expressly required by applicable law, each holder of Common Stock Series A and Common Stock Series B shall at every meeting of the stockholders be entitled to one vote in person or by written proxy signed by him for each share of Common Stock Series A and Common Stock Series B owned by him and shall be entitled and required to vote as part of a single class, i.e., Common Stock (without distinction as to Series A or Series B) upon all such matters as may come before the stockholders including without limitation the election of directors, which shall be decided by majority vote of the Common Stock present or represented by proxy and entitled to vote at the meeting. The stockholders of this corporation shall have no preemptive right to subscribe to any issue of shares of stock of this corporation now or hereafter made.

(e) Upon this amendment becoming effective, each holder of the outstanding shares of the old common stock shall thereupon be and become the holder of one share of the new Common Stock Series B for every share of the old common stock then held by him. Promptly after this amendment becomes effective each holder of the new Common Stock Series B shall have the right for a period of seventy five days and upon such terms and conditions as shall be prescribed by the Board of Directors of the corporation to exchange any portion of the Common Stock Series B owned by him into shares of Common Stock Series A on a share for share basis and any holder not exercising such exchange right within such seventy five day period shall not at any time thereafter be entitled to exchange any shares of Common Stock Series B into shares of Common Stock Series A.

CITIZENS   UTILITIES
COMPANY

December 31, 1955

Fellow Shareholders:

We have reached an important point in the career of our Company. And so I send you this personal message to emphasize the desirability of the approval you are asked to give in connection with a voluntary reclassification of the common shares of Citizens, covered in this letter and enclosures.

Most of you are aware that Citizens' record of the past ten years has not been achieved by blind adherence to orthodox approaches, methods and solutions to problems. As management, we have not been inhibited or deterred by tradition and precedent when there was no fundamental logic or reason for following these. As a company, we have pursued new and pioneering concepts and techniques when these indicated benefits to our Company and our fellow shareholders.

For a decade now, we have had to contend each year with the perennial problem of how best to finance Citizens' capital requirements. The increasingly large construction and acquisition budgets, resulting from the continuing expansion of our Company, necessitate substantial investment of funds each year to pursue our program. Our study of the problem over ten years has led us to the conclusion that Citizens' progress can continue best to be enhanced in the interests of its shareholders if the equity segment of our capital requirements are provided—*as much as possible*—through the use of retained earnings, maintaining the equity portion of our total capitalization at satisfactorily high levels; and minimizing public sale of additional shares of stock to finance expansion, because this latter course would result in the dilution of the individual shareholder's equity.

The disadvantages of a high cash dividend payout by a growing company—such as Citizens—are patent. Assuming that $1,000,000 of cash dividends were paid and the company paying it required—and could productively use—such amount of equity capital for expansion, it would have to issue at least $1,150,000 in new stock, at then current market prices, in order to recoup the $1,000,000 of cash dividends paid out. The difference, of course, arises from the direct expenses of registration, accounting and legal fees, and compensation to investment bankers for underwriting the issue. The shareholders of the company pursuing this course would, as a group, suffer dilution even greater than 15%. The dividends received would be subject to income taxes. Thus, as a group, the shareholders, after payment of income taxes, would retain appreciably less than the $1,000,000 of dividends paid with which to attempt to maintain their pro rata ownership of the company. This pro rata ownership could only be maintained by the purchase of all of the additional shares being offered to raise the required equity capital.

Obviously with materially less than $1,000,000 of the cash dividends retained after taxes, the shareholders, as a group, could not purchase the $1,150,000 additional common stock offered to recoup the funds paid out in dividends; and their pro rata ownership would necessarily suffer dilution accordingly. If, on the other hand, the cash dividend funds were retained and a stock dividend paid in its stead, the company would not have the additional $150,000 expense of the new stock flotation, would have the $1,000,000 required for equity capital expansion, and the shareholders' position would not be diluted at all.

For some months, we have been working intensively on what I think may properly be called a unique long-term solution of this problem. The method for achieving this result is a voluntary reclassification of the common shares of Citizens. The plan worked out calls for an amendment to our Company's Certificate of Incorporation. We are submitting the proposed amendment (copy attached to enclosed Notice of Special Meeting) with the unqualified recommendation of both our Board of Directors and management for approval by shareholders at a special meeting being called for January 27, 1956.

The plan provides that, after adoption of the proposed amendment to our Certificate of Incorporation, all of the shares of Common Stock now outstanding will automatically be reclassified into a new Series B Common Stock, upon which it is now intended that dividends will be paid *only and entirely in cash*. The amendment to the Certificate further provides that, for 75 days following adoption of the amendment, all shareholders will have the right to exchange all or any portion of what will then be their Series B (cash dividend) shares for an equal number of shares of a new Series A Common Stock, *upon which it is now intended that dividends will be paid only in shares of stock. The privilege of exchanging Series B (cash dividend) shares for Series A (stock dividend) shares will expire at the end of the 75-day period.* However, by its terms, the Series A (stock dividend) shares will thereafter be fully convertible, on a share for share basis, into Series B (cash dividend) shares, at all times subsequent to its issuance — except for the brief interval between the dates of the declaration of cash dividends on Series B Common Stock and the record dates set for determination of shareholders entitled to receive each such dividend.

The terms of the proposed amendment provide that the value of the shares of stock issued as dividends on the Series A shares will each year be equal to the cash dividends on the Series B shares.

The text of the proposed amendment contains a provision permitting the Directors to declare cash dividends on the Common Series A (in which event the same cash dividend is payable on the shares of Common Stock Series B). This provision has been included in the amendment in order to afford the Company flexibility in the event it should become necessary or desirable at any time in the future to declare a cash dividend on the Common Stock Series A for some reason which the Board of Directors cannot now anticipate. The Board of Directors has no present intention of declaring cash dividends on the Common Stock Series A. It is the present intention of the Board that only stock dividends will be declared on Common Stock Series A of a fair value equal each year to the cash dividends which may be declared on the Common Stock Series B.

To provide flexibility for future issuance of shares of stock for distribution as stock dividends or for other corporate purposes, it is proposed to provide for an authorization of 1,500,000 shares which will be designated as Common Stock Series A and 1,500,000 shares which will be designated as Common Stock Series B, of 33 1/3¢ par value each.

Adoption of this reclassification amendment will permit each shareholder thereafter, by exchange or non-exchange for Series A shares, to select the type (or combination of types) of dividend which he desires to receive—payable in shares of common stock, cash, or any combination thereof.

The reclassification proposed for your approval will be of real benefit to our Company. The measure of benefit will largely depend on the extent to which shareholders elect to receive Series A shares. The results of the shareholder survey on dividend policy which was conducted last spring gave us the conviction that a sufficient number of shareholders would elect to exchange for Series A shares to make the proposed reclassification worthwhile. In the interest of our Company, I urge you to make such election to the maximum extent possible. I would do so even though no direct, immediate benefit flowed to our shareholders. However, there is a direct, immediate benefit; and it is material. As you know, stock dividends as a general rule are not taxable under our income tax laws. We have obtained a ruling from the United States Treasury Department that the *receipt* of shares of stock as dividends on the Series A shares will not create income subject to taxation.

Here it may be appropriate to outline the general rules of taxation governing the disposition of stock dividends. In the case of nontaxable stock dividends, such as the shares of stock which will be issued as dividends on Series A Common Stock, the tax basis or cost of the original stock is allocated between the original stock and the shares received as a stock dividend. The holding period of the shares received as a stock dividend is determined by the purchase date of the underlying stock on which the stock dividend is received. Thus, if a shareholder sells the stock dividends received on Series A stock, the proceeds so received are taxable, but only at capital gains rates—and only to the extent that the proceeds of the sale exceed the adjusted tax cost basis of the shares sold. In addition, only one-half of a capital gain is subject to taxation if the original stock on which the stock dividends are received was purchased more than six months prior to the sale of the shares received as stock dividends. Thus, the capital gains treatment accorded the sale of stock dividends is of very real benefit to shareholders in all income brackets. As you know, the *maximum* tax rate on long-term capital gains is 25%. Hence, those shareholders who elect to receive Series A stock will not only advance the Company's interests; they will also benefit themselves.

We should also point out that the Treasury Department's ruling provides that no tax will be payable by any shareholder in connection with the reclassification of all shares of present common stock into the new Series B shares or upon the subsequent exchange of such Series B (cash dividend) shares for Series A (stock dividend) shares during the period allowed for the exchange. The Treasury Department has also ruled that no tax will be payable in connection with the subsequent conversion of Series A (stock dividend) shares into Series B (cash dividend) shares by any shareholder who elects to make such conversion.

With the exception of the dividend provisions above referred to, all other rights of the holders of the Common Stock Series A and the Common Stock Series B will be identical.

There is enclosed Notice of Special Meeting of the Shareholders of our Company to be held on January 27, 1956 at 2 o'clock in the afternoon Eastern Standard Time. There is also enclosed a Proxy for your use, in the event that you cannot attend the meeting in person. It is intended that the Proxies solicited will be voted in favor of the proposed amendment to the Company's Certificate of Incorporation, in order to effect the reclassification of the present outstanding shares of Common Stock into Series A and Series B shares.

If you cannot attend the meeting in person, will you please be sure to sign and return the enclosed Proxy at your very earliest convenience. No postage is required. We earnestly solicit the early return of our Proxy because we believe that the proposed reclassification will be of very great benefit to both our Company and our fellow shareholders. Your cooperation in prompt return of the Proxy will help us keep the cost of this meeting at a minimum.

If shareholder ratification is given to the proposal to amend the Company's Certificate of Incorporation to effect the reclassification of the shares of Common Stock into Series A and B shares, the Amendment to the Certificate will be filed promptly with the Secretary of State in Delaware, in which state our Company is incorporated. You will thereafter be notified of the effective date of the amendment, in order that you may promptly make your decision as to whether you will:

(a) retain the Series B (cash dividend) shares into which your present shares of Citizens' common will automatically be reclassified; or

(b) exchange the Series B (cash dividend) shares for Series A (stock dividend) shares during the period provided for such exchange.

Cordially yours,

Richard L. Rosenthal, *President*

The stockholders voted overwhelmingly in favor of the changes, which went into effect in 1956. A record of earnings per share and of cash and stock dividends from 1953 through 1965 is given in Table 2.

Table 2: Citizens Utilities Company
Record of earnings per share, cash and stock dividends
1953–1965

Year	Earnings (per share)*	Cash dividends (per share) (in dollars)	Stock dividends (per share) (in per cent)
		Old common†	
1953	$ .35	.18	3.0
1954	.38	.22	3.0
1955	.39	.23	3.0
		Series B‡	Series A
1956	.43	.45	6.5
1957	.49	.44	6.5
1958	.53	.50	5.25
1959	.61	.52½	3.75
1960	.71	.56	4.0
1961	.80	.60	2.4
1962	.88	.68	3.45
1963	.97	.74	3.7
1964	1.31	.80	3.72
1965	1.54	.99	3.3

*Earnings per share based on 2,625,359 total shares of Series A and B outstanding December 31, 1965.

†Cash dividends adjusted for 3% stock dividends and 2-for-1 stock split in 1959.

‡Cash dividends adjusted for 2-for-1 stock split in 1959.

Table 3 shows the approximate price record for the company's common stock. The prices are adjusted for stock dividends and for a 2-for-1 stock split in 1959. The adjusted prices show what a Series A and Series B holder would have paid in prior years for each share held at the end of 1965. Prices for 1965 are unadjusted market prices.

Table 3: Citizens Utilities Company
Approximate price record
Common stock 1953–1965
(Over-the-counter bid prices)

Year	Old common		Old common*		Old common†	
	High	Low	High	Low	High	Low
1953	$15\frac{1}{4}$	$10\frac{7}{8}$	7	5	$4\frac{3}{4}$	$3\frac{3}{8}$
1954	$18\frac{3}{4}$	$15\frac{5}{8}$	$8\frac{7}{8}$	$7\frac{1}{8}$	6	$4\frac{7}{8}$
1955	$17\frac{1}{4}$	$14\frac{1}{2}$	$8\frac{3}{8}$	7	$5\frac{3}{4}$	$4\frac{7}{8}$

Year			Series B‡		Series A§	
1956			$8\frac{1}{8}$	$6\frac{3}{8}$	$5\frac{5}{8}$	$4\frac{3}{4}$
1957			$8\frac{1}{8}$	$6\frac{1}{4}$	$5\frac{7}{8}$	$4\frac{1}{2}$
1958			$11\frac{3}{4}$	$6\frac{3}{4}$	$9\frac{1}{4}$	$5\frac{1}{4}$
1959			$15\frac{1}{4}$	$11\frac{3}{4}$	$13\frac{1}{4}$	10
1960			$17\frac{5}{8}$	$11\frac{7}{8}$	$16\frac{1}{4}$	$11\frac{1}{4}$
1961			$30\frac{3}{4}$	$17\frac{3}{4}$	$32\frac{1}{2}$	$16\frac{1}{2}$
1962			$27\frac{1}{2}$	16	29	15
1963			$24\frac{3}{4}$	$20\frac{1}{4}$	23	$19\frac{1}{4}$
1964			$26\frac{3}{8}$	$21\frac{1}{2}$	$25\frac{3}{8}$	$20\frac{3}{4}$
1965			$37\frac{1}{8}$	26	37	$26\frac{1}{4}$

*Adjusted for 2-for-1 stock split in 1959 and 3% stock dividends in 1953, 1954, and 1955.

†Adjusted for 2-for-1 stock split in 1959 and stock dividends 1953 through 1964.

‡Adjusted for 2-for-1 stock split in 1959.

§Adjusted for 2-for-1 stock split in 1959 and stock dividends 1956 through 1964.

The company's annual report for 1962 stated:

Since 1956, when our two-Series capitalization came into being, our Board of Directors has, as a matter of policy, confined its dividend declarations on the Series A shares to stock dividends payable in Series A stock. Similarly, the Board has confined declarations on the Series B shares to cash dividend payments. The Board has the power, under our Certificate of Incorporation, to declare cash dividends on both Series or stock dividends on both Series. However, our Board has indicated that so long as the current policy serves the best interests of both our Company and its shareholders, the Board intends to continue to declare stock dividends *only* on Series A shares; and cash dividends *only* on Series B shares.

The importance of limiting the payment of cash dividends in facilitating expansion is shown in the source and application of funds statement in Table 4. For comparison purposes, partial source and application statements are given in Table 5 for two public utilities of about the same size as Citizens, neither of which distributed any stock dividends during the period 1955–1965.

Table 4: Citizens Utilities Company
Sources of funds for additions to plant
1955–1965 inclusive

Source			Total funds
Earnings $22,739,872			
Depreciation 13,525,878			
Cash dividends paid 4,364,896			
Net cash generated from earnings			$31,900,854
Cash generated from sales of property, insurance recoveries and salvage of property retired			12,301,748

	As of 12-31-65	As of 12-31-54	
Change in long-term debt*	$21,481,557	$8,897,500	12,584,057
Change in current position	(3,085,367)	(129,350)	2,956,017
Change in customer advances	2,738,778	139,653	2,599,125
Change in deferred taxes	1,932,567	144,840	1,787,727
Change in operating reserves	1,623,612	8,024	1,615,588
Change in contributions in aid of construction	420,260	194,258	226,362
Change in deferred debits	912,461	310,103	(602,358)
Total cash generated			$65,369,120
Change in gross plant	71,052,905	20,834,808	$50,218,097
Property retirements (cumulative)			15,151,023
Gross additions to plant			$65,369,120

*Net of sinking fund applications and call of bonds.

Table 5: Citizens Utilities Company
      Partial source-and-application-of-funds statement for two public utilities
      compared with Citizens Utilities Company

Source	Citizens Utilities Company	California Pacific Utilities Company	Community Public Service Company
A. Plant additions			
1. Gross plant 12-31-54..............	$20,835,000	$19,507,000	$28,859,000
2. Increase in gross plant 1-1-55			
through 12-31-65	50,218,000	33,459,000	42,938,000
3. Percentage increase in gross plant			
1-1-55 through 12-31-65	241%	172%	149%
B. Funds raised from			
1. Earnings, less cash dividends, plus			
depreciation	$31,901,000	$12,848,000	$20,165,000
2. Increase from sale of debt 1-1-55			
through 12-31-65	12,584,000	11,433,000	17,024,000
3. Increase from sale of common stock			
or equivalents.................	-0-	10,820,000	-0-
4. Increase from sale of convertible			
preferred stock not converted......	-0-	-0-	-0-
5. Increase from sale of non-			
convertible preferred stock........	-0-	13,000	8,880,000
Total	$44,485,000	$35,101,000	$46,069,000
C. 1. Earnings per share—1954*	$ .38	$ 1.05	$ 1.13
2. Earnings per share—1965.........	1.54	1.50	2.14
3. Percentage increase—1965 vs. 1954*	305.3%	42.9%	89.4%
D. 1. Dividends per share—1954*	$ .22	$ .71¼	.67
2. Dividends per share—1965	.99	1.00	1.40
3. Percentage increase 1965 vs. 1954* .	350.0%	40.4%	109.0%
E. 1. Mean market price—1954*	7⅞	12⅜	14⅛
2. Mean market price—1965	†31⅜	31⅜	45¾
3. Percentage increase—1965 vs. 1954*	†301.6%	155.6%	245.1%
F. 1. Per cent common equity 12-31-54 ..	40.5	29.5	49.2
2. Per cent common equity 12-31-65 ..	54.9	49.0	21.1

*Adjusted for stock dividends and stock splits

†Series "B" common stock

Various financial data for Citizens are given in Tables 6, 7, and 8.

Table 6: Citizens Utilities Company
Consolidated balance sheet
December 31, 1965

Assets

Cash	$	997,866
Special deposits, prepayments and misc.		837,061
Receivables net		1,949,203
Materials and supplies		578,068
Current assets		$ 4,362,198
Property, plant, and equipment and intangibles	$71,052,905	
Less depreciation	14,570,992	
Fixed assets		56,481,913
Other assets and deferred debits		912,461
Total assets		$61,756,572

Liabilities

Accounts payable and accrued expenses, including taxes	$7,447,565	
Customers advances for construction	2,738,778	
Other deferred credits and operating reserves	1,623,612	
Deferred federal income taxes	1,932,567	
Contributions in aid of construction	420,260	
Current liabilities		$14,162,782

Long-term debt
Bank loans (prime rate—credit expires 12/9/66) 3,800,000
First mortgage and collateral trust

Bonds		3,198,000
$3\frac{1}{2}$% due 1972		2,225,000
$3\frac{1}{2}$% 1980		990,000
$3\frac{7}{8}$% 1982		2,251,000
$5\frac{1}{2}$% 1990		4,000,000
$4\frac{5}{8}$% 1991		4,000,000
$4\frac{5}{8}$% 1992		783,000

$4\frac{1}{2}$% debentures, due 1977
2%, 35-year mortgage note—Rural Electrification
Administration 234,557

Total long-term debt $21,481,557

Common stock
Authorized: 7 million shares   Series A
9 million shares   Series B
(both of $1 par value)

Issued: 1,885,323 shares Series A	$1,885,323	
740,036 shares Series B	740,036	
Capital surplus	10,281,830	
Earned surplus	13,205,044	
Owners equity		26,112,233
Total liabilities and equity		$61,756,572

Table 7: Citizens Utilities Company
   Consolidated statement of income
   Year ending December 31, 1965

Operating revenues:

Electric	$5,569,482
Gas	2,346,325
Water	4,183,788
Telephone	4,338,173
Cold storage and ice	231,964
Total	$16,669,732

Deductions from operating revenue:

Electricity and gas purchases	2,124,970
Operating and maintenance expenses	4,572,022
Depreciation	2,041,862
Taxes other than income taxes	1,440,066
Federal and state income taxes	1,677,489
Total	11,856,409
Net operating income	$ 4,813,323
Other income	53,676
Gross income	$ 4,866,999

Income deductions:

Interest on long-term debt	$1,010,180
Amortization of bond discount and expense	8,980
Other interest	14,077
Interest during construction	(229,282)
Miscellaneous	23,718
Total	827,673
Net income	$ 4,039,326

Table 8: Citizens Utilities Company
   Shares and dividends
   1956–1965

Year	Series B			Series A		
	No. of shares outstanding year end	Dividends per share	Total cash dividends	No. of shares outstanding year end	Stock dividends during year	
					No. shares	Value
1956	243,275	$ .90	$217,219	766,767	47,598	$ 658,486
1957	270,884	.90	236,601	788,275	49,125	679,722
1958	296,969	1.00	289,461	802,972	40,787	777,491
1959*	602,838	† .52½	314,770	1,657,593	‡60,554	854,479
1960	606,912	.56	338,894	1,720,349	66,837	962,274
1961	611,197	.60	366,581	1,757,466	41,408	1,067,500
1962	618,788	.68	417,001	1,810,864	60,995	1,119,523
1963	653,053	.74	472,215	1,843,376	66,780	1,352,663
1964	708,219	.80	544,937	1,856,117	67,913	1,458,554
1965	740,036	.99	718,699	1,885,323	61,025	1,830,866

*Stock split 2 for 1 on May 14, 1959

†Dividend of $.52½ paid before split and $.26½ after, so dividends for the year were $1.05 figured on each old share, or $.52½ figured on each new share.

‡The stock dividends for 1959 were entirely in new (post stock split) shares.

Litton Industries, Inc.

On February 10, 1966, Litton Industries mailed the following letter to its stockholders:

LITTON INDUSTRIES, INC.

February 10, 1966

To Our Stockholders:

At the annual Meeting held on December 4, 1965, the stockholders of Litton Industries authorized 8,000,000 shares of Preference Stock. The first issue of this new stock, to be known as Convertible Preference Stock, Participating Series, is being offered exclusively to stockholders in a voluntary exchange for Common Stock and Series A $3 Cumulative Convertible Preferred Stock owned by them as of the date of record.

The new Participating Series of Preference Stock is a security designed to provide each investor with an opportunity to participate fully in the growth of Litton. In addition, this new instrument offers an unusual range of choices that enable the investor to fulfill his individual investment goals each year by the selection of a cash return, increased equity position through an automatic reinvestment feature at no cost, or a combination of both.

The new Participating Preference Stock is convertible each year into an increasing number of Litton Common shares at a compound rate of more than 3% annually. In the first year each share of Preference Stock is convertible into one share of Common Stock; in the second year each share of Preference is convertible into 1.0309 shares of Common; in the third year 1.0628 shares; and by 1989, 2.0145 shares. Thus, without any action on his part and without tax or other costs, the investor in Participating Preference Stock will hold a security convertible into a continually increasing number of Litton Common shares.

The increasing conversion privilege offers the Preference holder an attractive alternative. He may sell up to 3% of his Preference shares each year without reducing the number of Common shares into which the remaining Preference Stock is convertible. Thus, in the second year, an investor holding 100 shares of Preference may sell three shares and receive a cash return. Even though he does this, the remaining 97 shares of Preference are still convertible into 100 Common Stock. The profit realized from the sale is taxable at capital gain rates.

Another key feature of the Preference Stock is an optional redemption feature designed to protect the investor by providing a cash return similar to that afforded by a fixed income security. This feature fixes a redemption value which increases each year from $51.65 in 1967 to $100.95 in 1989, in those years when the Board of Directors makes such redemption right available, a stockholder may sell to the Company up to 3% of his Preference shares at the price set forth in a schedule of prices.

When a cash dividend is paid on the Common, a cash dividend will also be paid on the Preference Stock, equal to the rate of the cash dividend on the Common multiplied by the conversion ratio at the time of the dividend.

To the extent that a stock dividend is paid on the Common in excess of 2 1/2% per year, an amount equal to the excess would be added to the conversion right of the Preference shares for that year.

In addition, the Preference stockholder participates in the affairs of Litton with one vote for each Preference share, the same voting right as one share of Common or one share of Preferred. In the event of liquidation, the new Preference has a prior claim over the Common of $25 per share.

In summary, the new Participating Preference Stock combines most of the benefits of both conventional convertible Preferred and Common Stock:

1. Full participation in the growth of Litton.
2. Automatic reinvestment in Litton without tax or other costs.
3. Opportunity for a cash return taxable at capital gain rates.
4. Stable return on investment.
5. Safety through priority in the event of liquidation.

Litton Common stockholders may exchange up to 12 1/2% of their shares for the new Preference issue on the basis of one Common share for one Preference share. Litton Preferred stockholders may exchange 100% of their shares on the basis of one Preferred share for two shares of the new Preference Stock.

I urge you to give this exchange offer your most thoughtful attention and to examine its benefits carefully. We regard it as another significant opportunity to serve the interests of our stockholders.

Sincerely yours,

CHARLES B. THORNTON,
Chairman of the Board of Directors

Exchange Offer

February 10, 1966

To the Stockholders of Litton Industries, Inc.:

By this Exchange Offer, Litton Industries, Inc. ("Company") hereby offers to issue to its stockholders as of the close of business on the above date shares of the Company's new Convertible Preference Stock Participating Series, par value $2.50 ("Participating Series") in exchange for shares of its $1 par value Common Stock ("Common Stock") and its Series A $3 Cumulative Convertible Preferred Stock ("Series A Preferred Stock") surrendered in accordance with this Exchange Offer.

A holder of the Common Stock of the Company may exchange up to 12 1/2% of the Common Stock of the Company held by him on the date of this Exchange Offer for shares of the Participating Series. The rate of such exchange will be 1 share of the Participating Series for 1 share of Common Stock. No fractional shares will be offered or issued.

A holder of the Series A Preferred Stock of the Company may exchange up to 100% of the Series A Preferred Stock of the Company held by him on the date of this Exchange Offer for shares of the Participating Series. The rate of such exchange will be 2 shares of Participating Series for 1 share of Series A Preferred Stock. No adjustment will be made for accrued dividends.

The details of this Exchange Offer and the instructions on the manner in which it may be accepted are set forth below together with descriptions of the Participating Series, the Series A Preferred Stock and the Common Stock of the Company.

Details of the exchange offer

The Exchange Offer is open exclusively to all holders of the Company's Common Stock and Series A Preferred Stock as of the close of business on the date of this Exchange Offer and is open to such holders from the date hereof until 3:30 P.M., Eastern Standard Time, March 10, 1966 (such period being hereinafter called the "Exchange Period").

The Exchange Offer may be accepted only by such holders and only by completing the enclosed Transmittal Form (red for Common and blue for Preferred) and surrendering it to the Exchange Agent (hereinafter named) together with Common or Series A Preferred Stock Certificate(s), as the case may be, representing at least the number of shares to be exchanged. THE EXCHANGE OFFER IS NOT TRANSFERABLE AND THE TRANSMITTAL FORM MUST BE SURRENDERED IN CONNECTION WITH THE EXCHANGE.

The shares of Common Stock and Series A Preferred Stock surrendered hereunder for exchange, upon receipt by the Exchange Agent, shall be deemed irrevocably deposited for exchange pursuant to the Exchange Offer and will not be returned. Shares of Common Stock and Series A Preferred Stock in excess of those needed to accomplish the exchange but included in the stock certificate or certificates delivered to the Exchange Agent in connection with the exchange will, however, be returned.

Fractional shares are dealt with as follows: All fractions of 5/8 or more will be rounded up to the next whole share, and all fractions of 4/8 or less will be rounded down to the next whole share, except that holders of 1, 2, 3 or 4 shares of the Company's Common Stock as of February 10, 1966 have been given the opportunity to exchange at least one share of Common Stock for one share of Participating Series.

Assume, for example, that a stockholder holds 100 shares of Common Stock on February 10, 1966 represented by one certificate. He will be eligible to exchange *up to* a maximum of 12 shares of Common Stock for 12 shares of the Participating Series. If he wishes to accept the Exchange Offer to the maximum extent and if his holdings of Common Stock are represented by the one stock certificate, he must surrender such certificate together with the enclosed Transmittal Form to the Exchange Agent indicating his acceptance of the Exchange Offer as to 12 shares. Only 12 shares of the Common Stock represented by the 100 share certificate will have been deemed irrevocably deposited for exchange. The other 88 shares will be returned. If the 100 share stockholder holds his shares in more than one certificate he should send in certificates most nearly equaling, but not less than, the number of shares to be exchanged.

The Company reserves the right to determine whether any holder of the Company's Common Stock and Series A Preferred Stock was in fact a holder of such stock on the date of this Exchange Offer and is entitled to participate therein, and further reserves the right to reject in its sole discretion any or all surrenders hereunder which in its judgment do not comply with the terms or purposes of the Exchange Offer.

Shareholders may accept this Exchange Offer as to any number of shares of Common Stock and Series A Preferred Stock *up to* the maximum number of whole shares eligible for exchange pursuant to the terms of this Exchange Offer.

All shares of the Participating Series issued in exchange for shares of Common Stock or Series A Preferred Stock will be issued as of March 10, 1966. Certificates for the Participating Series will be delivered in exchange for the irrevocably surrendered shares of Common Stock and Series A Preferred Stock as soon as possible after March 10, 1966. Certificates for shares of Common Stock and Series A Preferred Stock not needed to accomplish the exchange or not eligible for exchange hereunder will be returned as soon as possible after receipt of such shares by the Exchange Agent. No Participating Series shares will be delivered prior to the close of the Exchange Period.

The shares of Common Stock surrendered hereunder will be retired and returned to the status of authorized but unissued shares in accordance with the resolutions approved by the stockholders at the Annual Meeting held December 4, 1965. The shares of Series A Preferred Stock surrendered hereunder will also be retired and returned to the status of authorized but unissued shares in accordance with the resolutions of the Board of Directors in the manner provided by Delaware corporation law.

Description of Litton participating series

Authorized shares

Under Article FOURTH of its Certificate of Incorporation, as amended, the Company may issue up to 8,000,000 shares of its Preference

Stock with a par value of $2.50 per share. These shares may be issued in one series or a number of series as determined by the Board of Directors provided, however, that each share of a series must be identical with the other shares of the same series, and further, that shares of all series must be of equal rank and be identical with each other series except for certain provisions such as the designation, dividend rate and the redemption, liquidation and conversion rights that may be made different by the Board of Directors as set forth in Article FOURTH. The Participating Series which is the subject of this Exchange Offer is the first series of Preference Stock issued under Article FOURTH, as amended, approved by the stockholders on December 4, 1965.

Dividend rights

The holders of the Participating Series shall be entitled to receive cash dividends when and if cash dividends shall be declared on the Company's Common Stock. In such case, the rate of dividend on each share of the Participating Series shall be equal to the dividend declared on each share of Common Stock multiplied by the number of shares of Common Stock into which each share of the Participating Series is then convertible. Such dividend shall not be cumulative and shall be declared and paid to the holders of the Participating Series at the same time or times as declared and paid to the holders of the Common Stock. If and so long as the Company is in default with respect to any dividends payable on any series of the Preference Stock or the Preferred Stock, it may not pay any dividends (other than dividends payable in Common Stock) on its Common Stock.

Optional redemption provisions

(1) *Optional partial redemption.* The Company shall have the right, at its option, each calendar year beginning with 1967 to redeem shares of the Participating Series by offering to the holders of the Participating Series at the close of business on the first business day of January in any such year, the right, at the option of each holder thereof, to call upon the Company until the close of business on the last business day of January in any such year to redeem up to 3% of the shares of the Participating Series held by him on such record date at the following applicable optional redemption price per share:

Year	Redemption Price Per Share	Year	Redemption Price Per Share
1967	$ 51.65	1979	$ 74.43
1968	53.30	1980	76.65
1969	54.95	1981	78.87
1970	56.60	1982	81.47
1971	58.25	1983	84.07
1972	60.15	1984	86.67
1973	62.05	1985	89.27
1974	63.95	1986	91.87
1975	65.85	1987	94.90
1976	67.75	1988	97.92
1977	69.97	1989 and thereafter	100.95
1978	72.20		

Notice of such offer by the Company shall be given by mail not less than fifteen days prior to January 31 in such year to each stockholder of the Participating Series at the close of business on the first business day of January of such year. Such notice shall specify the maximum number of shares that may be redeemed, the applicable optional redemption price, the place of redemption and the expiration date of such offer. If such offer is made by giving notice as provided above each such holder shall have the right, at his option, at any time up to the close of business on the last business day of January in such year to require the Company to redeem, subject to the terms and provisions of this Section, up to 3% of the shares of the Participating Series held by him on such record date at the applicable optional redemption price per share set forth above upon the surrender and endorsement of the certificate or certificates covering the number of shares to be redeemed. No fractional shares or scrip representing fractional shares shall be issued upon any such partial redemption of the Participating Series. If the shares of any such holder to be redeemed shall include a fraction of a share, such fraction of a share shall be redeemed at the rate of the applicable optional redemption price per share set forth above and the remaining fraction of the whole share surrendered shall be paid for by the Company in an amount equal to such remaining fraction multiplied by the last sales price on the New York Stock Exchange per share of the Participating Series on the day of surrender. Upon such surrender and endorsement (unless the Company shall default in payment of the applicable optional redemption price) such holder shall cease to be a stockholder with respect to such shares and shall have no interest in or claim against the Company and shall have no rights with respect to such shares except the right to receive the moneys payable upon such redemption from the Company; and the shares represented thereby shall no longer be deemed to be outstanding. Any such offer by the Company for any such year shall terminate at the close of business on the last business day of January of such year and all such right to call upon the Company to redeem shares of the Participating Series shall cease and terminate at the close of business on the last business day of January of such year.

(2) *Total redemption.* All of the outstanding shares of the Participating Series shall be redeemable by the Company at any time after January 31, 1976 at the following redemption price per share: If redeemed during the calendar year

Year	Redemption Price Per Share	Year	Redemption Price Per Share
1976	$ 67.75	1983	$ 84.07
1977	69.97	1984	86.67
1978	72.20	1985	89.27
1979	74.43	1986	91.87
1980	76.65	1987	94.90
1981	78.87	1988	97.92
1982	81.47	1989 and thereafter	100.95

except that they shall be redeemable by the Company at any time prior to February 1, 1976 at the applicable price per share set forth in paragraph (1) of this Section in the event the Company recapitalizes, merges, consolidates, or voluntarily sells or transfers its property and assets as, or substantially as, an entirety to any other corporation for cash or stock (or both) of such other corporation (or of a parent, affiliate or subsidiary corporation of such other corporation), upon such date and notice (not less than 30 days) as shall be determined by resolution of the Board of Directors.

Liquidation rights

In the event of any liquidation, dissolution or winding-up of the affairs of the Company, the holders of the Participating Series will be entitled to receive, before any distribution is made on the Common Stock and on a parity with the Preferred Stock, $25 per share plus an amount equal to all dividends accrued and unpaid on each such share up to the date fixed for distribution.

Conversion rights

(1) *Option and rate of conversion.* At the option of the holder thereof on the stock books of the Company, the shares of the Participating Series shall be convertible, at any time on or after the date of first issuance of shares of the Participating Series, into shares of Common Stock of the Company at the following conversion rates per share: If converted during the calendar year

Year	Number of shares of Common Stock for each share of the participating series	Year	Number of shares of Common Stock for each share of the participating series
1966	1.0000	1978	1.4411
1967	1.0309	1979	1.4857
1968	1.0628	1980	1.5316
1969	1.0956	1981	1.5790
1970	1.1294	1982	1.6279
1971	1.1644	1983	1.6781
1972	1.2005	1984	1.7301
1973	1.2376	1985	1.7835
1974	1.2758	1986	1.8386
1975	1.3153	1987	1.8954
1976	1.3559	1988	1.9539
1977	1.3978	1989 and thereafter	2.0145

In case of a call for the redemption of all of the outstanding shares of the Participating Series such right of conversion shall cease and terminate at the close of business on the third day preceding the date fixed for redemption unless default shall be made in the payment of the redemption price.

(2) *Adjustment of conversion rate.* The conversion rates provided for in the table set forth in paragraph (1) of this Section shall be subject to the following adjustments:

(a) While any of the Participating Series shall be outstanding, in the event the Company shall declare and pay to the holders of the Common Stock a dividend or dividends in the Common Stock in any calendar year which in the aggregate exceeds or exceed 2 1/2% of the total number of shares of Common Stock outstanding at the close of business on the record date fixed for the determination of stockholders entitled to the latest such dividend in such calendar year (herein called "Common Stock dividend requiring adjustment"), the conversion rates in effect for the balance of such calendar year and thereafter shall be adjusted as follows:

(i) The conversion rate for such calendar year as set forth in the table in paragraph (1) of this Section shall be increased by adding to it the decimal equivalent of the amount of percentage of the Common Stock dividend requiring adjustment that is in excess of 2 1/2%. Such increased conversion rate is hereinafter referred to as the "adjusted conversion rate."

(ii) The conversion rate as set forth in the table in paragraph (1) of this Section for the calendar year following the year for which the adjusted conversion rate has been determined shall be increased to the product obtained by multiplying (x) the adjusted conversion rate by (y) the quotient resulting from the division of the unadjusted conversion rate for such calendar year as shown in such table by the unadjusted conversion rate for the previous calendar year as shown in such table.

(iii) The conversion rate for each calendar year thereafter as set forth in the table in paragraph (1) of this Section shall be increased to the product obtained by multiplying (x) the newly adjusted conversion rate of the previous calendar year determined in accordance with the formula set forth in (ii) above by (y) the quotient resulting from the division of unadjusted conversion rate for such calendar year as shown in such table by the unadjusted conversion rate for the previous calendar year as shown in such table.

(iv) All adjustments shall be carried out to four decimal places.

(b) Any dividend to holders of Common Stock in shares of Common Stock of 25% or more of the total number of shares of Common Stock outstanding at the close of business on the record date fixed for the determination of stockholders entitled to such dividend shall be considered in the same manner as a subdivision of outstanding shares of Common Stock and an adjustment in the conversion rate shall be made in accordance with the provisions of subparagraph (c) below with respect to subdivision of the outstanding shares of Common Stock.

(c) While any of the Participating Series shall be outstanding, in case the Company shall subdivide the outstanding shares of Common Stock into a greater number of shares of Common Stock or combine the outstanding shares of Common Stock into a smaller number of shares of Common Stock, the conversion rate in effect immediately prior to such subdivision or combination, as the case may be, shall be proportionately increased or decreased, as the case may require.

(d) No adjustment of the conversion rate shall be made by reason of the issuance of Common Stock in exchange for cash, property or service.

(3) *Recapitalization, consolidation, merger.* In case the Company shall be recapitalized, or shall be consolidated with or merged into, or shall sell or transfer its property and assets as, or substantially as, an entirety to any other corporation, proper provisions shall be made as a part of the terms of such recapitalization, consolidation, merger, sale or transfer whereby the holder of any shares of the Participating Series at the time outstanding immediately prior to such event shall thereafter be entitled to such conversion rights, with respect to securities of the corporation resulting from such recapitalization, consolidation or merger or to which such sale or transfer shall be made, as shall be substantially equivalent to the conversion rights herein provided for.

(4) *Fractional shares.* No fraction of a share of Common Stock shall be issued upon any conversion but, in lieu thereof, there shall be paid an amount in cash equal to the same fraction of the market value of a full share of Common Stock.

Voting rights

The holders of Participating Series and any other series of Preference Stock outstanding will be entitled to one vote per share on all matters upon which stockholders generally have the right to vote. If dividends on any series of the Preference Stock as to which the Board of Directors shall have determined an annual dividend rate are in default in an amount equivalent to six full quarterly dividends or three semiannual dividends on such series of the Preference Stock then outstanding, the number of directors of the Company shall be increased by two and the holders of the Participating Series and any other series of Preference Stock outstanding shall have the exclusive right, voting separately as a class (without regard to series) so long as such default continues, to elect such two additional directors.

Without the affirmative vote or written consent of at least two-thirds of the then outstanding Participating Series and any other series of Preference Stock, the Company may not (i) authorize any class of stock ranking either as to the payment of dividends or distribution of assets prior to any series of the Preference Stock, (ii) change the preferences or rights with respect to any series of the Preference Stock in any material respect prejudicial to the holders thereof, or (iii) purchase or redeem less than all of the then outstanding Preferred Stock and Preference Stock unless all dividends, if any, thereon shall have been paid or declared and a sum sufficient therefor set apart. However, no such vote or written consent will be required if, at or prior to (i) the time of the issuance of any such prior stock or (ii) the time any such change is to take effect or (iii) the time any such purchase or redemption is to take effect, as the case may be, provision is made for the redemption of all the then outstanding shares of all series of Preference Stock. In addition, no such class vote or written consent is required in connection with (a) any increase in the authorized number of shares of Common Stock, Preferred Stock or Preference Stock, (b) the authorization or increase of any class of stock ranking on a parity with the Preference Stock, or (c) the fixing of any of the particulars of shares of other series of Preference Stock that may be fixed by the Board of Directors with respect to the shares of such other series of Preference Stock.

Holders of the Participating Series and any other series of Preference Stock do not have cumulative voting rights, which means that the holders of more than 50% of the shares of Preferred Stock, Common Stock and the Preference Stock voting as one class for the election of directors can elect 100% of the directors, if they choose to do so, and in such event the holders of the remaining less than 50% of the shares voted for the election of directors will not be able to elect any person or persons to the Board of Directors.

Reissue of reacquired participating series

Shares of the Participating Series and any other series of Preference Stock which have been issued and reacquired in any manner will have the status of authorized and unissued Preference Stock and may be reissued as shares of the series of which they were originally a part or may be issued as shares of a new series or as shares of any other series, all subject to the conditions and restrictions of any series of Preference Stock.

Preemptive rights

No holder of the Participating Series and any other series of Preference Stock will be entitled as a matter of right as such holder to subscribe for or purchase any stock, obligations, warrants or other securities of the Company.

Description of Litton common stock

The existing provisions of the Company's Certificate of Incorporation, as amended, authorize the issuance of 39,000,000 shares of Common Stock of the par value of $1 of which 23,457,193 are outstanding (including 795,648 shares held as treasury stock); 260,308 shares of such Common Stock are reserved for issuance upon conversion of the Company's 4¾% Convertible Subordinated Debentures due June 1, 1974; 204,750 shares are reserved for issuance upon conversion of the Company's 5¼% Convertible Subordinated Debentures due December 1, 1974; 1,550,173 shares are reserved for issuance upon the conversion of the Company's 3½% Convertible Subordinated Debentures (including the Series A thereof) due April 1, 1987; and 1,856,154 shares are reserved for issuance upon conversion of the Company's outstanding Series A $3 Cumulative Convertible Preferred Stock.

Holders of Common Stock are entitled to receive such dividends as are declared by the Board of Directors and to cast one vote for each share on all matters voted by stockholders. The holders of Common Stock do not have cumulative voting rights. Shares of Common Stock have no preemptive or conversion rights, and such shares are not subject to any further calls or assessments.

The Company has paid 2½% Common Stock dividends in each of the calendar years 1959, 1960, 1961, 1962, 1963, 1964 and 1965. Under its Note Agreements with insurance companies and its Bank Credit Agreement, the Company may not pay cash dividends unless certain conditions are complied with. At the present time the Company is in compliance with these conditions. No cash dividends have been paid by the Company on its Common Stock because it has been the policy of the Company to use its earnings to finance expansion. The payment of future dividends in cash or stock will rest within the discretion of the Board of Directors and will depend, among other things, upon earnings, capital requirements, the financial condition of the Company and opportunities for reinvestment.

In the event of any liquidation, dissolution or winding-up of the affairs of the Company, the holders of the Common Stock will be entitled to receive pro rata all the assets of the Company available for distribution, after satisfaction of the prior preferential rights of the holders of Preferred Stock and of the Preference Stock and the payment or satisfaction of the other obligations of the Company.

Description of Litton preferred stock

The existing provisions of the Company's Certificate of Incorporation, as amended, Article FOURTH, authorize the issuance of 3,000,000 shares of Preferred Stock with a par value of $5 per share. Article FOURTH further provides that such shares may be issued in one series or a number of series as determined by the Board of Directors, provided, however, that each share of a series must be identical with the other shares of the same series and, further, that the shares of all series must be of equal rank and be identical with each other series except for certain provisions, such as the designation, dividend rate and the redemption, liquidation and conversion rights, that may be made different by the Board of Directors as set forth in Article FOURTH.

Pursuant to this authority vested in the Board of Directors, the Board, on December 6, 1963, provided for the issuance of a series of Preferred Stock of the Company designated "Series A $3 Cumulative Convertible Preferred Stock." A more particular description of the Preferred Stock and the Series A thereof, including its rights, qualifications and restrictions is set forth below.

Of the 3,000,000 authorized shares of $5 par value Preferred Stock, 928,077 shares of Series A Preferred Stock have been issued and are outstanding, including 27,141 shares held as treasury stock.

Dividend rights

Holders of the Preferred Stock are entitled to receive an annual cumulative cash dividend in the amount fixed by the Board of Directors prior to the first issuance of the particular series of Preferred Stock before any dividends (other than dividends payable in Common Stock) are paid on the Common Stock of the Company. The holders of the Series A Preferred Stock are entitled to receive such an annual dividend of $3 payable semiannually on July 15 and January 15. The $3 annual dividend on the Series A Preferred Stock commences to accrue from the dividend payment date next preceding the date of issue of such shares, unless such shares are issued between a dividend record date and payment date; in such event the dividend commences to accrue from the dividend payment date following the date of issue. Accumulations of dividends do not bear interest. If and so long as the Company is in default with respect to any dividends payable on shares of the Preferred Stock, it may not pay any dividends on any other class of stock (other than dividends payable in Common Stock). Subject to the foregoing, holders of Common Stock are entitled to receive such dividends as may be declared by the Board of Directors of the Company.

Redemption and liquidation rights

Shares of the Preferred Stock may be redeemed in whole or in part by the Company at such time and at such prices as the Board of Directors shall fix and determine in the resolution providing for the first issuance of a particular series, plus all dividends accrued and unpaid thereon up to the date fixed for redemption. Shares of the Series A Preferred Stock may be redeemed in whole or in part by the Company at any time after April 1, 1972 at $100 per share plus all accrued and unpaid dividends, except that they may be redeemed in whole or in part prior to that date by the Company at $100 per share (plus all dividends accrued and unpaid thereon up to the date fixed for redemption) at any time in the event the Company recapitalizes, merges, consolidates or voluntarily sells or transfers its property and assets as, or substantially as, an entirety to any other corporation for cash or stock of such other corporation (or of a parent, affiliate or subsidiary corporation of such other corporation), or both. The holders of the Series A Preferred Stock will have the right, in the event of any liquidation, dissolution or winding-up of the affairs of the Company, to receive $50 per share plus all dividends accrued and unpaid thereon up to the date fixed for distribution and no more. Earnings retained in the business are not restricted by the excess of the liquidation preference (at July 31, 1965 – $40,000,725) of the Preferred Stock over its par value, and there are no liquidation remedies available to any security holder before or after payment of any dividends that would reduce surplus to an amount less than the amount of such excess. There is no sinking fund applicable to the Preferred Stock. Neither the merger or consolidation of the Company, nor the sale, lease or conveyance of all or a part of its assets, is deemed to be a liquidation, dissolution or winding-up of the affairs of the Company.

There is no restriction on the repurchase or redemption of the Preferred Stock by the Company while there is any arrearage in the payment of dividends, except that the price to be paid by the Company upon such repurchase or redemption of the Series A Preferred Stock shall be $100 per share plus all dividends accrued and unpaid on such stock up to the date fixed for redemption or repurchase.

In the event of a partial redemption, the Preferred Stock will be redeemable either by lot or pro rata in such manner as the Board of Directors may determine, upon at least 30 days' but not more than 60 days' notice.

Conversion rights

The Company's Certificate of Incorporation, as amended, gives the Board of Directors authority to fix all of the terms and conditions relating to the conversion of shares of the Preferred Stock, other than the Series A Preferred Stock, into Common Stock or other stock of the Company. Each share of the Series A Preferred Stock is now (since the 2-for-1 split of Common Stock distributed January 31, 1966) convertible into two shares of Common Stock, at the option of the holder thereof at any time or, if called for redemption until the close of business on the third day preceding the date fixed for redemption. Upon conversion the holder thereof shall be entitled to receive all dividends accrued and unpaid thereon to the dividend date immediately preceding the surrender of such shares for conversion. The 2-for-1 conversion rate is subject to adjustment in certain events. In the event the Company declares and pays during any particular fiscal year of the Company (the fiscal year commences August 1 each year) dividends on the Common Stock in Common Stock which in the aggregate exceed three per cent (3%) of the total number of shares of Common Stock outstanding at the close of business on the record date for the determination of the stockholders entitled to receive the latest such Common Stock dividend in such fiscal year, the conversion rate in effect immediately prior to the record date fixed for the determination of stockholders entitled to such latest dividend shall be increased in the same percentage or ratio that the aggregate of all such Common Stock dividends during such fiscal year bears to the total number of shares of Common Stock outstanding at the close of business on the record date fixed for the determination of stockholders entitled to such dividend first declared and paid in such fiscal year. (Any dividend on the Common Stock in shares of Common Stock of 25% or more of the total number of shares of Common Stock outstanding at the close of business on the record date fixed for the determination of stockholders entitled thereto will be considered in the same manner as a subdivision of the Common Stock.) Upon any dividend or distribution on the Common Stock which would otherwise call for an adjustment in the conversion rate, the Company may, in the discretion of the Board of Directors, issue shares of Common Stock as an equivalent dividend or distribution on the Series A Preferred Stock and no adjustment in the conversion rate will be made.

In the event of a subdivision of the Common Stock into a greater number of shares of Common Stock or the combination of the Common Stock into a smaller number of shares of Common Stock, the conversion rate in effect immediately prior to such subdivision or combination will be proportionately increased or decreased, as the case may require, such increase or decrease to become effective immediately after the opening of business on the day following the day upon which such subdivision or combination, as the case may be, becomes effective.

In the event the Company shall be recapitalized, or shall be consolidated with, or merged into, or shall sell or transfer its property and assets as, or substantially as, an entirety, to any other corporation, appropriate provision shall be included as a part of the terms of such recapitalization, consolidation, merger, sale or transfer to entitle the holders of the Series A Preferred Stock outstanding at the time to such conversion rights with respect to securities of the corporation resulting therefrom as will be substantially equivalent to the conversion rights of the holders of such Preferred Stock immediately prior thereto.

No adjustment of the conversion rate will be made by reason of the issuance of Common Stock for cash, property or services. No fraction of a share of Common Stock will be issued upon any conversion, but in lieu thereof an amount, in cash equal to the same fraction of the market value of a full share of Common Stock will be paid.

Voting rights

The holders of Preferred Stock are entitled to one vote per share on all matters upon which stockholders generally have the right to vote. If dividends on the Preferred Stock are in default in an amount equivalent to six quarterly (or three semiannual) dividend payments on all shares of Preferred Stock of any series then outstanding, the number of directors of the Company shall be increased by two and the holders of the Preferred Stock shall have the exclusive right, voting separately as a class (without regard to series) so long as such default continues, to elect such two additional directors.

Without the affirmative vote or written consent of at least two-thirds of the then outstanding Preferred Stock, the Company may not (i) authorize any class of stock ranking either as to the payment of dividends or distribution of assets prior to the Preferred Stock, (ii) change the preferences or rights with respect to the Preferred Stock in any material respect prejudicial to the holders thereof, or (iii) purchase or redeem less than all of the then outstanding Preferred Stock and Preference Stock unless all dividends thereon if any, shall have been paid or declared and a sum sufficient therefor set apart. However, no such vote or written consent will be required if, at or prior to (i) the time of the issuance of any such prior stock or (ii) the time any such change is to take effect, or (iii) the time any such purchase or redemption is to take effect, as the case may be, provision is made for the redemption of all the then outstanding shares of Preferred Stock. In addition, no such class vote or written consent is required in connection with (a) any increase in the authorized number of shares of Common Stock, Preferred Stock or Preference Stock, (b) the authorization or increase of any class of stock ranking on a parity with the Preferred Stock, or (c) the fixing of any of the particulars of shares of other series of Preferred Stock or of any series of Preferred Stock that may be fixed by the Board of Directors.

Holders of the Preferred Stock do not have cumulative voting rights, which means that the holders of more than 50% of the shares of Preferred Stock, Common Stock and the Preference Stock voting as one class for the election of directors can elect 100% of the directors, if they choose to do so, and in such event the holders of the remaining less than 50% of the shares voted for the election of directors will not be able to elect any person or persons to the Board of Directors.

Reissue of reacquired preferred stock

Shares of Preferred Stock which have been issued and reacquired in any manner, will have the status of authorized and unissued Preferred

Stock and may be reissued as shares of the series of which they were originally a part or may be issued as shares of a new series or as shares of any other series, all subject to the conditions and restrictions of any series of Preferred Stock.

Preemptive rights

No holder of Preferred Stock will be entitled as a matter of right as such holder to subscribe for or purchase any stock, obligations, warrants or other securities of the Company.

The description of the Common Stock, Preferred Stock and Participating Series above set forth are not intended to be complete and are qualified, in their entirety, by the specific provisions of the Company's Certificate of Incorporation, as amended, and the resolutions of the Board of Directors providing for the issue of the Series A Preferred Stock and the Participating Series. Copies of these are available from the Exchange Agent or the Company on request.

Federal income tax aspects

A ruling has been received from the Internal Revenue Service that the proposed exchange of the Company's Common Stock and Series A Preferred Stock for shares of the Participating Series will constitute a tax-free recapitalization and that no taxable gain will be recognized to the Company as a result of the transaction. The ruling further states that no taxable gain will be recognized to the shareholders of the Company upon the exchange of their shares of Common Stock or Series A Preferred Stock (or shares of both classes, as the case may be) for shares of the Participating Series.

The basis of the shares of the Participating Series received in the exchange will be the same as the basis of the shares of Common Stock or Series A Preferred Stock surrendered in exchange therefor.

The Internal Revenue Service ruling also states that Section 306(a) (1) of the Internal Revenue Code will not apply to the proceeds of the disposition of the Participating Series. This means that if an investor sells his Participating Series, the amount of gain realized on such sale will be treated as capital gain unless such sale is in anticipation of redemption. Since the Internal Revenue Service rules only on pending transactions, a tax ruling as to the effects of future redemptions of the Participating Series (or sales in anticipation of such redemption) could not be issued at this time. However, it is the opinion of Messrs. Miller & Chevalier, Attorneys at Law, Washington, D.C., and also the opinion of the Company's Tax Counsel, that under present Internal Revenue Service policy proceeds from future redemptions (or sales in anticipation of such redemptions) of the Participating Series will be considered as having been received from the sale of such redeemed stock and any gain thereon treated as capital gain. If, and at such time as, the Board of Directors of the Company declares a voluntary redemption of a portion of the Participating Series, the Company will apply for a tax ruling confirming the above opinion.

Proposed listing on the New York stock exchange and Pacific Coast stock exchange

Application is being made by the Company for the listing upon notice of issuance of the Participating Series that may be issued hereunder, and the Common Stock into which it is convertible, on the New York Stock Exchange and the Pacific Coast Stock Exchange. The Common Stock and the Series A Preferred Stock of the Company are currently listed on such Exchanges.

Method of effecting exchanges

Morgan Guaranty Trust Company of New York, Corporate Trust Department, 23 Wall Street, New York, New York 10015, will serve as Exchange Agent for this transaction. Stockholders desiring to effect the exchange under this Exchange Offer should execute the accompanying Transmittal Form and forward it to the Exchange Agent together with the stock certificates representing the shares to be surrendered. *The attention of the stockholders is directed to the accompanying* **Instructions for Transmittal Form** *which should be carefully examined.* An envelope addressed to the Exchange Agent is enclosed for the convenience of Stockholders desiring to effect such exchange. Transmittal Forms properly signed and stock certificates must be received by the Exchange Agent not later than 3:30 P.M., Eastern Standard Time, on March 10, 1966.

By order of the Board of Directors

JAMES X. KILBRIDGE
Secretary

Chapter seven

Tax factors in the purchase and sale of a corporation

There are two obvious ways of selling the entire business of a corporation. One method is for the shareholders simply to sell their stock. In this case, the purchaser acquires entire ownership of the corporation and can either continue to operate it or liquidate it and take the assets into his own business or into a new corporation. We know what the tax consequences of a transaction like this will be to the selling shareholders. What they are selling is almost certainly a capital asset (unless of course they are in the business of buying and selling securities and the stock is an inventory asset). The transaction will then produce capital gain or loss, long- or short-term, depending on how long they have held the stock.

The second type of sale is an asset sale. The corporation simply sells all its assets to a purchaser, turning itself into a corporate shell, and holding cash or perhaps some other property that was paid for its assets. We know what the consequences of this transaction will be to the selling corporation; they will be essentially the same as the consequences to a proprietor on the sale of his proprietorship. The purchase price will have to be allocated to all the assets, the assets classified as capital, section 1231, or other assets, and a final gain and loss and tax liability calculated. This asset sale might be followed by liquidation of the corporation, probably with capital gain or loss to the shareholders.

Sale of assets

There are a few complications in both of these methods of sale. The second method, without a special provision in the Code, could involve double taxation if the corporation were to liquidate after selling its assets. The corporation would be taxed on any gains resulting from the sale of its assets, and then in the liquidation the shareholders would pay a capital gains tax on anything they received above the adjusted basis of their stock.

Tax experts discovered a way around this double taxation. Instead of selling its assets directly, the corporation would liquidate; then the shareholders who had received the assets from it would sell them. The shareholders would be taxed at capital gains rates at the time of liquidation, but the corporation itself would not be taxed. The sale of assets by the shareholders would not produce gain or loss.

This transaction was a rather risky one, as the U.S. Supreme Court decision in *Commissioner* v. *Court Holding Company*[1] proved. The Court held in that case that the corporation was liable for tax on the sale of its assets even though technically the assets were distributed to the shareholders in a liquidation and were then sold by the shareholders. The corporation had negotiated the sale of its sole asset, an apartment house, to a purchaser, and an oral agreement was reached concerning the terms of the sale. It was after the agreement was reached that the corporation decided not to go through with the sale but rather to liquidate and have the shareholders sell. This course of action was followed, and the shareholders conveyed the property to the purchaser according to the terms that had already been agreed upon between the corporation and the purchaser. The Supreme Court upheld the conclusion of the Tax Court that the sale really had been made by the corporation rather than the shareholders and that the liquidation and technical sale by the shareholders was a mere formality that would be ignored.

The Supreme Court reached an opposite conclusion, however, in *United States* v. *Cumberland Public Service Company*.[2] In this case, the tax advisers had been more careful and the corporation had never at any time entered into negotiations for the sale of its assets. There was a genuine liquidation, and the shareholders negotiated the sale. The moral seemed to be that good tax advice could lead to avoidance of double taxation but that carelessness or ignorance would be severely penalized. And, of course, no matter how good the tax advice, in many cases it simply would be impractical for the shareholders as a body to negotiate and bring about the sale of all the assets of a substantial corporation.

The dilemma was resolved in 1954 when section 337 was put into the new Code. Section 337 permits the corporation to negotiate and actually carry out the sale of assets but relieves it of tax liability if the sale is followed by a liquidation.

Read section 337 carefully and notice exactly how section 337(a) brings about the tax relief. Does it eliminate all the tax liabilities

---

[1] 324 U.S. 331 (U.S. Supreme Court, 1945).

[2] 338 U.S. 451 (U.S. Supreme Court, 1950).

of the corporation resulting from the sale of assets? Does it eliminate recapture of depreciation, for example, under sections 1245 and 1250? (Read Regulations, section 1.1245 – 6(a) and (b).)

We will discuss later in this chapter some of the limitations of section 337. We turn now to the other method of selling a corporate business: a sale of stock by the shareholders.

Sale of stock

The sale of stock generally creates no problems for the seller. The purchaser, however, may face some disadvantages in terms of the adjusted basis of the assets he has bought. Suppose, for example, that the depreciable assets of the corporation have adjusted bases considerably below fair market value. The purchaser has bought the corporation, and so long as the assets remain in the corporation, their adjusted bases will be unchanged and the corporation will continue to take depreciation at the same rate and on the same basis. This may seem rather unattractive to the purchaser, who has paid a price reflecting the high market value of the assets. Suppose he liquidates the corporation and absorbs the assets into his own business. We have seen (in Chapter six) that this liquidation can be tax-free under 332, at least if the purchaser is a corporation; and in a section 332 liquidation, the basis of the assets distributed is generally not changed. The liquidation, then, would appear to be useless to the purchaser as a means of increasing the depreciable basis of the assets. However, the Tax Court reached a different conclusion in *Kimbell-Diamond Milling Company* v. *Commissioner.*[3] The purchaser in that case paid $110,000 for the stock of the corporation, with the purpose of obtaining the corporation's assets. Immediately after the stock purchase, the corporation was liquidated in a tax-free liquidation under an earlier version of section 332. In this case, the basis of the assets in the corporation's hands was $140,000 *greater* than the purchase price of the stock, and the purchaser sought to use this higher basis in computing its depreciation deductions. The court upheld the Commissioner's conclusion that the basis should be only $110,000 since "the purchase of the stock and subsequent liquidation must be considered as one transaction, namely, the purchase of the corporation's assets, which was the purchaser's sole intention."

The result of this decision seems attractive to the purchaser where the assets are worth more than their adjusted basis in the corporation purchased, but unattractive where they are worth less as in the *Kimbell-Diamond* case. You can appreciate that arranging which rule would apply to a transaction – the *Kimbell-Diamond* rule or the literal section 332 rule – would be a tricky business. The Tax Code was amended in 1954 to take care of this dilemma, too, by the addition of section 334(b)(2). When this section applies, the purchaser can substitute his price paid for stock for the basis of the assets received in the liquidation of the subsidiary.

---

[3] 14 T.C. 74 (U.S. Tax Court, 1950), affirmed 187 F. 2d 718 (U.S. Court of Appeals, 5th Circuit, 1951), cert. den. 342 U.S. 827.

Section 334(b)(2) simply brings about the *Kimbell-Diamond* result when the conditions of the section are met.

Avoidance of sections 337 and 334(b)(2)

At this point, you should be able to see that sections 337 and 334 (b)(2) together make a sale of stock followed by liquidation about equivalent to a sale of corporate assets followed by liquidation for both the seller and the purchaser, at least where the conditions of those two sections are met.

Does section 1245 create a tax difference between the two transactions?

It is possible that the parties will not want either of these sections to apply. For example, if the method of sale chosen is a sale of assets by the corporation, it may be that the corporation has some loss carry-overs that will absorb gains; or it may be that the sale of assets will produce losses rather than gains, and there may be no reason for wanting to avoid recognition of gain or loss through section 337. In the case where the sale is a sale of stock and where the purchaser is interested in liquidating his newly purchased corporation, he may wish to avoid section 334(b)(2) if the assets actually have a higher basis in the original corporation than the price paid for the stock of that corporation. (This was the situation in the *Kimbell-Diamond* case.) In this situation, section 334(b)(2) will produce a reduction in basis, which the purchaser naturally wants to avoid. The purchaser could, of course, simply continue to operate the original corporation as a subsidiary, enjoying the high basis of the assets in the subsidiary. But an obvious way to avoid the application of either section 337 or 334(b)(2) would be simply to fail to comply with some of the conditions stipulated in the section or in the Regulations. It is not always easy, however, to know exactly what the limitations are.

Read the Regulations corresponding to section 337 and consider this example. A corporation has two assets, one with an adjusted basis of $5000 and a market value of $50,000 and the other with an adjusted basis of $70,000 and a market value of $25,000. The corporation has income or gains for the year which could be offset by a loss recognized on the asset with the lower value. Is it possible for the corporation to sell this asset and recognize a loss and then to sell the other asset and avoid recognition of gain under section 337, if a liquidation follows soon after the sale?

As you can see, section 334(b)(2) also contains a number of rather technical requirements. One that you might not notice is a requirement that the stock of the subsidiary be obtained by "purchase." This means that section 334(b)(2) does not apply where the stock in the subsidiary was acquired in a tax-free reorganization, a topic we will be coming to.

Loss carry-over

So far we have talked as though the purchaser's only concern is for the basis of depreciable assets he is acquiring, either directly or through the medium of a corporation. But other tax attributes of the corporation whose business is to be sold may be equally important, especially any loss carry-over. Sections 269, 381, and 382 deal with the passing of loss carry-overs to successor corporations. Of course if the purchaser simply buys a corporation and continues to operate it, it will come with all its loss carry-overs intact. But more often, the purchaser would like to extract the loss carry-over from the corporation he has purchased and use it to offset profits in another corporation. Section 381 describes the kinds of transactions that can effect this transfer of loss carry-over. Notice that although the purchaser gets the benefit of section 334(b)(2) for depreciable assets when he liquidates his subsidiary, he does not get the benefit of section 381.

Tax-free corporate reorganizations

We have looked so far at sales of corporations or of all their assets that result in at least capital gains taxation, where gains are realized on the sale of assets or stock. The Code includes a number of sections which permit a corporation to acquire the stock or assets of another corporation in a transaction that is tax-free to the seller in that it postpones the recognition of gain or loss for tax purposes. We have already encountered similar provisions (in Chapter three), relating to exchanges of like property, for example, or involuntary conversion of property, or contributions of appreciated assets to a corporation in return for its stock.

Section 368 is the fundamental section of the group we are going to discuss. It defines "reorganization." The other sections in the group do not as a rule refer explicitly to section 368, but they all describe the consequences of a "reorganization," which means a transaction falling within the section 368 definition.

The section describes six different kinds of reorganization. We have already seen an example of a section 368 (a)(1)(E) reorganization (which we shall for convenience call an E reorganization) in the Litton Industries case. The important reorganizations, for tax purposes, are the A, B, and C reorganizations, and these are the ones we will discuss.

There are many ways in which two corporations can be put together. Corporation X could buy all the assets of Corporation Y. Corporation X could buy all the stock in Corporation Y and either operate Y as a subsidiary or liquidate it into X. Corporation Y could be merged into Corporation X with the former stockholders of Corporation Y receiving stock in Corporation X in exchange for their X stock. Or both Corporations X and Y could be merged into a new Corporation Z with the old stockholders of both X and Y receiving stock in Z. Section 368(a)(1)(A) is designed to apply to any one of these transactions as long as it is authorized under a state corporation statute. Sometimes it is feasible to come under this subsection and sometimes it is not, depending on the transaction the parties want to bring about and the particular state law that applies. We will focus our discussion on sections 368(a)(1)(B) and (C). The B and C types of reorganization are the most interesting ones since they do not require any state statutes for their tax consequences and they illustrate the two important alternatives in bringing about a combination of two corporations.

Sections 354, 356, and 358 describe the tax consequences to shareholders who give up shares of stock in a reorganization in exchange for new stock or securities (or other kinds of payment). Notice that section 354 deals with the simple case, where no gain or loss is recognized. This could be the consequence of an A or B or C reorganization (a C reorganization where a corporation disposes of its assets for stock and then liquidates, passing the stock to its own shareholders). Section 356 deals with the case where some gain or loss is recognized (and notice that gain may be treated as a dividend rather than as capital gain). Section 356 could apply to an A or C reorganization (where there is a liquidation to shareholders following the sale of assets) but not to a B reorganization. Section 358 tells us what the basis will be of whatever payment the shareholders receive in the reorganization.

Sections 357, 358, and 361 apply to the corporation disposing of assets in an A or C reorganization. Section 361 states the general rule with respect to recognition of gain or loss. Notice that it is analogous to sections 354 and 356, the two sections dealing with recognition of gain or loss to shareholders. Section 361(b)(1) distinguishes between cases where the sale of assets is followed by a liquidation and those where there is no liquidation.

Section 357 describes the tax consequences where part of the payment for assets takes the form of an assumption of liabilities. Section 361 talks about "other property or money" as part payment but says nothing about assumption of liabilities, and section 357 fills the gap. Finally, section 358 furnishes the basis rules for what the corporation received in exchange for its assets.

Section 362 establishes the basis of the assets exchanged, in the hands of the new owner. Notice that section 358(e) makes it clear that section 358 applies to the corporation that gave up its assets for stock (as in a C reorganization) and not to the corporation that acquired the assets, while section 362(b) explains that it applies to the latter corporation.

We have now referred to seven sections of the Code relating to reorganizations, and it may be helpful to show, in the form of a diagram, which sections apply to the parties in a B or C reorganization.

B Reorganization

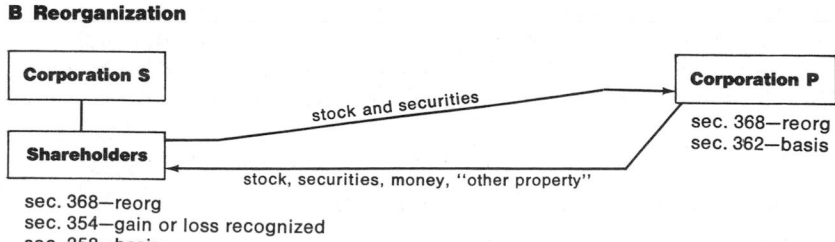

Corporation S

stock and securities

Corporation P

sec. 368—reorg
sec. 362—basis

Shareholders

stock, securities, money, "other property"

sec. 368—reorg
sec. 354—gain or loss recognized
sec. 358—basis

C Reorganization

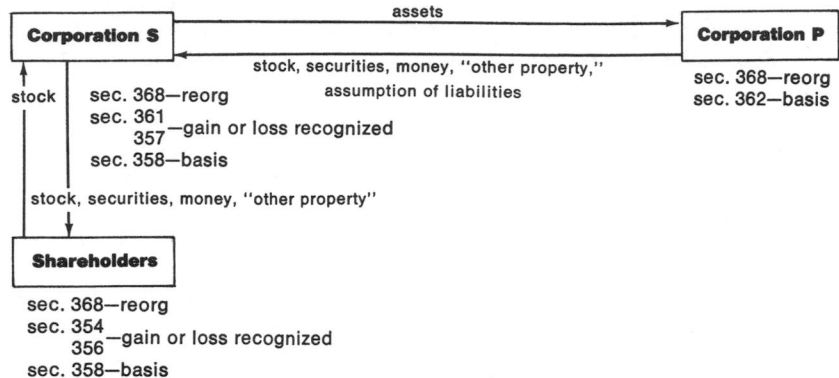

Meeting the requirements of section 368 can sometimes present difficult problems of interpretation. The Regulations under section 368 contain a reference to "continuity of interest," an important requirement. The courts have established two tests for continuity of interest. According to the *Southwest Natural Gas Company* v. *Commissioner*[4] decision, the corporation giving up its assets in a C reorganization or the shareholders giving up their stock in a B reorganization must end up with a "material interest in the affairs of the transferee corporation," and the retained interest must represent "a substantial part of the value of the property transferred." The second test is satisfied when the shareholders exchanging their stock receive common stock of the surviving company representing 25 per cent of the value of the assets transferred. The Internal Revenue Service, in a 1966 statement, said that the test is satisfied if the shareholders receive stock worth at least 50 per cent of the value of all the former stock of the corporation they gave up.[5]

The Regulations also refer to the "business purpose" rule. The rule was first expressed in *Gregory* v. *Helvering*.[6] In this case, a corporation wished to distribute shares in a subsidiary to its own shareholders without having the distribution taxed as dividends. The shareholders formed a new corporation and the parent corporation gave its stock in its subsidiary to the new corporation in exchange for the stock in the new corporation, distributing the latter to its shareholders. In other words, the shareholders turned in their stock in the new corporation in exchange for stock in the subsidiary. All the technicalities for a tax-free reorganization were met, but the Supreme Court concluded that the new corporation served no business purpose and simply treated the entire set of transactions as equivalent to a distribution of the stock in the subsidiary as a dividend.

Notice the strict terms imposed in section 368 for a B reorganiza-

---

[4] 189 F. 2d 332, (U.S. Court of Appeals, 5th Circuit, 1951), cert. denied 342 U.S. 860.

[5] Revenue Procedure 66–34, 1966–34, Int. Rev. Bull. 22.

[6] 293 U.S. 465 (U.S. Supreme Court, 1935).

tion. The purchasing corporation may transfer only its *voting* stock in exchange for the stock it acquires. The rule for C reorganization was the same until section 368(a)(2)(B) was enacted in 1954. This may seem to make the C reorganization more attractive than B. But note that if this exception from the strict rule is used, voting stock must be given for at least 80 per cent of *all* and not just "substantially all" of the assets of the selling corporation. The rule covering assumption of liabilities in this special case may also cause trouble. The Regulations provide examples.

We have referred to section 361 which states the general rule that gain or loss is not recognized to the corporation selling its property in a reorganization in exchange for stock or securities. This section does not, of course, apply to the corporation that gives stock or securities in exchange for assets. No section of the Code specifically applies to this corporation, but section 1032 states that where stock is exchanged for property "no gain or loss shall be recognized on the receipt of money or other property in exchange for stock (including Treasury stock) of the corporation." And even if the purchasing corporation were to give securities or cash in addition to stock for the assets it acquired, there should be no recognition of gain since this would be simply a purchase of assets case and the purchaser is not taxed at the time of the purchase.

You should recall our discussion of section 306 in connection with the so-called "preferred stock bail-out" (in Chapter six). If preferred stock were received in a tax-free reorganization, the recipient might sell this and yet retain effective control of a corporation through common stock. In other words, a sort of by-product of the reorganization might be disposition of significant corporate assets putting cash in the shareholder's pocket through the issue and sale of preferred stock. If you look at section 306(c)(1)(B) you will see that preferred stock received in a tax-free reorganization is designated "Section 306 stock" and therefore suffers from all the disabilities of preferred stock received as a stock dividend.

> *Suppose that in a section 368(a)(1)(C) reorganization P corporation exchanges $1,200,000 worth of its voting stock plus $200,000 in cash and $100,000 worth of notes for all of the assets of S corporation, worth $1,500,000 and with a basis to S of $1,000,000. How much gain is recognized to S; to P? What is the basis of the assets received by P; of the stock and notes received by S?*

> *Suppose P corporation exchanges $1,500,000 worth of its common stock for all the assets of S corporation, worth $1,750,000, with a basis to S of $1,000,000, but subject to a liability of $250,000 which is assumed by P. Is gain or loss recognized to S or to P? What will be the bases of the assets to P and the stock to S?*

> *Suppose a shareholder of S corporation, in a section 368(a)(1)(B) reorganization, gives up one share of stock with a basis of $90 in exchange for one share of stock in P corporation worth $100 plus cash of $10 and a note worth $30. What gain is recognized by the shareholder? What is the basis of what he receives? What is the basis to P of this share which it has received?*

Wilcox Corporation

Karl Wilcox owns 65 per cent of the common stock of the Wilcox Corporation, his son David owns 30 per cent, and his daughter Linda owns the remaining 5 per cent.

Karl is sixty-eight years old and anxious to retire from active management of the company. David is vice-president but in Karl's opinion is not capable of taking over the company. The management of a much larger corporation, Statesman Manufacturing Inc., with a New York Stock Exchange listing, has offered to purchase the gross assets of the Wilcox Corporation for $1,030,000 in cash or for 15,000 shares of Statesman. The shares are currently selling at about $70. In such a sale the Wilcox Corporation would use part of the proceeds to pay off its liabilities.

Karl has been assured that David will be taken on as a vice-president of Statesman if the deal goes through, and David is satisfied with this arrangement.

The price of $800,000 is based on an appraisal of the Wilcox assets, which Karl and David think is fair. Receivables are valued at $150,000 and inventory at $185,000. Land is appraised at $175,000, buildings at $140,000, and equipment at $320,000.

The Wilcox Corporation balance sheet is shown in Exhibit 1. The depreciation shown on the books is the same as that taken for tax purposes. Net income after taxes last year was $100,000.

Karl is concerned about his future income. He will give up a $25,000 salary when he retires (he will receive no pension), so the income from the proceeds of sale will be important. He is satisfied with stock in Statesman, but he has been advised that it might be better for him and his children to sell their stock to Statesman rather than have the Wilcox Corporation sell its assets. The Statesman management has indicated a willingness to discuss a stock purchase but has warned that the price may be lower. The current dividend on Statesman stock is $1.70 per share. This is unchanged from five years ago when it was raised from $1.30. Earnings at that time were $3.50 a share and have risen fairly steadily to $4.70 at present.

Karl Wilcox founded his company in 1931 on a $15,000 investment. Over the years he has given stock to his son and daughter to bring their interests to 30 per cent and 5 per cent.

What alternative methods do you see for arranging a sale of the Wilcox business to Statesman?

How much should Statesman pay for the Wilcox stock, if $800,000 is the right price for the net assets?

Using the price you have calculated for a stock purchase, decide which method is best for Karl Wilcox.

Do you see any reasons why what is best for Karl may not be best for David and Linda, in terms of tax consequences?

Exhibit 1: Wilcox Corporation
Balance sheet

Assets

Cash		$ 60,000
Receivables		160,000
Inventory		170,000
Land		150,000
Buildings	$405,000	
less depreciation-reserve	340,000*	
Net		65,000
Equipment	$415,000	
less depreciation-reserve	200,000†	
Net		215,000
Total assets		$820,000

Liabilities

Current	$180,000
Notes	50,000
Common stock	15,000
Earned surplus	575,000
Total liabilities and capital	$820,000

*Straight-line depreciation

†Sum-of-the-years digits depreciation. Amount written off on equipment since December 31, 1961, is $87,000.

Revenue Ruling 61–156[7]

Advice has been requested whether the transaction described below should be treated, for Federal income tax purposes, as a sale of corporate assets to a newly organized corporation followed by the liquidation of the

[7]*Cumulative Bulletin*, 1961–2, 62.

"selling" corporation under sections 337 and 331 of the Internal Revenue Code of 1954, or whether the transaction should be treated as a reorganization within the meaning of section 368 of the Code.

Within a 12-month period following the adoption of a plan of complete liquidation, a corporation sold substantially all of its assets to a new corporation formed by the management of the selling corporation. The "purchasing" corporation paid 18,000x dollars for the assets as follows:

(a) 2,025x dollars in shares of its stock equal to 45 percent of all the shares to be issued,
(b) 4,975x dollars in long-term notes, and
(c) 11,000x dollars in cash obtained through a first mortgage borrowing on the assets acquired.

Immediately thereafter, the new corporation sold shares of its stock, equal to 55 percent of all the shares to be issued, to the public through underwriters.

The "selling" corporation was then completely liquidated, paying off its funded and unfunded liabilities and distributing the balance of its assets, including the 45 percent stock interest in the purchasing corporation, the long-term notes, and cash to its shareholders. As a result of the transaction, the business enterprise continued without interruption in the corporate form with a substantial continuing stock interest on the part of those persons who were shareholders in the selling corporation.

Section 1.331-1(c) of the Income Tax Regulations provides as follows:

A liquidation which is followed by a transfer to another corporation of all or part of the assets of the liquidating corporation, or which is preceded by such a transfer may, however, have the effect of the distribution of a dividend or of a transaction in which no loss is recognized and gain is recognized only to the extent of "other property." See sections 301 and 356.

In this case, if the issuance of stock to the new investors is disregarded, there is clearly a mere recapitalization and reincorporation coupled with a withdrawal of funds. The withdrawal would be treated either under section 356(a) of the Code as "money or other property" received in connection with a reorganization exchange of stock for stock, or under section 301 of the Code as an unrelated distribution to the shareholders.

The issuance of stock to new investors can be disregarded as being a separate transaction, since even without it the dominant purpose—to withdraw corporate earnings while continuing the equity interest in substantial part in a business enterprise conducted in corporate form—was fully achieved. The issuance of stock to new investors was not needed to implement the dominant purpose and, therefore, the rest of the transaction was not fruitless without it and so dependent on it.

The transaction was shaped so as to make it essentially "a device whereby it has been attempted to withdraw corporate earnings at capital gains rates by distributing all the assets of a corporation in complete liquidation and promptly reincorporating" them. See Conference Report No. 2543, 83d Cong., to accompany H.R. 8300 (Internal Revenue Code of 1954), page 41.

It was not intended by Congress that such a device should obtain the benefits of section 337 and avoid dividend taxation. In substance there was no reality to the "sale" of corporate assets or to the "liquidation" of the selling corporation, since each was only a formal step in a reorganization of the existing corporation. The entire transaction was consummated pursuant to a plan of reorganization which readjusted interests in property continuing in a modified corporate form. Sections 1.368-1(b) and 1.368-2 (g) of the regulations.

The newly formed "purchasing" corporation was utilized to effect, in substance, a recapitalization and a change in identity, form or place of organization of the "selling" corporation and, at the same time, to withdraw accumulated earnings from the corporate enterprise for the benefit of the shareholders, while they nevertheless continued a substantial equity interest in the enterprise.

The fact that the shareholders of the "selling" corporation own only 45 percent of the stock of the "purchasing" corporation because of the public stock offering does not dispose of the reorganization question. A surrender of voting control, or ownership of less than 50 percent of the stock of a newly-formed corporation, does not in itself mark a discontinuity of interest. In *John A. Nelson* v. *Helvering* 296 U.S. 374, Ct. D. 1062, (1936), the Supreme Court of the United States held that there was a "reorganization" even though the shareholders of the acquired corporation received less than half of the stock of the acquiring corporation and received only nonvoting preferred stock therein. It is necessary only that the shareholders continue to have a definite and substantial equity interest in the assets of the acquiring corporation.

In view of the foregoing, it is held that the transaction here described constitutes a reorganization within the meaning of sections 368(a) (1) (E) and (F) of the Code. No gain or loss is recognized to the "selling" corporation on the exchange of property, as provided by section 361 of the Code. The basis of the assets in the hands of the "purchasing" corporation will be the same as in the hands of the "selling" corporation, as provided in section 362(b) of the Code. No gain or loss is recognized under section 354 of the Code on the exchange of the stock of the "selling" corporation for stock of the "purchasing" corporation pursuant to the plan of reorganization.

With regard to the stockholders withdrawal of money and other property from the corporate solution, it is necessary to determine whether such withdrawal is to be treated as "boot" received as part of the consideration for their stock in the "selling" corporation in accordance with section 356 (a) of the Code or as a separate dividend distribution taxable in accordance with the provisions of section 301 of the Code. See sections 1.301-1(1) and 1.331-1(c) of the regulations and *J. Robert Bazley* v. *Commissioner* 331 U.S. 737, Ct. D. 1687, C.B. 1947-2, 79, rehearing denied and amended. 332 U.S. 752 (1947).

Under section 356(a) (1) of the Code, gain would be recognized to the shareholders of the "selling" corporation upon the surrender of their shares of stock in exchange for stock of the "purchasing" corporation, its long-term notes, cash, and other assets, but in an amount not in excess of the sum of cash and the fair market value of the long-term notes and other assets received. Under section 356(a) (2) of the Code, such gain would be taxable as a dividend to each shareholder to the extent of his ratable share of the undistributed earnings and profits of the corporation accumulated after February 28, 1913; the remainder, if any, would be treated as gain from the exchange of property. Under section 301 the distribution would be taxable as a dividend to the same extent as a dividend formally declared in the same amount.

In this case, viewing the issuance of stock of the "purchasing" corporation to new investors as a transaction separate from the reorganization, it is concluded that the distribution to stockholders of the "selling" corporation of the cash, long-term notes, and other assets should be treated as a distribution under section 301 of the Code.

In view of the conclusions reached herein, reconsideration has been given to Revenue Ruling 56-541, C.B. 1956-2, 189, which holds under similar circumstances that a nontaxable corporate sale of assets was effected under section 337 of the Code and that distributions to the shareholders were to be treated as in full payment in exchange for their stock under a plan of complete liquidation of the old corporation. The conclusions reached in the instant case are equally applicable to the question involved in Revenue Ruling 56-541. Accordingly, Revenue Ruling 56-541, C.B. 1956-2, 189, is revoked.

Under authority of section 7805(b) of the Code, this Revenue Ruling will be applied retroactively in any case in which transactions were consummated prior to August 21, 1961, in reliance on the Service's position as published in Revenue Ruling 56-541 and a retroactive application would be to the taxpayer's detriment.

Mace Instruments, Inc.

On December 10, 1964, Mace Instruments, Inc., acquired all the outstanding common stock (there were no other classes of stock) of Walter and White, Inc., for 50,000 shares of its own voting common stock in a tax-free reorganization. The 50,000 shares were worth $2,500,000.

Mace Instruments manufactures electronic control devices for use in aircraft and industrial processes and hoped to integrate the activities of Walter and White, a manufacturer of thermostatic controls used with heating systems. Within a few months, however, the Mace Management realized they had bought a "lemon." They discovered the two companies were actually engaged in quite different types of business, that the Walter and White management was not nearly so capable as it had seemed, and that Walter and White products were rapidly losing ground in a competitive market.

The management of Mace was therefore highly receptive to inquiries received in March 1965, from Carlson Heating Systems, Inc., indicating an interest in purchasing Walter and White, Inc. It was clear from the outset that the price would be well below $2,500,000, and the accountants advising Mace were opposed to a sale of stock. They pointed out that while Mace, with taxable income of about $4,000,000 a year, could make good use of ordinary business losses, the company had realized no capital gains in 1965 and was unlikely to realize any significant capital gains for some years. Hence the Mace management insisted that any sale would have to be a sale of assets rather than stock.

Carlson offered to pay $1,361,792 in cash and to assume the $286,524 liabilities of Walter and White, Inc., for all of the assets of Walter and White except its cash $72,415. Carlson prepared an allocation of the price to the assets which is shown below together with the adjusted basis of the assets to Walter and White.

Table 1: Walter and White, Inc.
Allocation of price to assets

Asset	Adjusted basis to Walter and White, Inc.	Allocation of purchase price
Accounts receivable and prepaid expenses	$ 221,864	$ 221,864
Inventory	420,445	312,425
Stock of subsidiary #1*	82,254	264,000
Stock of subsidiary #2*	210,000	115,955
Land†, buildings, other fixed and depreciable assets	1,162,537	734,072
Total	$2,097,100	$1,648,316
Less liabilities assumed	286,524	286,524
Grand total	$1,810,576	$1,361,792

*The stock in both subsidiaries had been acquired by Walter and White, Inc., in the 1940's.

†The land was used in the business. All of the land, buildings and other fixed and depreciable assets had been held by Walter and White, Inc., for over a year.

The management of Mace was satisfied with the amount of the offer. If the assets were sold, however, either they could be sold directly by Walter and White, Inc., to Carlson or they could be distributed to Mace in a liquidation and then sold to Carlson. Mace had no use for the Walter and

White corporation once the assets had been disposed of. The management was primarily concerned about tax consequences and the superiority of ordinary losses to capital losses, although some of the executives were wondering whether they could have made a mistake in refusing to sell the stock of Walter and White, Inc.

Walter and White had a loss carry-over of $2510 from 1964 (its earnings and profits at the end of 1964 were $125,604), and in the first five months of 1965 it had lost approximately $4000. Section 381 of the Code offered the possibility that these losses could be used by Mace. For both Mace Instruments and Walter and White the taxable year was the calendar year.

The Board of Directors of Mace met on June 3, 1965, to make a final decision.

Sherman Manufacturing Company, Inc.

The Sherman Manufacturing Company is presently family-owned and largely family-managed, and it has been so since its founding in 1900. Over the years, however, some of the stock has come into the ownership of family members who have no part of the management. The owner-managers are seeking some way to concentrate control equitably in the hands of some of the managers.

Ownership

The company was founded in Rhode Island in 1900 by John Sherman, who was its president and sole stockholder until his death in 1935. He left his 1500 shares in equal portions to his three sons, John, Jr., William, and Edward. John, Jr., who was president of the company until his death in 1955, left 250 shares to his widow Ellen and 125 shares each to his sons James and Kenneth. William, who is now chairman of the board, still owns his 500 shares as does Edward, who is treasurer of the company.

Management

William has almost nothing to do with the company, except to preside at infrequent directors' and shareholders' meetings. He is sixty-eight years old, married, but childless. Edward, who is sixty years old, plays an active role but expects to retire in five years. He has an only child, Carlton, who is twenty-seven years old and assistant controller of the company. James is thirty-one years old and in charge of the company's marketing. Ellen has no interest in the operations of the company. Kenneth likewise has no interest; he owns a ranch in Arizona.

The president of the company is Art Carter, who is not related to any of the Shermans. He was brought in when John died in 1955, because at the time none of the family was believed competent to run the business. He has done a good job and is at present very important to the company's continued success. But he is apprehensive about his future. He sees the possibility of his being ousted to make way for James or Carlton, and he wants to share in ownership of the company. His salary is $40,000 a year, and he feels unable to save any significant portion of it. The company does have a pension plan which should pay him about $20,000 a year after age sixty-five (he is forty-eight at the present time). The plan is funded with life insurance.

The company

Operations of the company have been quite successful. Total assets are about $1,750,000, liabilities about $850,000, and equity (represented entirely by the 1500 shares of common stock) about $900,000. Earnings have been about $350,000 before taxes, on sales of about $4,000,000 and are rising at about 10 per cent a year.

There is no market for the company's stock and hence no market value. But on John's death in 1955 the Internal Revenue Service accepted book value, at that time $400 per share, as the correct value for estate tax purposes. The stock has never paid any dividends, because until 1955 all the stockholders were drawing salaries and needed no dividend income. Ellen and Kenneth have been pressing for dividends since 1955, but the company has used all its earnings for modernization and increased promotion, and those in control have been in no need of dividends. (Ellen is living fairly comfortably on the proceeds of her late husband's life insurance, and Kenneth's ranch is prospering; but neither can see any point in holding stock that pays no dividends.) William is paid $30,000 a year, Edward $35,000, James $9,500, and Carlton $8,500. William is not included in the pension plan, and the others expect he will draw his salary until his death. All the others will receive pensions on retirement.

Planning goals

Edward, James, and Carlton are agreed on the following objectives:

(1) James and Carlton are the only members of the family who will be engaged in management after Edward retires. They should ultimately have equal share ownership and between them they should control the company.

(2) The voting power of Ellen and Kenneth should be eliminated, both because they are only a nuisance at the present time and because it would be undesirable for their shares to pass to unfriendly hands.

(3) Art Carter is almost indispensable to the company at the present and will be for at least five years. He should be guaranteed future

employment as long as he is competent to manage, and he should be enabled to acquire some stock ownership. But he should be prevented, if possible, from passing his stock to outsiders.

(4) William's and Edward's stock should not be allowed to pass to outsiders, and on or before their deaths it should be either retired by the company, passed to James and Carlton, or somehow have its voting power removed. (Edward expects to pass the full *value* of his ownership to his widow and to Carlton. None of the three knows exactly what William plans to do with his estate, but they are not counting on his leaving anything to James or Carlton.)

Relations between Ellen and Kenneth and the other members of the family are a little strained, and those two can hardly be expected to give up their voting rights unless they receive something in exchange. The three men feel that some dividend payments would be possible, but they feel there is no point in paying unneeded dividends to William and Edward. James and Carlton are not quite so affluent, but although they would not object strongly to dividends (Carlton has no stock at the present, of course), they would rather see earnings retained and reinvested.

The stock owned by Ellen, Kenneth, and James has a basis, for tax purposes, of $400 a share. That owned by William and Edward has a basis of $80.

Chapter eight

Depreciation and the investment tax credit

In making up the profit and loss statement for a business, we show depreciation as an expense, under the assumption that the cost of certain assets should be charged against the income which they help to produce over the years. The depreciation charged for tax purposes follows the same principle—the tax deduction for the outlay on a depreciable asset is spread over the useful life of the asset. But the rate at which an asset is written off for ordinary bookkeeping purposes is chiefly a function of proper accounting procedures, while the rate at which depreciation is taken for tax purposes is determined largely by the Internal Revenue Code. There is generally no reason to expect that the depreciation shown on the operating statement of a business will be the same as the depreciation claimed for tax purposes.

Method of depreciation

Section 167 of the Tax Code is the starting point for a discussion of depreciation. Notice the three standard methods by which depreciation can be taken: straight line, declining balance, and sum-of-the-years digits. The method of depreciation is one of three important elements in determining a depreciation deduction. The other two are the salvage value and the useful life of the asset, which we will discuss later in this chapter.

Until the introduction of the 1954 Code, depreciation was generally taken for tax purposes on a straight line basis. The 1954 Code, however, introduced two methods of "accelerated" depreciation: declining balance and the sum-of-the-years digits. Declining balance is sometimes referred to as double declining balance, since the rate at which depreciation is taken on the declining balance is twice the normal straight line rate. For example, if an asset has a useful life of five years, straight line depreciation would call for writing off 20 per cent of the depreciable cost each year. Under double declining balance as authorized in section 167, 40 per cent of the cost could be written off in the first year, 40 per cent of the undepreciated balance in the second year, and so on. The Regulations for section 167 describe in some detail how these depreciation methods work.

Notice the limitations in section 167 on the use of accelerated depreciation. Some of the distinctions that are drawn in the Code in prescribing depreciation rules are those between new and old property, tangible and intangible property, and personal and real property. Real property is, in general, buildings and land (land, of course, is not depreciable at all), while personal property is all other property. Distinctions are also drawn on the basis of the expected useful life of an asset.

On the basis of section 167, you might conclude that used equipment can be depreciated only on a straight line basis. However, the Regulations in section 1.167(b)-0(b) authorize the use of 150 per cent declining balance, as a pre-1954 depreciation method that is still "reasonable." In the example given above of declining balance depreciation, if the asset were used property the deduction would be 30 per cent a year, rather than 40 per cent, on the declining balance.

It should be clear that both the declining balance and the sum-of-the-years digits methods of depreciation will give a "faster" write-off than straight line depreciation. That is, more depreciation is taken in the early years of the asset's life and less taken in the later years. The present value of the taxes saved by depreciation deductions will then be greater for the two methods of accelerated depreciation. Which of these two methods is the faster will depend on a number of factors; it is not possible to say generally that one is faster than the other. The following tables show some comparisons for the four methods of depreciation:

Table 1: Comparison of depreciation methods

Example A

Depreciation on an asset put into service at the end of 1967, with cost $10,000, salvage 0, and useful life 12 years:

Year	Straight line depreciation	Double declining balance*	Sum-of-the-year digits	150% declining balance†
1968	$833.33	$1666.67	$1538.46	$1250.00
1969	833.33	1388.89	1410.26	1093.75
1970	833.33	1157.41	1282.05	957.03
1971	833.33	964.50	1153.85	837.40
1972	833.33	803.75	1025.64	732.72
1973	833.33	669.79	897.43	641.13
1974	833.33	558.16	769.23	560.99
1975	833.33	558.16	641.02	490.87
1976	833.33	558.16	512.82	429.51
1977	833.33	558.16	384.61	375.82
1978	833.33	558.16	256.41	328.84
1979	833.33	558.16	128.20	2301.91

Present value at the beginning of 1967, of depreciation, discounted at 5 per cent:

$7034.33	$7508.60	$7659.95	$7107.91

Example B
Depreciation on an asset put into service at the end of 1967, with cost $10,000, salvage $2,000, and useful life 8 years:

1968	$1000.00	$2500.00	$1777.78	$1875.00
1969	1000.00	1875.00	1555.56	1523.44
1970	1000.00	1406.25	1333.33	1237.79
1971	1000.00	1054.69	1111.11	1005.71
1972	1000.00	791.01	888.88	817.13
1973	1000.00	373.04	666.66	663.92
1974	1000.00	-0-	444.44	539.43
1975	1000.00	-0-	222.22	337.56

Present value at the beginning of 1967, of depreciation, discounted at 5 per cent:

$6155.44	$6725.96	$6504.92	$6487.32

*Switch over to straight line when this becomes advantageous.

†Undepreciated balance is written off in final year—abandonment is assumed.

Salvage value

The Regulations under section 167 indicate how to take salvage value into consideration in calculating depreciation. Notice that salvage is not taken into account for declining balance depreciation, but total depreciation may not be taken beyond the salvage value. Section 167(f) of the Code permits a taxpayer to ignore small amounts of salvage under certain circumstances. This is a concession that was made in 1962 in connection with the introduction of section 1245. (This section has been discussed before and will be discussed again in this chapter.) It governs the recapture of depreciation when an asset that has been depreciated is sold.

Some problems arise in the estimation of salvage value, but they are generally of far less importance than the problems concerned with choice of the method of depreciation and useful life.

Useful economic life of an asset

Until 1962, the economic life of an asset, which affects the rate of depreciation for tax purposes, was a subject for negotiation between the taxpayer and the Internal Revenue Service, with "Bulletin F," last revised in 1942, the only official guide to what was acceptable. In 1962 the Treasury published Revenue Procedure 62–21, containing a new set of depreciation "Guidelines" and rules.

The Guidelines group business assets into about seventy-five classes and authorize a useful life for each class, which is generally considerably below the corresponding useful life suggested in Bulletin F. This liberalizing measure was partly the result of generally increasing rates of obsolescence and of asset turnover, to the extent that the Internal Revenue Service was becoming rather embarrassed about the lives suggested in Bulletin F. And it was partly the result of a desire to encourage capital investment by providing more attractive tax write-offs. It is something of a paradox that when the 1954 Internal Revenue Code was drawn up under a Republican administration, something like the Guidelines was not introduced for fear that such a concession to business by Republicans might have unfortunate political results. Reform had to wait for eight years until a Democratic administration could show its concern for business by publishing the Guidelines.

Although the Guideline lives themselves are not complicated, the rules governing them are, and they have become considerably more so since 1962. The complexity of the rules stems from the Treasury's unwillingness to permit a taxpayer to enjoy the advantages of the short Guideline lives unless the actual useful lives of his depreciable assets turn out to be no longer, or not much longer, than the Guideline lives. There has been a good deal of debate about this principle. A number of commentators argue that it should make no difference at all what the actual lives of a taxpayer's assets turn out to be. This is the practice in Canada, for example, where depreciation is all taken on a declining balance basis and the percentage to be applied is prescribed by asset classes. The actual useful life of an asset is irrelevant to the classification and hence to the rate at which depreciation is taken. The argument in favor of the Treasury position is that the Guidelines were designed at least in part to encourage investment and rapid replacement; this purpose is defeated if investors can have the advantage of the short Guideline lives without rapid replacement.

When the Guidelines were introduced, the Treasury said that any taxpayer who could justify a class life shorter than the prescribed Guideline life would be permitted to use that shorter class life. A taxpayer who had been using a life longer than the Guideline life would be permitted to switch to the Guideline life. And for a three-year "grace period" the taxpayer would be free to use the Guideline life without justifying it on the basis of his experience. That is, for three years he would not have to worry whether the actual useful lives of his assets were in fact somewhat longer than the Guideline lives; he could continue to use the Guideline lives for depreciation purposes.

But in Revenue Procedure 62–21 the Treasury first established the "reserve ratio test" that would be applied beginning at the end of three years. When the Revenue Procedure was published, a good many businessmen and tax experts believed that at the end of the three-year period these tests would be abandoned. There was considerable hope that Congress would intervene within the three years and by statute abolish the reserve ratio test. Congress did not act, however, and in 1965 the Treasury found itself in a rather awkward position. Many businesses had been happy to take depreciation based on the Guideline lives, making little or no effort to bring their actual replacement policy in line with these lives, partly in the hope that the tests would be abandoned by 1965. A day of reckoning was approaching and the Treasury was not pleased at the prospect of having to challenge thousands of depreciation schedules. The taxpayers' hope was partly fulfilled when the Treasury backed down and in 1965 proposed a new set of tests designed to soften and delay the impact of the reserve ratio test.

The reserve ratio test is mathematically a fairly complicated procedure designed to establish whether a taxpayer's retirement and replacement practices concerning assets in a Guideline class are consistent with the class life he is using for depreciation purposes. The reserve ratio is actually the ratio of the total depreciation on assets still in use to the original cost of those assets; it is a measure of how depreciated the assets actually are, for tax purposes. If this ratio is too high, then the taxpayer has been taking too much depreciation. Deciding whether the ratio is too high requires comparison with a standard, and Revenue Procedure 62–21 includes a number of tables showing what the reserve ratio should be, depending on the rate of growth in the taxpayer's assets, the method of depreciation used, and the time period over which the test was applied.

As noted above, the reserve ratio test was not to be enforced until 1965. In addition, any taxpayer whose reserve ratio did not meet the test in 1965 would be given a number of years to bring his reserve ratio within the permissible limit, provided that each year his reserve ratio moved closer to the limit. And the "adjustment table" established a lengthening of depreciable lives for taxpayers who failed the test.

In 1965, when it became clear that a great many taxpayers could not meet the reserve ratio test, Revenue Procedure 65–13 was published. This publication provided an alternative to the reserve ratio table, called the "Guideline Form." The Guideline Form overcomes one of the disadvantages of the reserve ratio table, a disadvantage which must certainly have unfairly caused some taxpayers to fail to meet the reserve ratio test. The reserve ratio test assumes an even rate of growth in assets, while the Guideline Form makes allowance for an individual taxpayer's pattern of asset growth. The 1965 Revenue Procedure also introduced two rules to assist taxpayers who could not meet the reserve ratio test. The "transitional allowance rule" increases the flexibility already built into the permissible ranges of the reserve ratio test. A second rule, called the "minimal adjustment rule," modifies the adjustment table of the 1962 Revenue Procedure. The adjustment table showed what would be done if a taxpayer failed to meet the reserve ratio test and authorized the Internal Revenue Service to increase the estimated life used by a taxpayer by as much as 25 per cent in a single year. The minimal adjustment rule permits an increase of only 5 per cent or 10 per cent in a year, depending on by how much the taxpayer fails to meet the reserve ratio test.

There are other technicalities associated with the Guidelines. Perhaps the best way to demonstrate the complexity of the whole business is to point out that Revenue Procedure 62–21 is ninety-two pages in length and Revenue Procedure 65–13 is seventy pages. Considering that virtually all of the complications concern the reserve ratio test and the way in which it is to be applied, it is perhaps unfortunate that the test is used at all.

Special depreciation provisions

Note in passing sections 171, 174, and 178 of the Code, dealing with the write-off of bond premiums, research expenses, and leasehold improvements. Section 179 is of more general interest. This section was added to the Code by the Small Business Tax Revision Act of 1958 and was clearly aimed at strengthening small enterprises. Notice the kinds of assets that qualify for this additional first-year depreciation allowance and the way in which these assets must be acquired.

*If a partnership acquired an asset and took the additional deprecia-
tion authorized by section 179, and then the partnership were incorporated, could the corporation in its first year of existence also
claim an additional first-year allowance under section 179? If a
parent corporation were to liquidate a subsidiary, could the parent
claim the additional first-year allowance on assets received from the
subsidiary in the year following liquidation?*

Depreciation recapture

We have already referred to section 1245 (in Chapter three) dealing
with the recapture of depreciation. The section was added to the Internal
Revenue Code in 1962, and it is not coincidental that the Guidelines
were published in the same year. The Treasury was not willing to liberalize depreciation deductions unless something was done about the loophole which permitted a taxpayer to convert ordinary income into capital gain through depreciation and resale of an asset at more than its depreciated value. The Treasury had, in fact, been concerned about this
loophole since 1954 when accelerated depreciation was first introduced.

Notice the definition, in section 1245(a)(3) of "section 1245 property." The real estate lobbies fought long and hard to have buildings
excluded from the definition. It was not until 1964 that depreciation
recapture was applied to buildings, through section 1250, which will be
covered in Chapter eleven. The real estate interests paid a price, however, for the exclusion in 1962: The Guidelines did not shorten the depreciable lives on buildings; in fact, some of these lives were lengthened
from the old Bulletin F lives.

Elevators and escalators were added to section 1245 property in
1964. There had been considerable doubt about whether an elevator or an
escalator was a structural component of a building or whether it was
personal property. As we will see, the provisions of section 1245 are
rather closely integrated with the provisions of section 48 governing the
investment tax credit. The Treasury had taken the position that elevators
and escalators are structural components of a building and hence were not
eligible for the investment tax credit. In 1964, Congress decided they
should be eligible for the investment tax credit and amended section 48.
At the same time, it concluded that they should also be subject to depreciation recapture and hence adopted the 1964 amendment to section
1245.

The investment tax credit

We noted above that one purpose of the depreciation Guidelines was
stimulation of investment and rapid replacement of depreciable assets.
The investment tax credit, also introduced in 1962, is an even clearer
demonstration of a policy favoring capital investment. What this tax credit
does, in effect, is permit a taxpayer to subtract, not from his taxable
income *but from the income tax itself*, a percentage of his investment in
assets qualifying for the tax credit. Sections 46, 47, and 48 of the Code
deal with the investment tax credit. Section 48 tells what investments
qualify for the credit.

Compare the description in section 48(a)(1) with that in section 1245(a)(3). The credit and the recapture provision show a substantial degree of correlation: Congress was consciously attempting to give a tax benefit through section 48 but to curb abuses of this benefit in section 1245. Section 46 describes how large the tax credit will be, and section 47 takes care of cases where property is disposed of and it turns out that the taxpayer really did not deserve the credit.

In 1966, when there were signs that the United States economy needed dampening rather than stimulating influences, the administration decided to remove the incentive of the investment tax credit. Section 48 was therefore amended to suspend the credit with respect to property acquired between October 10, 1966, and December 31, 1967. (Accelerated depreciation was also suspended with respect to this property.) Judging from the fact that the credit itself had a very much delayed effect on capital investment, it seems likely that the suspension also had a delayed effect. In fact, by early 1967 the administration had decided to restore the credit, and it was restored effective March 9, 1967.

Commissioner v. Indiana Broadcasting Corp.[1]

Mercer, District Judge: The single contested issue presented on this petition is the question whether a television network affiliation contract for a two-year term, which is automatically renewable, in the absence of termination by the affirmative act of either of the parties, for an unlimited number of successive two-year terms is a depreciable asset.

The purpose of the depreciation allowance permitted under the Code is to enable a taxpayer to recover the cost of a wasting asset used in his business by charging the diminution in the asset's value each year as a deduction from the gross income that year. *Detroit Edison Co.* v. *Commissioner* 319 U.S. 98; *Friend* v. *Commissioner*, 7 Cir., 119 F. 2d 959, cert, denied 314 U.S. 673. The end to be achieved "is to approximate and reflect the financial consequences to the taxpayer of the subtle effects of time and use on the value of his capital assets." *Detroit Edison Co.* v. *Commissioner, supra*, at 101.

---

[1]350 F. 2d 580 (U.S. Court of Appeals, 7th Circuit, 1965).

Intangible assets will not usually be a proper subject of the depreciation allowance unless the useful life of the asset is definitely limited or unless the intangible asset has value in the production of income for only a limited period of time, the duration of which can be estimated with reasonable accuracy. 26 CFR section 1.167(a)(3).[2] Although the Internal Revenue Code contains no specific reference to intangible assets in that regard, the Treasury Regulation, first adopted under the Revenue Act of 1918, remained substantially unchanged through successive re-enactments of the Code and the Regulation has thereby acquired the force and effect of law. *Helvering* v. *Winmill* 305 U.S. 79, 83; *Old Mission Co.* v. *Helvering* 293 U.S. 289, 293, 294; *United States* v. *Dakota-Montana Oil Co.* 288 U.S. 459, 466.[3]

The Tax Court found that the contracts in issue were depreciable assets which could be depreciated by use of the straight line method over an estimated valuable life of twenty years. The Commissioner filed this petition to review the determination.

Taxpayer, Indiana Broadcasting Corporation, acquired all of the assets of WISH-TV in Indianapolis, and WANE-TV in Fort Wayne, Indiana, in November, 1956, by its purchase of all of the issued and outstanding stock of Universal Broadcasting Company, Inc., the prior owner of the two television stations. Among the assets acquired by the taxpayer were the two CBS[4] network affiliation contracts, one with respect to station WISH-TV and the other with respect to station WANE-TV. Each of those contracts was dated March 30, 1956, and had been renewed prior to taxpayer's acquisition of the Universal assets for terms ending, respectively, on August 18, 1958, and September 26, 1958. Each contract provided that thereafter it would be automatically renewed for additional two-year periods, unless the contract was terminated in writing by either of the parties thereto not less than six months prior to its then termination

---

[2]The applicable Regulation provides:
"If the intangible asset is known from experience or other factors to be of use in the business or in the production of income for only a limited period, the length of which can be estimated with reasonable accuracy, such an intangible asset may be the subject of a depreciation allowance. Examples are patents and copyrights. An intangible asset, the useful life of which is not limited, is not subject to the allowance for depreciation. . . ." 26 CFR, sec. 1.167(a)(3).

[3]Applying the Regulation, the courts have allowed depreciation over the term thereof of the value of real estate leases and baseball player contracts, which, though renewable, could be renewed beyond the specified life of the contract only by renegotiation. E.g., *Bonwit Teller & Co.* v. *Commissioner*, 2 Cir., 53 F. 2d 381; *Commissioner* v. *Pittsburgh Athletic Co.*, 3 Cir., 72 F. 2d 883; *Helvering* v. *Kansas City American Assoc. Baseball Co.*, 8 Cir., 75 F. 2d 600. Also recognized as proper subjects for depreciation have been street railway and motor coach franchises which were for fixed terms and not automatically renewable. E.g., *Cleveland Railway Co.* v. *Commissioner* 36 B.T.A. 208; *Pasadena City Lines, Inc.* v. *Commissioner* 23 T.C. 34.

Examples of intangibles which have been held not to be the proper subject of a depreciation allowance are a FCC broadcasting license, *KWTV Broadcasting Co.* v. *Commissioner*, 5 Cir., 272 F. 2d 406; renewable liquor licenses and saloon permits, *Tube Bar Inc.* v. *Commissioner*.

[4]The three existing television networks are designated throughout this option by the following initials: CBS for Columbia Broadcasting Company, and NBC for National Broadcasting Company, and ABC for American Broadcasting Company.

date. Both of those contracts were still in force at the time of the trial of this action.

The consideration paid by the taxpayer for the Universal assets was $11,098,800.67. Of that amount the taxpayer allocated $4,000,000 to the CBS affiliation with WISH-TV and $625,000 to the CBS affiliation contract with WANE-TV. In each of its taxable years ending, respectively, on November 30, 1957, 1958 and 1959, taxpayer claimed deductions for depreciation on the $4,625,000 allocated to the CBS contracts. The Commissioner disallowed the deductions and assessed a deficiency against the taxpayer for each of those taxable years. The taxpayer filed a petition in the tax Court for a redetermination of the deficiencies charged by the Commissioner.

At the trial below, the parties stipulated into evidence an 84-page exhibit which shows the history since 1948 of affiliation contracts of all television networks in each of 84 television market areas which had three or more television stations in operation on December 31, 1962. That exhibit showed the date when each station in each area began operation and the duration of all network affiliation contracts in each of the 84 areas.

Using that history, taxpayer's statisticians prepared a two-pronged life expectancy table, i.e., the aggregate termination experiences reflected by all NBC and CBS contracts and the selected CBS experience. The latter was based upon CBS contract experience only for periods after which in any market area there had been at least one other station in operation for at least twelve months, which was neither affiliated with NBC nor owned and operated by ABC. The latter area of experience was selected because it is limited to CBS contracts after there were sufficient stations in each particular market area to permit CBS to select between its affiliated station and at least one station which was neither owned by nor affiliated with either NBC or ABC.

Those tables showed 88 terminations of NBC and CBS affiliation contracts from 1948 through 1962, and, on the selected CBS side, 19 terminations of CBS affiliations from 1948 through 1962.

The theory of the statistical tables compiled was that an annual rate of contract termination for each pertinent period could be obtained by dividing the total number of years commenced by all of the affiliation contracts during a given period into the total number of contract terminations occurring during the same period. Using that termination rate, taxpayer's witnesses testified that the average life expectancy of any given contract could be determined by applying the Poisson-Exponential Theory of Failure. The crux of that theory is that the percentage of failure of items to which it is applied is a constant. For example, assuming a termination rate from the table of 5 percent per year, 95 percent of the whole group would survive at the end of one year, 5 percent of that 95 percent would fail to survive the second year and so on.

Adopting that theory, and applying it with some modification to the statistical history, the Tax Court found that an estimated useful life of the WISH and WANE CBS affiliation contracts could be determined with reasonable accuracy, and that use of the straight-line method over 20 years was a reasonable basis for depreciation of the contracts.

We think that the Tax Court erred in its findings that an estimated useful life of these contracts could be determined with reasonable accuracy.

The validity of the statistical analysis is more apparent than real because the analysis ignores the facts of life of the television broadcasting industry. Factors must be taken into account which show conclusively that these affiliation contracts, while in force, are not only not wasting assets but are assets of a constant, or even expanding, value. There are also factors which argue strongly for the perpetual duration of the contracts, at best, or at least for a wholly unpredictable life. We think those factors which we hereinafter explore show that each contract is more unique than generic, which makes it questionable whether any meaningful general experience could ever be shown.

There are 12 VHF channels and 70 UHF[5] channels available upon which television broadcasting stations may operate. Those channels are variously allocated by the FCC[6] to particular cities or broadcast areas upon the basis of population and other factors. Each such channel may be utilized for commercial broadcasting pursuant to licenses granted to applicants by the FCC.

In 1945 there were 6 commercial television stations operating within the continental United States, all VHF. By September, 1948, the number of VHF stations had increased to 108, at which point a period of time known in the industry as "the freeze" began. From September, 1948, to July 1, 1952, the freeze period, the FCC processed no applications for television broadcasting licenses. The number of VHF commercial stations increased each year after the freeze was lifted to a total of 474 stations as of January 1, 1963.

UHF licensing was first authorized by the FCC at the end of the freeze, and the number of the UHF channels in actual use has been variable, but limited.[7]

Relevant to this case, the FCC allotted to Indianapolis four VHF channels, all now in use, and three UHF channels, none of which is in use. Fort Wayne was allotted four UHF channels, three of which are now on the air. WISH-TV began operating on July 1, 1954, and WANE-TV[8] began operating in September, 1954.

The revenue of television broadcasters is derived from charges for broadcast time paid by advertisers. The rates charged by stations for advertising time vary from area to area, and from station to station within a given area, according to the estimated size of the audience of the partic-

---

[5]Very High Frequency; Ultra High Frequency.

[6]Federal Communications Commission.

[7]Because few early television receivers were equipped to receive UHF broadcasts, UHF stations in operation reached a high of 121 stations in 1954, and then declined in number to 76 stations in 1960. By January 1, 1963, the number of such stations had increased to 90 under the impetus of legislation and rules requiring all channel capability for new television receivers.

[8]First licensed as WINT-TV.

ular station. The charges of a single station may vary according to its usual audience for different hours of the day. Therein lies the value of network affiliation; attractive programs draw a large audience, a large audience attracts advertisers and advertisers are revenue.

The sources of available programming are three-fold, namely, locally produced programs, motion pictures and other filmed material purchased by a station from distribution sources other than the networks and network programming. The latter is of two types, namely, sponsored network programs and non-sponsored, or sustaining, programs furnished by the networks to their affiliated stations.

Throughout the history of television, network programs have been the most valuable source of programming for a station. Their value is three-fold. First, network programming tends to have a national audience appeal which attracts a large number of viewers. Secondly, network programs are delivered to affiliated stations without charge[9] whereas a non-affiliated station must produce or purchase all program material at substantial cost.[10] Finally, it is frequently impossible for a non-affiliated station to buy programming at any cost which can compete effectively against the network programs.

At all material times, CBS was the dominant network in audience appeal, with NBC and ABC following in that order.

Thus a network affiliation contract is something of value, and a CBS affiliation contract is something of the greatest value in any given market area.[11] At the time of the trial of this case, the value of a CBS contract was essentially equivalent to the value of all of the other combined assets of an operative station owning such a contract.

It seems, therefore, certain that any non-affiliated station now on the air, or any station which might begin operating, in taxpayer's market areas would covet taxpayer's affiliation contracts. However, the side of the slate which taxpayer's witnesses omitted from their opinion testimony, and which we believe the court below omitted from its evaluation of the evidence, militates strongly against the success of any covetous overtures to CBS by any competing station.

The first element which the court below overlooked is the state of flux which has affected this young industry,[12] with its consequent effect upon the industry history of contracts. Through the freeze period it was

---

[9]There is no charge for programming, except that for recorded programs, the networks do charge the affiliated station for the recording furnished.

[10]In a given market area, the cost of the operation of various stations, exclusive of the cost of programs, is substantial and approximately equivalent. This factor then has a very real bearing upon the profits to be realized by a station.

[11]Assuming all other factors to be equal, including the facilities to reach an audience, the Indianapolis experience of 1958 indicates a basis for comparison. In that year WISH-TV had net income of $1,195,695, as compared to $754,000 for the NBC affiliate, $199,777 for the ABC affiliate and a loss of $241,293 for a non-affiliated station.

[12]Though a few stations began commercial operation in 1945, 1948 may be called the year of the birth of the industry.

not uncommon for a single station to have affiliation contracts with two or more networks.[13] There simply were not enough stations in many areas, and the networks found outlets for their programs where they could, even if they had to share the spotlight with one or more competing networks. As new stations came on the air after the freeze a large number of affiliation contracts were terminated as the networks sought exclusive area affiliations. In the period 1953 to 1955 which immediately followed the freeze 49 NBC and CBS contracts were terminated.[14] All of those terminations entered into the statistical analysis of the aggregate experience and many of them affected the selected CBS statistics. The stipulated exhibit strongly suggests that the period of flux yet continues in the industry, and that it colors the industry history to such an extent that there is grave doubt that any reliable norm of contract expectation could be found at this time. We think it certain that any such norm built upon the evidence in this case would be pure guesswork, and we see no statistical validity in the life expectancy tables upon which the decision below rests.

It is likewise clear that the stipulated exhibit graphically refutes the existence of a basic premise upon which the Poisson theory relies, namely, that the life expectancy of all contracts is the same regardless of the length of duration of the contract. Of the 88 contract terminations included in taxpayer's aggregate experience analysis, 50 percent were terminated before they had been in force for four years, and 80 contracts, or approximately 91 percent of the group, were terminated before they had been in force for seven years.[15] Only three of those contracts were terminated after they had been in force for more than nine years. Of those three, one was terminated by the local station, not by the network. A second, terminated by CBS, was the contract of a station affiliated with both CBS and NBC, and located in a market area in which CBS had then contracted an exclusive affiliation with another station. The record contains no hint as to the background for the termination of the third of those contracts. The summary of industry history is undoubtedly subject to varying interpretations, each of arguable validity, but we think it necessary to conclude that the premise that a contract in its ninth year, for example, is no more immune from termination than is a contract in its first year is not one of such arguable interpretations. A very high degree of stability is reflected in the history of contracts which have continued in force for more than eight or nine years. Whatever its worth in other areas, the Poisson-Exponential theory has no application in this case.

---

[13]WISH-TV was affiliated with NBC, ABC and the now inoperative Dumont Network, as well as with CBS, in its first year of operation. WANE-TV was affiliated with both CBS and ABC from 1954 to 1957.

[14]That number represents about 55 percent of the terminations considered in compiling the life expectancy tables adopted by the court below.

[15]No reason for termination is shown as to any of those contracts, though the timing of the termination does suggest that a very substantial number of them were terminated when exclusive affiliation facilities first became available to the networks.

Another factor which taxpayer's statistician did not consider at all[16] and a factor which the court below largely overlooked, is the CBS policy in the renewal of its contracts.

CBS policy, as outlined by a network bulletin in evidence, stresses "present affiliation with a station" as a "substantial factor" governing the CBS decision when any contract is ripe for renewal because of general business considerations and because an audience tends to associate the network with its established outlet. CBS is "reluctant to disturb" the existing affiliation, and, unless a new station shows "substantial superiority in significant areas, the fact of present affiliation controls."

Factors deemed significant by CBS in determining questions of affiliation with a local station are the station's clearance of network programs for broadcast,[17] the qualifications of management, including newspaper ownership of the station, multiple station ownership and location of the station in the principal city of its market area.

The record reveals that taxpayer is managed by experienced persons in the field, and that it is owned in common with the New York Herald-Tribune and three other corporations operating television stations in Tulsa, Houston and Sacramento.[18] Its stations are located in the principal cities of its respective market area.[19] Its stations have a record of broadcasting network programs about 63 percent of their total broadcast time and during an average 95 percent of the "prime time" hours.[20] Though the factor of contemporaneous ownership of CBS-affiliated radio facilities is now considered inconsequential by CBS, it may be noted that taxpayer operates radio stations affiliated with CBS in both Indianapolis and Fort Wayne.[21]

Clearly taxpayer attached substantial significance to the renewal prospects of its contracts and purchased the stations with the expectation

---

[16]He professed to have no knowledge of the television industry in general and of network affiliation practices in particular. He testified that he based his evaluation and testimony solely upon the data contained in the contract-history exhibit.

[17]Non-clearance and delay of broadcast of network programs evidencing a disinterest in those programs which unreasonably impairs the ability of CBS to serve national advertisers will "generally" outweigh the disadvantages of disrupting an existing relationship because of the network's need "to effect substantial clearance."

[18]All of those stations are affiliated with CBS under contracts ranging in date from November, 1949, to March, 1955.

[19]Of present significance, the only non-affiliated station in the Indianapolis market area is located outside the City of Indianapolis. The record reveals that that station has had contracts with NBC and ABC terminated for that reason as new stations began broadcasting from Indianapolis, the central city of the market area.

[20]From 7:30 p.m. through 11:00 p.m.

[21]Whatever significant relationship the selected CBS experience may bear to taxpayer's situation, particularly in Indianapolis, the table is meaningless because it lacks any reference to the cardinal factor of the reason for the several terminations included therein. Without knowledge of the reason for each contract termination, there is totally lacking any basis for the comparison of taxpayer's situation to the situation which evoked any of those several CBS terminations.

that the contracts would be continued in force indefinitely. It appears that that expectation will be realized by it in the light of the already substantial duration of the contracts and of pronounced CBS policy governing contract renewals. There is nothing to suggest that CBS will change its policy, or that at any reasonably predictable time the one party or the other will cause the contracts to be terminated. Moreover, unlike an asset having a declining value with the passage of time, these contracts probably will have a constant value, or even an increasing value in years to come.

In the single previous case dealing with the issue before us it was held that the taxpayer had failed to adduce any evidence to prove that network affiliation contracts had a useful life capable of reasonable calculation. *Westinghouse Broadcasting Co.* v. *Commissioner* 36 T.C. 912, aff'd 3 Cir. 309 F. 2d 279, cert. denied 372 U.S. 935. Taxpayer argues that the stipulated industry-history exhibit supplies the deficiency held to exist in *Westinghouse.* There is no merit to that position. That exhibit suggests, and the record as a whole persuasively indicates, that taxpayer's contracts may be expected to remain in force for a wholly unpredictable period of time.

We think that a close analogy to this case is found in *Nachman* v. *Commissioner*, 5 Cir., 191 F. 2d 934. There the taxpayer paid $8,000 for a city liquor license having five months of a one-year term unexpired. Although the license itself contained no provision relative to renewal, the evidence indicated that the city, in issuing licenses from year to year, gave preference to holders of existing licenses over other applicants for the limited number of licenses authorized. The court affirmed the Tax Court's decision holding, inter alia, that the license was indefinite in duration and, therefore, a non-depreciable capital asset.

The *Nachman* rationale was applied in *Gant* v. *Commissioner*, 6 Cir., 263 F. 2d 558,[22] *KWTX Broadcasting Co.* v. *Commissioner*, 5 Cir., 272 F. 2d 406,[23] and *Coca Cola Bottling Co.* v. *Commissioner*, 6 B.T.A. 1333.[24]

We think that the reasoning of those cases is sound and that the present case cannot be factually distinguished therefrom. Where there is no reasonable basis for the prediction of the expected valuable life of an intangible asset, it follows that the asset is not the proper subject of depreciation allowance.

The Tax Court's findings that the estimated useful life of these contracts is ascertainable with reasonable certainty and that these contracts are depreciable assets are clearly erroneous. The decision of the Tax Court is therefore reversed.

Reversed.

---

[22]That case involved a gasoline distributorship agreement for a fixed term which contained no specific renewal covenant except the customary usage in the trade.

[23]This case involved a three year FCC license to operate a television station, and the factor that the FCC had never refused to renew an existing license.

[24]This case involved a Coca Cola franchise with no guarantee of renewal except industry practice.

Exhibit 1: Racine Stone and Gravel Company
Balance sheet as of March 31, 1962
(dollar figures in thousands)

	1958	1959	1960	1961	1962
Assets					
Current assets:					
Cash......................	$ 627	$ 1,524	$ 826	$ 505	$ 2,581
Securities.................	506	558	573	372	373
Acc'ts receivable—net	608	824	894	872	776
Inventories	628	700	598	840	698
Prepaid expenses............	3	7	10	15	24
Total current assets	$ 2,372	$ 3,613	$ 2,901	$ 2,604	$ 4,452
Investments.....................	573	232	73	62	87
Other assets....................	-0-	562	873	823	542
Property, plant and equipment......	11,480	12,054	13,492	15,445	15,560
Less depr. and depl. allowances.	3,883	4,472	4,959	5,646	6,191
Net plant....................	$ 7,597	$ 7,582	$ 8,533	$ 9,799	$ 9,369
Total assets....................	$10,542	$11,989	$12,380	$13,288	$14,450
Liabilities					
Current liabilities:					
Notes payable—1 year	$ 41	$ 31	$ 3	$ 200	$ 200
Acc'ts payable	541	511	312	489	453
Salaries, wages, payroll taxes ..	-0-	-0-	-0-	-0-	-0-
Taxes	348	825	524	60	550
Total current liabilities	$ 930	$ 1,367	$ 839	$ 749	$ 1,203
Long-term debt:					
Notes payable	-0-	-0-	70	870	658
Reserve for compensation					
liability	227	232	223	217	199
Stockholders' equity:					
Common Stock (par value					
$50 per share:					
Authorized—60,000 shares.					
Outstanding—40,927 shares) ..	2,011	2,011	2,011	2,022	2,037
Capital surplus..................	1,100	1,101	1,101	1,117	1,141
Retained earnings	6,274	7,278	8,135	8,318	9,212
Less stock in treas.	-0-	-0-	-0-	(5)	-0-
Total equity	$ 9,385	$10,390	$11,248	$11,452	$12,390
Total liabilities	$10,542	$11,989	$12,380	$13,288	$14,450

Racine Stone and Gravel Company

The Racine Stone and Gravel Company was founded at the turn of the century for purposes of supplying ballast (crushed stone) to the Great Northern Railway System. The company operates at present in Wisconsin, Illinois, and Minnesota, and since 1963 its major product has been bituminous concrete or blacktop.

The company is a closely held corporation, owned by two families. Both of the families play an active part in management. There are 60,000 authorized shares of stock, 41,000 of which were outstanding at the end of 1962. Book value per share is slightly over $300, although the company's bank places a value of $150 on Racine stock for purposes of estate planning. Financial statements are given in Exhibits 1 and 2.

Exhibit 2: Racine Stone and Gravel Company
Statement of operations 1958–1962
(Years ending March 31)
(dollar figures in thousands)

	1958	1959	1960	1961	1962
Net sales	$9,333	$10,060	$10,733	$10,157	$11,743
Less:					
Cost of goods sold	6,506	6,356	6,750	7,277	7,327
Depreciation	749	832	851	942	992
Depletion	11	12	11	15	15
Total cost of sales.	$7,266	$ 7,200	$ 7,612	$ 8,234	$ 8,334
Total	$2,067	$ 2,860	$ 3,121	$ 1,923	$ 3,409
Other income	$ 51	$ 54	$ 55	$ 56	$ 29
Other expenses.	993	1,019	1,210	1,331	1,432
Net income before taxes.	1,125	1,895	1,966	648	2,006
Income taxes.	435	875	907	265	910
Net income	$ 690	$ 1,020	$ 1,059	$ 383	$ 1,096

Company planning

In 1961, management expressed as one of its goals the expansion of the company's plant and equipment at a rate of about $1,385,000 annually. In the preceding ten years, retained earnings had averaged $700,000 and depreciation about $800,000. In 1961, preliminary steps were taken to make a public offering of common stock, but negotiations were broken off in early 1962 because of a sharp decline in the stock market. However, new opportunities for expansion through acquisitions emphasized the need for funds, and the company continued to think of the possibility of "going public."

1962 depreciation changes

In early 1963, Racine's Treasurer, Albert Jameson, and Controller, Robert Goodman, were analyzing the effect on the company of the Treasury Department's new Revenue Procedure 62–21. This procedure set up new guidelines for depreciation which, in many cases, enable a corporation to recover the cost of an asset in a shorter time than was possible under the Treasury's old Bulletin F.

Jameson had contacted the company's public accounting firm, seeking advice on the best way to adjust current depreciation practices in order to take advantage of the new rules. Excerpts from the reply follow:

Dear Mr. Jameson:

As a result of the study that you wished us to make, we have decided that the following would be the most effective way in which to organize Racine's accounts for the application of the new depreciation guidelines.

In the first place, we note that both the Office Furniture and Fixture Account and the Building Account are being depreciated at rates equal or shorter than the guideline lives. Therefore, depreciation calculations should not be altered in either of these accounts.

We suggest that the remaining assets be divided into three major categories, as shown in Exhibits 3 4 and 5. Exhibit 3 shows our suggested organization of the Transportation Account, which until now has been depreciated on a six-year basis under the sum-of-the-years digits method. Exhibit 3-A shows our recommended handling of trucks and automobiles, in a new Automotive account. Under guidelines, all trucks should continue to have a six-year life. Automobiles, however, should be depreciated on a four-year basis. We recommend four years rather than the three-year guideline life in order to take advantage of the seven percent investment tax credit. In arranging the accounts for a changeover, it will also be necessary under the guideline rules to transfer certain production equipment from the Automotive Account to the Stone and Sand Plant Account. This adjustment has been recorded in Exhibit IV-B. In summary, the assets in the Transportation Account would be distributed among the new Automotive Account and the Stone and Sand Plant Account.

Exhibits 4 and 5 show the Stone and Sand Plant Account and the Bituminous Concrete Plant Account both of which have been using a twenty-five-year life with sum-of-the-years digits depreciation for some property and straight line depreciation for some. The Stone and Sand Plant assets now qualify under a ten-year guideline class, and the Bituminous Concrete assets under a fifteen-year class. Both sum-of-the-years digits and straight line methods of deprecia-

Exhibit 3-A: Racine Stone and Gravel Company
Current transportation equipment account
(On sum-of-the-years digits)
(Years ending March 31)

Account	1958	1959	1960	1961	1962	1963
Asset account						
Balance—beginning of year	$ 919,369	$1,039,357	$1,331,157	$1,450,009	$1,606,693	$1,561,957
Additions	292,817	215,993	335,023	366,562	183,204	
Transfers and deductions	(47,882)	277,824	(85,260)	(57,341)	(18,235)	
Fully depreciated	(124,947)	(202,017)	(130,911)	(152,537)	(209,705)	
Balance—end of year	1,039,357	1,331,157	1,450,009	1,606,693	1,561,957	
Depreciation account						
Balance reserve—beginning of year	500,326	607,341	798,272	860,423	939,442	989,021
Provisions for year	272,598	264,634	259,634	275,925	274,945	
Transfers and deductions	(40,636)	92,211	(66,572)	(44,369)	(15,660)	
Fully depreciated	(124,947)	(165,914)	(130,911)	(152,537)	(209,706)	
Balance—end of year	607,341	798,272	860,423	939,442	989,021	
Net assets—end of year	$ 432,016	$ 532,885	$ 589,586	$ 667,251	$ 572,936	

Exhibit 3-B: Racine Stone and Gravel Company
Recommended automotive account 3/31/62
(After transfer of $1,320,827 cost and $864,309 depreciation reserve to stone and sand plant account)
(On sum-of-the-years digits basis)

Item	Year of acqui-sition	Original cost	Deprecia-tion resv. 3/31/62	Net asset 3/31/62	Remaining life (pres. schedule) at 3/31/62	Remaining life* (guidelines) at 3/31/62
Automobiles	1957	$ 2,367	$ 2,310	$ 57	.5	.333
(4 year	1958	8,843	8,001	842	1.5	1.000
life under	1959	29,407	23,105	6,302	2.5	1.667
guidelines;	1960	68,411	42,349	26,062	3.5	2.333
6 years under	1961	55,487	22,460	33,027	4.5	3.000
present method)	1962	41,702	5,943	35,759	5.5	3.667
	1963	50,000(est.)				
Totals		$256,217	$104,168	$102,049		
Trucks	1957	-0-	-0-	-0-	.5	.5
(6 year	1958	-0-	-0-	-0-	1.5	1.5
life under	1959	9,727	7,643	2,084	2.5	2.5
present method	1960	16,500	10,214	6,286	3.5	3.5
and guidelines)	1961	5,522	2,235	3,287	4.5	4.5
	1962	3,164	452	2,712	5.5	5.5
	1963	5,000(est.)				
Totals		$ 39,913	$ 20,544	$ 14,369		

*Note: to convert from six-year lives to four-year lives, multiply remaining life by 4/6. In general, multiply remaining life under old method by $\frac{\text{new life}}{\text{old life}}$ to get remaining life under new method.

(The Guideline life for automobiles is three years, but the company's accountants suggest using four years and claiming the tax credit.)

Exhibit 4-A: Racine Stone and Gravel Company
Current stone and sand plant account
(On sum-of-the-years digits and straight line—25 years)
(Years ending March 31)

Account	1958	1959	1960	1961	1962	1963
Asset account						
Balance—beginning of year	$6,380,848	$7,316,947	$7,630,191	$8,228,631	$9,300,775	$9,516,468
Additions	998,857	260,974	826,818	997,134	212,136	
Transfers and deductions	(11,100)	179,431	(189,820)	117,378	153,125	
Fully depreciated	(51,658)	(127,162)	(38,577)	(42,369)	(149,568)	
Balance—end of year	7,316,947	7,630,191	8,228,631	9,300,775	9,516,468	
Depreciation account						
Balance reserve—beginning of year	1,856,544	2,144,978	2,549,683	2,869,132	3,321,094	3,684,539
Provision for year	349,570	411,168	424,557	452,456	472,091	
Transfers and deductions	(9,478)	95,020	(66,551)	41,875	40,922	
Fully depreciated	(51,658)	(101,483)	(38,557)	(42,369)	(149,568)	
Balance—end of year	2,144,978	2,549,683	2,869,132	3,321,094	3,684,539	
Net assets—end of year	$5,171,969	$5,080,508	$5,359,499	$5,979,681	$5,831,929	

Exhibit 4-B: Racine Stone and Gravel Company
Recommended stone and sand plant account   3/31/62
(After transfer of $1,320,827 cost and $864,309 depreciation reserve from transportation account)
(On sum-of-the-years digits basis)

Item	Year of acqui-sition	Original cost	Deprecia-tion resv. 3/31/62	Net asset 3/31/62	Remaining life (pres. schedule) at 3/31/62	Remaining life* (guidelines) at 3/31/62
Automotive Equipment (Now becomes part of sand plant account. Life under present method is 6 years; under guidelines 10 years)	1957	$267,203	$260,841	$ 6,362	.5	.83
	1958	223,856	202,536	21,320	1.5	2.5
	1959	155,956	118,588	37,368	2.5	4.2
	1960	219,033	134,628	84,405	3.5	5.8
	1961	324,875	129,156	195,719	4.5	7.5
	1962	129,904	18,560	111,344	5.5	9.2
	1963	200,000(est.)				
Totals		$1,520,827	$864,309	$456,518		
Sand Plant Life under present method 25 years; under guidelines 10 years)	1955	$609,894	$307,511	$302,383	17.5	7
	1956	175,797	78,056	97,741	18.5	7.4
	1957	972,150	373,495	598,655	19.5	7.8
	1958	998,858	321,217	677,641	20.5	8.2
	1959	265,563	65,882	199,681	21.5	8.6
	1960	376,473	70,283	306,190	22.5	9.0
	1961	666,642	87,270	579,372	23.5	9.4
	1962	207,769	9,852	197,917	24.5	9.8
	1963	400,000(est.)				
Totals		$4,673,146	$1,313,566	$2,959,580		

*Note: to convert from six-year lives to four-year lives, multiply remaining life by 4/6. In general, multiply remaining life under old method by new life/old life to get remaining life under new method.

Exhibit 4-C: Racine Stone and Gravel Company
Current stone and sand plant account   3/31/62
(On straight line depreciation. Life under present
method is 25 years; under guidelines, 10 years)

Year of acquisition	Original cost	Depreciation reserve 3/31/62	Net asset 3/31/62
1936	$ 11,600	$ 11,600	$ -0-
1937	70,250	69,548	702
1938	50,414	47,883	2,531
1939	118,740	108,123	10,617
1940	89,444	77,696	11,748
1941	107,686	89,719	17,967
1942	21,997	17,250	4,747
1943	37,109	27,080	10,029
1944	22,040	15,539	6,501
1945	85,675	57,301	28,374
1946	159,519	92,663	66,856
1947	415,758	247,408	168,350
1948	543,435	305,038	238,397
1949	347,425	211,774	135,651
1950	376,123	168,220	207,903
1951	674,685	325,340	349,345
1952	624,997	234,240	390,757
1953	330,470	119,734	210,736
1954	177,265	66,939	110,326
1955	2,532	846	1,686
1959	417	75	342
1960	466,442	46,644	419,798
1961	506,049	30,248	475,801
1962	3,250	65	3,185
1963	300,000(est.)		
Totals	$5,543,322	$2,370,973	$2,872,349

Note: In no case can depreciation in one year exceed 10 per cent of original cost. In the case of assets which are more than 10 years old and less than 90 per cent depreciated, depreciation up to 10 per cent of cost may be taken in the first year under new guidelines. The rest, if it does not exceed 10 per cent, may be written off in the following year.

   Example: 1940: 10 per cent × $89,444 = $8,944. The maximum depreciation write-off equals $8,944. Thus,
in 1963 depreciation can be: $8,944
in 1964 depreciation can be: 2,804
                               ———————
                              $11,748

Exhibit 5-A: Racine Stone and Gravel Company
Current bituminous concrete plant account
(On sum-of-the-years digits and straight line—25 years)
(Years ending March 31)

Account	1958	1959	1960	1961	1962	1963
Asset accounts						
Balance—beginning of year	$1,978,456	$2,518,771	$2,457,176	$2,880,468	$3,457,969	$3,558,985
Additions	471,606	338,056	579,103	692,687	117,309	
Transfers and deductions	68,709	(46,578)	(111,639)	(94,223)	28,058	
Fully depreciated	-0-	(353,073)	(44,172)	(20,963)	(44,351)	
Balance—end of year	2,518,771	2,457,176	2,880,468	3,457,969	3,558,985	
Depreciation accounts						
Balance reserve—beginning of year	744,036	863,758	839,724	893,619	1,040,272	1,211,282
Provision for year	120,305	149,225	158,495	196,115	214,142	
Transfers and deductions	(583)	(11,267)	(60,428)	(28,499)	1,219	
Fully depreciated	-0-	(161,993)	(44,172)	(20,963)	(44,351)	
Balance—end of year	863,758	839,724	893,619	1,040,272	1,211,282	
Net assets—end of year	$1,655,013	$1,617,452	$1,986,849	$2,417,697	$2,347,703	

Exhibit 5-B: Racine Stone and Gravel Company
      Recommended bituminous concrete plant account 3/31/62
      (On sum-of-the-years digits basis. Life
      under present method is 25 years; under guidelines, 15 years)

Year of acquisition	Original cost	Depreciation reserve 3/31/62	Net asset 3/31/62	Remaining life (pres. schedule) at 3/31/62	Remaining life* (guidelines) at 3/31/62
1955	$ 30,211	$ 15,152	$ 15,059	17.5	10.5
1956	31,368	13,947	17,421	18.5	11.1
1957	273,806	105,694	168,112	19.5	11.7
1958	515,835	165,862	349,973	20.5	12.3
1959	334,317	85,381	248,936	21.5	12.9
1960	529,100	98,417	430,683	22.5	13.5
1961	673,877	76,664	597,213	23.5	14.1
1962	135,427	5,534	129,893	24.5	14.7
1963	400,000(est.)				
Totals	$2,923,941	$566,651	$1,957,290		

*See Note—Exhibit 3-B

Exhibit 5-C: Racine Stone and Gravel Company
      Current bituminous concrete plant account 3/31/62
      (On straight line depreciation. Life under
      present method is 25 years; under guidelines, 15 years)

Year of acquisition	Original cost	Depreciation reserve 3/31/62	Net asset 3/31/62
1930	$ 5,000	$ 5,000	$ -0-
1937	80,978	80,403	575
1938	26,575	25,211	1,364
1939	27,145	24,702	2,443
1940	59,288	51,831	7,457
1941	8,022	6,657	1,365
1942	2,075	1,760	315
1943	66	50	16
1944	4,154	2,950	1,204
1945	112,160	74,762	37,398
1946	169,506	106,658	62,848
1947	110,761	65,066	45,695
1948	139,839	76,930	62,909
1949	86,669	46,470	40,199
1950	78,589	36,937	41,652
1951	47,721	20,520	27,201
1952	27,206	10,610	16,596
1953	17,515	6,094	11,421
1954	450	141	309
1961	31,325	1,879	29,446
1963	30,000(est.)		
Totals	$1,065,044	$644,631	$390,413

See Note to Exhibit 4-C before calculating new straight line depreciation.

tion should be continued. Our exhibits have separated those assets subject to each method.

In our last discussion, we were in agreement that Racine should claim the maximum depreciation allowable. This additional depreciation, however, may adversely affect the company's depletion allowances. Racine is allowed, under section 613 of the 1954 Tax Code, to deplete its raw material reserves at a rate of the lesser of 5 percent of gross income or 50 percent of net income. This is done on a plant by plant basis. Income and depreciation figures for Racine's plants entitled to depletion are given in Exhibit 6.

Additional depreciation resulting from a changeover to guidelines must be reflected in Racine's accounts kept for *tax* purposes. Additional calculations should be made to assist in determining whether or not it should also be reflected for financial reporting purposes. . . .

The only feasible way in which to apply guideline rates, given the state of Racine's records, would seem to be on a year-by-year basis. Records of each year's acquisitions, beginning in 1930, seem to be adequate for this purpose. . . .

Exhibit 6: Racine Stone and Gravel Company
Income and depreciation data for plants having depletion

Data	Horseshoe	Greenville	Westerly	Warwick	Rumford
Gross income	$899,480	$1,466,366	$499,400	$1,059,060	$1,492,460
Income before depreciation	266,877	185,292	124,586	158,102	571,145
Depreciation (old method)	86,215	77,397	26,912	25,306	50,438
Depreciation guidelines (estimated)	156,911	140,863	48,980	46,057	91,797

Chapter nine

International operations

Section 61 of the Internal Revenue Code states that the United States taxes income "from whatever source derived." Although there are special provisions governing the taxes on income from foreign sources, the general principle is that a United States taxpayer is taxed on his world-wide income. Furthermore, the United States citizen (or business enterprise incorporated in the United States) cannot escape United States taxation by moving abroad. Again there are special provisions for the taxation of a U.S. citizen residing outside the United States, but the general principle is that U.S. income tax follows a citizen wherever he goes.

Under Tax Code section 61, the United States taxes U.S. residents on their world-wide income whether or not they are citizens. And it taxes persons who are neither U.S. citizens nor U.S. residents on their income from United States sources. Section 871 taxes individuals in this category — nonresident aliens — and section 881 taxes corporations.

These principles are not followed by all countries. Canada and the United Kingdom, for example, use a residence rather than a citizenship test, and they do not attempt to tax their citizens who have assumed foreign residence. And the United Kingdom taxes a foreign resident in the United Kingdom only on earned income actually received in the United Kingdom. It does not tax him on income sent directly, for example, to a bank account outside the United Kingdom. Almost all countries, however, tax income to foreigners derived from sources within those countries.

The detailed treatment of taxation of foreign income to U.S. citizens and taxation of foreigners receiving United States income has undergone considerable change in the last few years. Following the Second World War, the policy of the United States was to make it very attractive for

United States citizens to work abroad and to invest their money abroad; substantial tax concessions were available to these citizens. As the United States began to run into balance of payments difficulties, however, the policy shifted. Beginning in 1962, changes have been made in the Code with the specific purpose of restraining the outflow of investment capital. And the significant tax advantages enjoyed by those who moved abroad are now regarded as unreasonable and have been cut back. The important changes to the Internal Revenue Code were made in 1962, 1964, and 1966.

Taxes on the individual U.S. citizen or resident

We begin with a discussion of the individual income tax with respect to foreign earnings and foreign investment income. This subject is of particular concern to corporations sending employees abroad for periods of time and, of course, to any individual who has investments in foreign countries.

Foreign earned income

Section 911 of the Code provides a partial exemption for the foreign earnings of a U.S. citizen who is either resident abroad or actually present in foreign countries for a long enough period; the section 911 exemption, however, has been steadily narrowed. Until 1962 all foreign-earned income of U.S. citizens resident abroad for an uninterrupted period of at least a full taxable year was exempt from U.S. income tax. Dollar limits were imposed in 1962, and these limits were reduced in 1964.

Residence is a rather tricky concept. It is not necessary for a U.S. citizen to move to a foreign country with the intention of permanently living there in order to establish a foreign residence. The Internal Revenue Service takes the position that it is sufficient that a citizen intend to work in the foreign country "for an indefinite period" and that he set up "permanent quarters" there. This will pose some problems for the U.S. citizen who is sent abroad for a limited period of time by his employer.

In general, what time periods do you think are appropriate for a foreign tour of duty by a U.S. citizen, considering section 911?

The foreign earnings of a U.S. citizen, to the extent they are not exempt from U.S. taxes under section 911, will normally be subject both to foreign income tax and to U.S. income tax. The Code mitigates, and frequently eliminates, the effect of this double taxation through a choice of a deduction or a tax credit. Section 164 permits the taxpayer, in computing his taxable income, to deduct foreign income taxes. Section 901 offers the alternative of the so-called foreign tax credit.

In general, which choice is the more attractive?

The following table shows the tax calculations for an unmarried U.S. citizen resident in Canada with a gross income of $35,000 for Canadian tax purposes. It is assumed that he has established three consecutive years of residence in Canada.

Table 1: Alternative tax calculations for U.S. citizen resident in Canada

Items	Using deduction (sec. 164)	Using foreign tax credit (sec. 901)
Gross income (for Canadian tax)	$35,000	$35,000
Taxable income (for Canadian tax)	32,000	32,000
Canadian income tax, including old age security tax — 1967 rates	12,290	12,290
Exempt from U.S. income tax	25,000	25,000
Gross income (for U.S. tax)	10,000	10,000
Deduction for Canadian tax $\frac{10}{35}$ × $12,290 (sec. 265(1) and 164)	3,510	
Other deductions and exemptions (assumed)	2,000	2,000
Taxable income (for U.S. tax)	4,490	8,000
U.S. tax (before foreign tax credit) — 1967 rates	800	1,630
Limit on credit for Canadian tax $\frac{8000}{8000}$ × 1,630		1,630
Net U.S. tax	800	0

The section 901 credit is limited by section 904. Under what circumstances would you choose the per-country limitation, and under what circumstances would you choose the overall limitation? (Before 1954, the tax credit was subject to both limitations simultaneously. In 1954, the overall limitation was eliminated, but it was restored in 1961 with the one-time choice.)

Before leaving the subject of foreign-earned income, we ought to point out that there may be difficulty in establishing the treatment of fringe benefits. Notice that section 911 defines foreign-earned income. There are specific references elsewhere in the Code to the treatment of contributions to a pension plan for U.S. citizens working abroad. These are quite complicated and will not be discussed here. They are something to keep in mind, however, when an employee is sent abroad.

Foreign investment income

There is no exemption for foreign investment income of a foreign resident as there is for foreign-earned income under section 911. Hence only the deduction for foreign taxes under section 164 or the foreign tax credit under section 901 will mitigate the effect of double taxation. The calculation of the deduction or credit will be very similar to that shown in Table 1.

Most countries impose a tax on investment income flowing out of the country. This means that in general a U.S. citizen resident in the U.S. and investing in a foreign country will be subject to some foreign tax on the income flowing back to him in the United States. The most common rate of tax imposed on an outflow of investment income from a country is 15 per cent. (The United States imposes a tax of 30 per cent on investment income flowing out of the United States to foreigners. An exception occurs when the outflow is subject to a tax treaty, in which case the rate is generally 15 per cent).

Assuming that foreign investment income will be subject to a 15 per cent foreign tax, how much income must the U.S. recipient have for the tax credit to eliminate the effect of the foreign tax? In other words, how much income must the U.S. investor have before he can ignore the presence of a 15 per cent foreign tax on his foreign investment income?

Tax treaties and the individual

The United States has tax treaties with a number of foreign countries. One of the purposes of these treaties, as noted above, is to limit the tax imposed by each country, subject to the treaty, on outflows of investment income. The usual rate established in tax treaties is 15 per cent. In addition, tax treaties are likely to reduce the impact of income taxes on a citizen of one country who works in the other. For example, within certain limits Canada does not tax the income earned in Canada by a U.S. resident who is there for a short period of time, and the United States does not tax the United States-earned income of a Canadian resident who is in the United States for a short period of time.

In addition to treaties governing income taxes, the United States has treaties with many countries governing estate taxes. In general, a U.S. citizen who is either working abroad or investing abroad should be aware of the income taxes and the estate taxes in the country where he is located or is investing, the U.S. treatment of foreign income and foreign assets in an estate, and the terms of any income tax treaty and any estate tax treaty between the United States and the foreign country.

The interest equalization tax

This tax is actually an excise tax on the purchase of foreign securities, but it deserves to be discussed along with income taxes on foreign investment. It was first proposed in 1963 and became law in September 1964, retroactive to July 1963. The tax was entirely motivated by balance of payments problems. The most obvious way to encourage an inflow of investment funds and discourage an outflow is to raise domestic interest rates. Unfortunately, raising domestic interest rates may not fit in with domestic economic policy. In 1963, the administration was increasing short-term interest rates to attract short-term funds into the United States, but it was reluctant to increase long-term interest rates and hence discourage long-term borrowing and capital investment by United States business.

The interest equalization tax was originally aimed at the purchase of long-term foreign securities, both debt and equity. The objective was to increase the effective interest rates foreigners would have to offer to U.S. investors, without raising rates for domestic borrowers. The tax was initially designed to add about 1 per cent to the interest cost of foreign borrowers. For example, the foreign seller of a twenty-eight-and-one-half-year bond would have had to offer a 6 per cent coupon to provide a United States purchaser with a yield of almost exactly 5 per cent on his purchase price plus 15 per cent tax. The tax rate was set initially at 15 per cent on foreign equity securities, and ranged from 2.75 per cent to 15 per cent on foreign debt securities, depending upon the maturity. Purchases after July 18, 1963, up to December 31, 1965, were subject to the tax.

The measure was envisioned as a temporary one to deal with a temporary balance of payments problem. However, the tax has been extended twice, to 1967 and to July 31, 1969. The rates have also been increased. A 1967 amendment authorizes a rate as high as 22.5 per cent on equity securities and a maximum of 1.58 per cent to 22.5 per cent on debt securities, depending upon the maturity. The President was given authority to establish rates below the maximum, and by Executive Order, from August 29, 1967, these have been set at 18.75 per cent for equity securities and from 1.31 per cent to 18.75 per cent for debt securities.

The tax is a rather complicated one; it is dealt with in sections 4911 through 4931 of the Code. Much of the complication stems from the need to plug loopholes and from exceptions to facilitate foreign investment that the administration felt was still necessary. Sections 4915 and 4916 deal with what are probably the most important exceptions.

The interest equalization tax has been denounced as, in effect, a form of foreign exchange control. The United States has prided itself on the free convertibility of the U.S. dollar and the freedom of U.S. citizens to send money abroad in any quantity and at any time. The tax does not represent a prohibition against conversion of U.S. dollars or the sending of funds abroad, but it does attach a penalty, and it is hard to see the tax as something entirely different from foreign exchange controls. One of the consequences of the tax has certainly been to strengthen enormously the capital markets in various foreign countries. It is now feasible to raise amounts of money in foreign financial centers that would not have been thought possible a few years ago.

Foreign operations of a corporation

A U.S. corporation carrying on business in a foreign country will normally set up either a foreign branch or a subsidiary. The branch does not involve any new corporate entity; it is simply a part of the U.S. corporation. Consequently, for U.S. tax purposes, the results of its operations are simply added in with the results of all operations of the corporation. Any foreign income taxes paid because of the branch operations will be either deductible under section 164, or creditable under section 901, as in the case of foreign taxes paid by an individual. A foreign subsidiary, on the other hand, is a foreign corporate entity and apart from the effect of some special provisions introduced to the Internal Revenue Code in 1962, its operations will not be subject to U.S. taxes. When dividends are received by the U.S. parent corporation from its foreign subsidiary, of course these will be includible in the income of the parent. A tax credit, however, is available to reduce the U.S. tax burden.

The indirect foreign tax credit

We have already discussed the tax credit under section 901 of the Code. This credit is available to corporations as well as to individuals, but it relates only to foreign taxes paid directly by the U.S. taxpayer. In the case of the U.S. parent corporation receiving dividends from its foreign subsidiary, if any taxes are imposed by the foreign country on those dividends—that is, if taxes are imposed on the parent company—which will generally be the case since most countries impose a 15 per cent tax on the outflow of dividends, then this tax may be credited against United

States taxes, under section 901. But in the case of the corporate parent, there is another tax credit available through section 902 — the indirect credit. This credit reflects the fact that the dividends paid by the foreign subsidiary to its U.S. parent are paid out of income that has already been reduced by foreign taxes on the foreign subsidiary. Section 902 gives the U.S. parent some tax relief for the taxes that were paid by the subsidiary. Section 902 is rather complicated and must be read in conjunction with section 78, which requires the U.S. parent to include in its income not simply the dividend received from its foreign subsidiary but the pre-foreign tax income of the subsidiary which produced the dividend. Section 78 achieves what is called "grossing up" the dividend and was added to the Code in 1962 when section 902 was rewritten. The effect of the two sections is illustrated in the table below.

Table 2: Foreign tax credit calculation

Profit before tax of Canadian subsidiary	$100
Income after Canadian tax (at 52%)	48
Dividend to parent	25
Plus "gross up" under section 78, ($\frac{25}{48}$) × 52	27
Total income for U.S. tax calculation	52
Canadian tax on dividend, imposed on parent (at 15%)	3.75
U.S. income tax before credits (at 48%)	25
Direct tax credit under section 901	3.75
Indirect tax credit under sections 901 and 902	27
Net U.S. income tax	-0-
Canadian taxes not credited	5.75

In the example, because the Canadian tax rate is higher than the U.S. tax rate, there will be no U.S. tax to pay. But the total tax burden will be higher than that represented by U.S. taxes alone. This illustrates the point that the foreign tax credit results in the taxpayer paying the higher of the domestic and foreign tax rates.

Tax havens

Until 1962, the situation described applied to all operations through foreign subsidiaries. The important point was that U.S. income taxes did not apply at all until dividends were remitted to the U.S. parent, and then the tax depended upon the dividends. So long as the earnings of a foreign subsidiary were retained in the subsidiary, there was no U.S. tax to pay, and it soon became evident that earnings could be shifted from one foreign operation to another without the payment of U.S. taxes. This is where the tax haven became important. For example, a U.S. corporation might set up a holding company in the Bahamas where there is no income tax. The holding company might in turn control operating subsidiaries in several foreign countries. The earnings of any one of those subsidiaries could be transmitted back to its parent, the holding company in the Bahamas, with no payment of income tax by the holding company or the

U.S. parent. These dividends could then be remitted from the Bahamas to any other foreign operation. The Bahamas formed the tax haven, and the holding company in the Bahamas was the tax haven company. Not until some of the profits of the foreign subsidiaries were remitted back to the U.S. parent by the Bahamas holding company would there be any U.S. taxes to pay.

The tax changes in 1962, with respect to operations of foreign subsidiaries, reflected dissatisfaction both with the advantages available for foreign operations that were not available for domestic operations and with the outflow of investment capital from the United States. The Treasury argued that it was unfair for a company with purely domestic operations to pay heavier taxes than were paid by a company with foreign operations. One answer to this, of course, was that it is unfair for an American-owned operation in a foreign country to pay heavier taxes than a foreign-owned operation in that country. But the balance of payments problem was important enough to convince the Administration that foreign investment had to be discouraged and particularly that the use of tax havens had to be blocked.

The controlled foreign corporation

Sections 951–964, dealing with so-called "controlled foreign corporations," were added to the Code in 1962. A controlled foreign corporation is one incorporated in a foreign country and one where over 50 per cent of the total voting stock is owned, at any time during the corporation's taxable year, by United States stockholders; each of these stockholders must own 10 per cent or more. The treatment of controlled foreign corporations and their parent corporations is extremely complicated; we will outline it below.

For taxable years beginning after 1962, certain undistributed income of the controlled foreign subsidiary is included for tax purposes in the gross income of the parent and in the income of any other stockholders owning 10 per cent or more of the subsidiary. This imputation of income takes place only if the subsidiary was a controlled foreign corporation for an uninterrupted period of thirty days or more in the taxable year, and only if the stockholder was such on the last day of the year on which the subsidiary was a controlled foreign corporation.

The undistributed income of the subsidiary that is to be imputed to the parent consists of three elements: the subsidiary's "Subpart F income," its previously excluded "Subpart F income" withdrawn from investment in "less-developed countries," and the increase in the subsidiary's earnings invested in United States property.

Subpart F income is made up of two components. One is income from insurance of United States risks and is not discussed here; the other is "foreign base company income" and consists of three further categories: foreign personal holding company income, foreign base company sales income, and foreign base company services income.

Foreign personal holding company income is essentially investment income and includes dividends, interest, rents, and royalties. However, rents and royalties from the active conduct of a trade or business and received from a person other than a "related person" are not included. And dividends, interest, and gains from sales of stock and securities, derived from the conduct of banking and financing and not received from a "related person," are not included.

The second category of foreign base company income, foreign base company sales income, is income derived from the purchase and sale of goods where the goods are purchased from or sold to, or purchased or sold on behalf of, a related person, but only if the goods are manufactured or produced outside the foreign country and are also for use or consumption outside the foreign country. That is, the income that is being taxed is income derived from running a sales operation in a country that is not concerned with goods produced in that country or consumed in that country.

The third category, foreign base company services income, is income from technical and managerial services performed for or on behalf of a related person and outside the country of the foreign subsidiary. This provision is aimed at the establishment of service subsidiaries to avoid tax, just as the preceding provision is aimed at the use of sales subsidiaries.

Once these three categories of foreign base company income have been determined, certain exclusions come into operation. First, dividends and interest from "qualified investments in less-developed countries" are excluded from foreign base company income as are net gains from the sale or exchange of these investments, up to the increase in the year of investments in less-developed countries. In other words, investment income from less developed countries is not included so long as it is reinvested in less developed countries. Second, income derived from the operation of aircraft or ships in foreign commerce is not included in foreign base company income. And third, if the foreign base company income (before excluding the investment income from, and reinvested in, less-developed countries) is less than 30 per cent of the subsidiary's gross income, then none of the gross income is treated as foreign base company income. This means that a substantial amount of incidental income for the subsidiary may fall within the usual definition of foreign base company income but still not be taxed to the parent. But if the foreign base company income exceeds 70 per cent of the subsidiary's gross income, then all the gross income is treated as foreign base company income.

As indicated above, even with balance of payments problems the United States was enough concerned with the capital needs of less-developed countries to make special provision for them. Countries are designated "less-developed" by Executive Order.

We have now established the scope of foreign base company income, which with income from the insurance of United States risks makes up Subpart F income which, in turn, is taxed to the parent corporation. Certain exclusions apply to the determination of Subpart F income. First, any income from sources inside the United States is not included in Subpart F income of the foreign subsidiary if the subsidiary is engaged in trade or business in the United States. Second, Subpart F income for a year may be no more than total earnings and profits of the subsidiary for the year, reduced by losses carried over from taxable years since 1959. And the parent need not include any of the subsidiary's Subpart F income if there is a sufficient distribution of earnings by the subsidiary.

There are many more details in the calculation of income of the subsidiary that is to be attributed to the parent. But from the foregoing it should be clear that the legislation was aimed at the accumulation of income in tax haven corporations, while permitting a good many foreign business operations conducted through subsidiaries to continue on the same tax basis as before. In fact, the Administration had asked for much greater taxation of income of foreign subsidiaries but Congress had refused to tax anything except obvious tax haven operations. The net result is that the old advantages of the tax haven are about gone, while no serious penalty has been introduced on regular foreign operations through a subsidiary. But the provisions are so complicated that a great deal of work is generally necessary to establish whether or not income of a foreign subsidiary is caught under any of the controlled foreign corporation provisions.

The interest equalization tax

We discussed the interest equalization tax above in connection with foreign investment by individuals. The same tax applies, of course, to foreign investment by corporations. But as you have already seen, there are exclusions from the tax that will take care of most of the foreign business investments of a United States corporation. This does not mean that such investments are free of all controls; a set of regulations went into effect in 1968 to limit foreign direct investment. But these regulations are not tax provisions.

Pricing in transactions between related companies

It may seem obvious that if U.S. income tax rates are substantially different from the rates in other countries, there is an incentive to arrange the prices in transactions between foreign and domestic entities of the same business in such a way as to maximize income in the low tax country and minimize income in the high tax country. Section 482 was put into the Code to control the arbitrary setting of prices in order to bring about desirable tax effects. There are certainly some opportunities for shifting income back and forth across a national boundary, but the opportunities are not unlimited.

United States taxation of U.S. income of foreigners

We noted above that the United States taxes residents of the U.S., no matter what their citizenship, on their world-wide income. And it taxes persons who are neither U.S. citizens nor U.S. residents on their income from United States sources.

The tax treatment of U.S. source income of foreigners was substantially changed by the Foreign Investors Tax Act of 1966. We have already seen several examples of United States tax legislation in aid of a deteriorating balance of payments. All of this legislation, until 1966, was concerned with penalizing the exports of capital from the United States. The Foreign Investors Tax Act is the first example of incentive legislation designed to lure capital into the United States.

In October 1963, President John F. Kennedy appointed a Task Force to consider ways of encouraging foreign investment in the United States. The chairman of the Task Force was Henry H. Fowler, now Secretary of the Treasury, and the tax recommendations of the Task Force underlie much of the 1966 legislation.

The distinction between business and investment income from United States sources

Section 871 describes the tax imposed on individuals who are neither citizens nor residents of the United States, but who derive income from United States sources. Notice the distinction drawn in the section between income "effectively connected with the conduct of a trade or business within the United States" and income which is not so connected. Until 1966, the distinction was drawn between foreigners who carried on business in the United States and those who did not. This meant that the tax treatment of the investment income of a foreigner depended upon whether that foreigner did business in the United States. At present, the tax treatment of the investment income of a foreigner depends only on whether the income itself is connected with a trade or business in the United States. Sections 881 and 882 deal with the United States income of foreign corporations, again distinguishing between income connected with a United States business and income not connected.

These three sections apply in the absence of a tax treaty. The United States has treaties with a number of countries, in most cases substituting a 15 per cent rate for the tax on investment income, rather than the 30 per cent rate stipulated in section 871(a) and 881(a). Under the old version of section 881, some foreign corporations found it worth-while to maintain minimal business operations in the United States, in order to have substantial investment income from United States sources taxed as business income rather than investment income. The objective was to take advantage of the 85 per cent dividends-received deduction available to a corporation under section 243 of the Code. This meant that at a 48 per cent corporate tax rate, the foreign corporation would be taxed at only 7.2 per cent on its dividend income from United States sources. Without the business operations in the U.S., it would be taxed at 30 per cent under section 881 or at 15 per cent under a treaty.

Under the new form of section 881, what happens to this tax-avoiding strategy?

What strategy will a foreign corporation now have to adopt in order to reduce its taxes on U.S. source dividends to 7.2 per cent?

The definition of "effectively connected" is contained in section 864, almost all of which was added to the Code in 1966. Notice section 864(b) (2) dealing with foreigners who trade in securities in the United States through a U.S. broker. Until the 1966 legislation, it was not at all clear whether a foreigner who gave discretionary authority to a U.S. broker to deal in securities for him was therefore carrying on business in the United States. This was important since the tax treatment of the foreigner's investment income from the United States, and the tax treatment of any capital gains realized in the United States, depended on whether or not he was doing business there.

> *What is the present consequence to a foreigner of making use of a U.S. broker with complete discretionary authority?*

Sections 861 and 862 determine whether income is treated as if from sources within the United States or from sources outside the United States. Section 861(a) (F) (1), and sections 861(c) (1), (2), and (3) are of particular interest. Until 1966, all deposits of foreigners in United States banks were treated as if located outside the United States for tax purposes. This was a very attractive arrangement for many foreigners and also, of course, for United States banks. In 1966 Congress decided it was not fair to give foreigners this special treatment. However, it did feel that *foreign* branches of United States banks should be able to continue to operate as essentially foreign banks. And it was concerned about the impact on the balance of payments of eliminating the tax advantage to foreigners of deposits in domestic branches of United States banks. The sections referred to above represent a compromise between the practicalities of the balance of payments and the congressional desire for greater fairness.

Section 861(a) (1) (C) and (D), and section 861(a) (2) (B) deal with the rather special cases of dividend and interest payments by a foreign corporation to foreigners, where the foreign corporation derives substantial income from United States sources.

> *Is it reasonable for the United States to impose any taxes on dividend and interest payments by a foreign corporation to foreigners?*
>
> *Why would the United States be concerned about taxing these payments, and what is accomplished by the conditions in the sections?*

Eli Lilly and Company v. the United States[1]

PER CURIAM: This case was referred to Trial Commissioner Lloyd Fletcher with directions to make findings of fact and recommendation for conclusions of law. Since the court is in agreement with the opinion,

---

[1]372-F. 2d-990 (United States Court of Claims, 1967).

findings and recommendation of the commissioner, with modifications, it hereby adopts the same, as modified, as the basis for its judgment in this case, as hereinafter set forth. Plaintiff is therefore not entitled to recover and petition is dismissed.

Commissioner Fletcher's opinion, as modified by the court, is as follows:

It has been said that:
Of all the areas of executive decision, pricing is perhaps the most fuzzy. Whenever a price problem is discussed . . . , divergent figures are likely to be recommended without a semblance of consensus. Oxenfeldt, "Multi-stage Approach to Pricing," 38 Harv. Bus. Review 125 (July, August 1960).

This novel and difficult case presents a study in that "fuzzy" area of pricing. The taxpayer, hereinafter referred to as "Eli Lilly," has adopted a pricing policy on its products destined for international markets which results in its selling organizations receiving the bulk of the overall profits from sales abroad. That policy disturbs the Government only insofar as it involves Eli Lilly's products sold in the Western Hemisphere (other than the United States). Because one of Eli Lilly's selling subsidiaries qualifies as a Western Hemisphere trade corporation and therefore enjoys a reduced rate of tax on its income, the Government asserts that Eli Lilly's pricing policy results in tax avoidance and does not clearly reflect the incomes of the related organizations. Accordingly, the Government has endeavoured to counter Eli Lilly's pricing policy by making use of a relatively compact section of the Internal Revenue Code of 1954 containing words of delusive simplicity. It reads in its entirety as follows:

Sec. 482. Allocation of income and deductions among taxpayers.

In any case of two or more organizations, trades, or businesses (whether or not incorporated, whether or not organized in the United States, and whether or not affiliated) owned or controlled directly or indirectly by the same interests, the Secretary or his delegate may distribute, apportion, or allocate gross income, deductions, credits, or allowances between or among such organizations, trades, or businesses, if he determines that such distribution, apportionment, or allocation is necessary in order to prevent evasion of taxes or clearly to reflect the income of any of such organizations, trades, or businesses. (26 U.S.C. 1958 ed., Sec. 482.)[2]

Before describing the manner in which the Commissioner of Internal Revenue has allocated income between Eli Lilly and its subsidiaries, it is necessary to review briefly the history and development of Eli Lilly's

---

[2]Section 45 of the Internal Revenue Code of 1939, as amended (26 U.S.C. 1952 ed., Sec. 45), applicable to the years 1952 and 1953, is substantially the same as section 482 of the 1954 Code quoted above.

international trade including a description of the methods adopted by the company for conducting such foreign business during the years at issue, 1952 through 1957.

Eli Lilly is an Indiana corporation. It is a long-established and well-known manufacturer and seller of pharmaceuticals, biologicals, and related products, including certain agricultural and industrial products of a similar nature.[3] Prior to 1940, the management of Eli Lilly appears to have given only sporadic attention to the development of a significant international market for Lilly products. During 1940, however, J. K. Lilly, Jr., who was head of domestic marketing, assumed responsibility for export sales also. He initiated studies to determine what could be done to improve Eli Lilly's position in foreign markets. One result was the formation within Eli Lilly of an Eastern Hemisphere sales division and a Western Hemisphere sales division. That method of reorganization proved unsatisfactory because company personnel continued to devote their major energies to domestic matters and tended to treat the new international divisions as stepchildren.

By June of 1943, Mr. Lilly had decided that the best way to develop the international market was through subsidiary corporations. Whereupon, Eli Lilly formed under the laws of Indiana two wholly-owned subsidiaries, Eli Lilly International Corporation (International) to service business in the Eastern Hemisphere and Eli Lilly Pan-American Corporation (Pan-American) to service foreign business in the Western Hemisphere.[4] Eli Lilly personnel with prior experience in the respective hemispheres were placed in charge of the new corporations.

The matter of pricing Lilly products to the new subsidiaries was then made the subject of extensive consideration. Following discussions and studies of numerous unique factors applying to sales of pharmaceuticals in foreign markets, Eli Lilly's management decided to price its products to International and Pan-American on what is best described as an incentive or motivation basis. A very substantial discount off domestic prices, increasing with volume was applied to sales to the subsidiaries with the thought that such favorable treatment would be an incentive to expansion and growth of the foreign markets.

These original intercompany arrangements were worked out by Eli Lilly's management primarily for what it considered to be sound business reasons. At first, no consideration appears to have been given to the subject of taxes. However, in February 1944, the subject was considered, and an application was made to the Commissioner of Internal Revenue for ruling as to Pan-American's status under the West Hemisphere trade corporation provisions of the 1939 Code. Based on the facts submitted, the Commissioner issued a favorable ruling to Pan-American.

---

[3] It manufactures and sells nearly 1,000 different products. Primarily they comprise what are known as "ethical" drugs which are those sold to the ultimate consumer on prescription only. This tends to make Eli Lilly a comparatively high-cost manufacturer.

[4] Not long after, Eli Lilly also organized other wholly-owned subsidiaries to operate specifically in Mexico, Argentina, and Brazil. Previously, it had organized subsidiaries in England and Canada.

No significant change in the above arrangements occurred until 1946. In that year it was decided to change the merchandise flow to foreign markets. Instead of selling directly to its several subsidiaries, Eli Lilly decided to use International as its exclusive distributor for export of its products throughout the world. Under this new arrangement, all merchandise destined for exports was purchased from Eli Lilly by International and sold by the latter either to Pan-American, to other subsidiaries, or directly to unrelated wholesalers in the Eastern Hemisphere. The pricing policy adopted on sales to International was a discount of 60 per cent from domestic prices on finished and packaged merchandise, and at Eli Lilly's cost plus 15 per cent on bulk merchandise.

That pricing policy continued through 1948, when, during an audit of Eli Lilly's tax returns, the Internal Revenue Service first proposed to reallocate income of International and Pan-American to Eli Lilly. This dispute involving earlier years was compromised, and for 1949, 1950, and 1951 Eli Lilly transferred merchandise to International and prepared its tax returns on the basis of that settlement for the earlier years.

In the year 1952, Eli Lilly reexamined its position on pricing to International. It had become apparent that Pan-American and International were finding it difficult to make profits. Prices were demoralized in the antibiotic field and streptomycin was being purchased by Eli Lilly and sold at a loss because of its difficulties in manufacturing that product. Also, there was a continuing tax problem under section 45 of the 1939 Code (now section 482 of the 1954 Code, *supra*), and the company's accountants and tax attorneys told management that the existing pricing arrangement flowing from the settlement described above had placed Eli Lilly at a substantial disadvantage taxwise with respect to the rest of the industry. Accordingly, studies were made during the year 1952 and advice was obtained to determine what action should be taken with respect to the transfer price from Eli Lilly to International. This study was participated in by the highest management officials of Eli Lilly. They found that if Eli Lilly continued to price on the basis of the composite average which it had used during the years 1949, 1950, and 1951, resulting from the earlier settlement, International and Pan-American would have operated at losses during the year 1952.

The pricing policy finally established for the year 1952 differed somewhat from the policy which had been used in the years 1944 through 1948. The price arrangement which had been in effect from 1944 through 1948 had been considered in terms of a discount off domestic net trade prices which was the common denominator at that time in maintaining inventory controls. The price which was determined in 1952 was a cost-oriented price which made no provision for a specific monetary profit to Eli Lilly. All sales by Eli Lilly to International under this policy were priced to effect a recovery of the manufacturing cost of goods sold, plus royalties payable by Eli Lilly to third parties, plus all operating expenses incurred by Eli Lilly incident to the servicing of the export business.

This management decision took into consideration all of the factors which were considered originally in 1943 and 1944 in determining the appropriate prices to International and to Pan-American but with the benefit of the experience that had been obtained since 1944 in conducting export operations. It also took into consideration the continuing tax problem under section 45 referred to above.

Under this policy, all merchandise was transferred to International at the same price regardless of whether the final destination of the merchandise was to be in the Eastern Hemisphere or in the Western Hemisphere. However, International's price policy for goods purchased by it from Eli Lilly was different with respect to goods destined for the Eastern Hemisphere as compared to those destined for the Western Hemisphere. International had many wholesale distributors located in the Eastern Hemisphere, and it sold Lilly products to those distributors at the 'Interex' net trade price less 15 per cent. The Interex net trade price was approximately the same as the domestic net trade price being the suggested price to the retailer.

All products destined for foreign countries in the Western Hemisphere, however, were sold by International to its sister, Pan-American. On these sales International priced to Pan-American on a basis designed to effect a recovery of International's cost of goods sold, plus allocable administrative and selling expenses attributable to sales to Pan-American as determined by International's accountant. That allocation of expenses was based on a 3-factor formula which took into account total sales of the two companies and their total number of distributors and sales representatives. As in the case of sales by Eli Lilly to International, no provision was made for a specific monetary profit to International on its sales to Pan-American.

It is obvious, of course, that one result of the above-described intercompany pricing method was to assemble in Pan-American nearly all the taxable income derived from sales of Lilly products in foreign countries within the Western Hemisphere. Since Pan-American was entitled as a qualified Western Hemisphere trade corporation to the preferential treatment conferred on such corporations by sections 921–922 of the 1954 Code, the resulting tax advantage flowing to the affiliated corporate group from such pricing method is equally obvious.

But, says Eli Lilly, there is nothing wrong in this. It vigorously asserts, and on this record has satisfactorily proved, that sound business reasons primarily motivated its pricing policy on goods destined for foreign markets. Accordingly, it insists that any resulting tax advantage is nothing more than was intended by Congress when it enacted the Western Hemisphere trade corporation provisions of the Internal Revenue Code referred to above.

The Government disagrees. It does not dispute Eli Lilly's right to organize internally in any way company management may desire, nor does it question Pan-American's status as a qualified Western Hemisphere trade corporation. But for tax purposes, says the Government, section 482, *supra*, and the regulations issued thereunder, require it to intervene and determine the "true taxable income" of each of the controlled group. The regulation to which the Government points is section 1.482-1 of Treasury Regulations on Income Tax (26 C.F.R. Sec. 1.482-1) which reads, in pertinent part:

(b) *Scope and Purpose.* (1) The purpose of section 482 is to place a controlled taxpayer on a tax parity with an uncontrolled taxpayer, by determining, according to the standard of an uncontrolled taxpayer, the true taxable income from the property and business of a controlled taxpayer. The interests controlling a group of controlled taxpayers are assumed to have complete power to cause each controlled taxpayer so to conduct its affairs that its transactions and accounting records truly reflect the taxable income from the property and business of each of the controlled taxpayers. If, however, this has not been done, and the taxable incomes are thereby understated, the district director shall intervene, and, by making such distributions, apportionments, or allocations as he may deem necessary of gross income, deductions, credits, or allowances, or of any item or element affecting taxable income, between or among the controlled taxpayers constituting the group, shall determine the true taxable income of each controlled taxpayer. The standard to be applied in every case is that of an uncontrolled taxpayer dealing at arm's length with another uncontrolled taxpayer.[5]

During the course of his audits covering the 1952 through 1957 tax returns of Eli Lilly, International, and Pan-American, an Internal Revenue agent became convinced that Eli Lilly's intercompany pricing arrangements did not clearly reflect the respective taxable incomes of the related organizations and resulted in unwarranted tax avoidance. He decided that section 482, the above-quoted regulation, and Revenue Ruling 15, 1953-1 C.B. 141, required him to allocate items affecting taxable income between the controlled taxpayers in an effort to determine their true taxable incomes. His task under the above regulation, as he saw it, was to determine what Eli Lilly's prices would have been if its sales of Lilly products to International had been made at arm's length instead of to a controlled subsidiary. For this purpose he adopted as a measuring stick Eli Lilly's profit experience on its domestic sales to its uncontrolled wholesale distributors. On the basic assumption that the same profit earned by Eli Lilly on its domestic expense dollars should be earned by it on its foreign trade expense dollars, he first computed the percentage figure which Eli Lilly's net income from domestic sales bore to its expenses on those sales. He reasoned that, if International's cost·of goods purchased from Eli Lilly were increased by such a percentage figure, the results under the intercompany agreements would be (1) to increase Eli Lilly's sales (and thereby its taxable income) in a like amount and (2) to increase Pan-American's cost of goods purchased from International (thereby decreasing Pan-American's taxable income) in a like amount.

However, in discussing the matter with Eli Lilly's representatives, the agent became aware of certain flaws in his basic assumption that Eli Lilly should earn the same profit on its sales to International as it earned on its domestic sales to wholesale distributors. It became apparent to him

---

[5]The regulation promulgated under section 45 of the 1939 Code was substantially the same. See Treas. Reg. 118, Sec. 39. 45–1.

that the sales were not entirely comparable, the major difference being that International was one large customer to whom Eli Lilly could be expected to sell its goods in quantity at a lower profit than to its numerous domestic wholesalers.

In an effort to take this difference into account, the agent did something to which Eli Lilly points, among other things, as clear proof of arbitrary and unreasonable action. He simply applied one-half of Eli Lilly's profit percentage for domestic sales to the cost of goods sold to International. However, he applied the full percentage to the allocated expenses.[6] His only explanation for cutting the percentage figure in half when applied to cost of goods sold was to the effect that Eli Lilly's representatives had agreed with him that such reduction fairly reflected International's status as a single large customer. However, while the record shows earnest efforts were made to arrive at a settlement, it shows equally that Eli Lilly's representatives did not agree with any of the agent's theories of reallocation and, indeed, consistently contended that no reallocation at all was required or permissible under the law. It appears that the agent misinterpreted the nature of tentative concessions made in the course of exploring settlement possibilities. In any event, although the above-mentioned adjustments (and all others) made by the agent to his computed profit percentages were concessions in Eli Lilly's favor, it has seized upon them as demonstrating that his entire method of allocation (which was ultimately reflected in the Commissioner's deficiency notices) was arbitrary and based on subjective consideration with no discernible standards.

There is some merit to Eli Lilly's complaint in this respect, for it is apparent that a taxpayer subjected to a section 482 allocation will be severely handicapped in opposing any method of allocation where it contains a subjective element such as merely cutting a computed percentage figure in half. The difficulty with this contention is that, whatever criticism may be directed to the agent's methodology, Eli Lilly has failed, in my judgement, to prove that he arrived at an unreasonable result. As the Tax Court has said in analyzing a section 482 (then section 45) allocation:

> Although the method of allocation used by the respondent, based on the gross income of each company, might appear to be arbitrary, we can not say, on any evidence before us, that it led to arbitrary and unreasonable results. Our concern is more with the ultimate results arrived at by the Commissioner than the methods which he uses. (*Leedy-Glover Realty and Insurance Co.*, 13 T.C. 95, 107 (1949).)

The reasonableness of the result of the reallocation in this case seems to me apparent from a comparison of total book profits enjoyed by the three companies on sales of Lilly products in the Western Hemisphere both before and after the reallocation. It shows that, during the six years involved, prior to the reallocation, Pan-American received a share of

---

[6]The agent also made some other adjustments to the percentage figures for years which appeared to have unusual circumstances such as 1952 when Eli Lilly was experiencing production difficulties with streptomycin.

the total profits from Western Hemisphere sales ranging from 92.84 per cent to 97.68 per cent; Eli Lilly's share of such profits ranged from 0.61 per cent to 5.65 per cent; and International's share ranged from 0.70 per cent to 2.08 per cent. After the reallocation Pan-American's share of such profits was still high and ranged from 62.07 per cent to 74.56 per cent, while Eli Lilly's share had increased to a range of from 22.90 per cent to 28.30 per cent, and International's share ranged from 0.53 per cent to 9.63 per cent.

Hence, the lion's share of the profits from Western Hemisphere sales remained in Pan-American even after the reallocation, and to this extent it continues to enjoy (as it properly should) the tax benefits which flow from its Western Hemisphere trade corporation status. To accept Eli Lilly's contention that this is not enough, and that its cost-oriented pricing policy must be accepted, would require the court to ignore the provisions of Treas. Reg. 1.482-1, *supra*, which states that the standard to be applied in a section 482 allocation is that of "an uncontrolled taxpayer dealing at arm's length with another uncontrolled taxpayer." It must surely be obvious that, if International were an "uncontrolled" purchaser from Eli Lilly, it would not have been able to buy Lilly products for the prices paid by it in this case. It is equally obvious that, being a large volume purchaser, an "uncontrolled" International could expect to buy Lilly products at prices somewhat less than the suggested retail price minus 15 per cent paid by Lilly's domestic wholesale distributors. But, how much less? The revenue agent roughly split the difference, and Eli Lilly justifiably complained of such subjectivity. Yet, in electing simply to defend its cost-oriented pricing policy to its subsidiary, Eli Lilly has failed to meet its admittedly difficult burden of proving what it would have charged a volume purchaser, such as International, if it were an "uncontrolled" purchaser. In a refund suit such as this, the taxpayer in order to prevail must go further than proving arbitrary action by the Commissioner of Internal Revenue. In addition, the taxpayer must prove the correct amount of the tax and resulting overpayment. *Helvering* v. *Taylor*, 293 U.S. 507 (1935); *Lewis* v. *Reynolds*, 284 U.S. 281 (1932); *United States* v. *Pfister*, 205 F. 2d 538 (8th Cir., 1953). See, also, Plumb and Kapp, *Reallocation of Income and Deductions Under Section 482*, 41 Taxes 809, 830 (December, 1963).

Eli Lilly appears to recognize its burden in this respect but insists that it has fully carried that burden by proving the arm's-length character of its sales to International. It points to sizable sales made during the period involved to unrelated purchasers of Lilly products in bulk form. Those unrelated purchasers were industrial or agricultural consumers and the Defense Procurement Agency of the United States Government. In several instances, sales were made to those purchasers at prices less than were being charged to International, and Eli Lilly contends that such bulk sales were much more comparable to its sales to International than were the sales used by the revenue agent for comparison, i.e., the sales to domestic wholesalers. In showing such admittedly arm's-length sales at prices less than the International sales, Eli Lilly insists that it has borne its burden of proving that no allocation whatever was permissible under section 482.

Crucial to this argument, of course, is the assertion of comparability between sales to International and to the aforesaid bulk purchasers. However, those sales were not sufficiently comparable to establish an arm's-length criterion. In contrast to the foreign market, the bulk market was secondary, or marginal, and provided a convenient outlet for surplus capacity. Eli Lilly utilized such capacity by bidding low for Defense Procurement Agency and industrial contracts on a well-known theory used in pricing products at lower figures for a marginal market. The government market was also marginal in that sales made to the Government were, as described by Eli Lilly's president, "casual" in contrast to the regular and continuing sales made in the foreign market. Such sales also differed in that they comprised raw chemicals, semi-processed and finished drugs in large drums without an identifying trademark, whereas sales to International for the most part were in the form of finished and packaged goods with the Lilly trademark affixed, as was true in the case of domestic sales.

Sales made to International were tailored into the production planning of Eli Lilly. Unlike the casual bulk sales market, the foreign market was under consistent development and promotion by the responsible executives at Eli Lilly. From the time in 1940 that J. K. Lilly, Jr. assumed responsibility for the export sales division and initiated a study to determine the proper method of organization for international trade, Eli Lilly sought to cultivate the growth of its international operations. The keen interest in this market continued through the years at issue. It is clear that management viewed the sales made to International for the foreign market as an important and integrated part of the entire Eli Lilly production operation. Consequently, this market was not marginal in nature. It was more comparable to the domestic market generally even though not as large.

In its briefs Eli Lilly places great emphasis on the importance of the many business reasons which motivated its intercompany pricing policies. There is no doubt that the record here clearly establishes the existence of sound and well-considered business reasons for the pricing policies adopted. There is also no doubt that serious consideration was given to the "continuing tax problem" under section 45, now section 482, and surely management would have been considered derelict in its duties if it had not considered such an important problem. Nonetheless, there is ample credible testimony that the predominant reasons for Eli Lilly pricing policies were those connected with its management's efforts to expand and develop the foreign market.

Eli Lilly's eminent counsel argue, in effect, that this should be the end of the matter, that a finding of business motivation effectively removes section 482 from the Government's arsenal. Consequently, they say, Eli Lilly's "position is and has always been that no amount should be reallocated."

I am unable to agree that the existence of valid and sound business purposes for intercompany arrangements will thus devitalize section 482. In another connection, this court has stated that no such dispositive effect will be accorded to a valid business reason for a given transaction. See

Neff v. *United States*, 157 Ct. Cl. 322, 305 F. 2d 455 (1962), vacating and withdrawing 157 Ct. Cl. 304, 301 F. 2d 330, cert. denied, 372 U.S. 913 (1963) where the court said at 157 Ct. Cl. 327:

> Even assuming that the sole force motivating the redemption was as plaintiffs contend, the desire to raise additional capital to support corporate operations, we would view the distribution as one by its nature essentially equivalent to a dividend. Although such motivation would undoubtedly constitute a valid corporate purpose, we do not find the presence of valid corporate purpose, dispositive. *Holsey et al.* v. *Commissioner of Internal Revenue*, 258 F. 2d 865, 869 (1958); *Northrup* v. *United States*, 240 F. 2d 304, 307 (1957). While the absence of any valid corporate purpose as motivating the redemption might constitute substantial evidence indicating that the redemption distribution was essentially equivalent to a dividend, we do not believe that the presence of such corporate purpose establishes, per se, nonequivalence.

It will be recalled that section 482 states that its purposes are two-fold. First, the Commissioner may resort to it "in order to prevent evasion of taxes." Secondly, he may resort to it whenever he deems it necessary "clearly to reflect the income" of the related organizations. Here, the facts show that Eli Lilly's shift to its subsidiaries of a part of the income which it had earned from its manufacturing operations was done predominantly for business reasons. Hence, the applicability of the first purpose mentioned above is dubious. However, the shift resulted in a failure to reflect clearly Eli Lilly's income from manufacturing, and this is enough to warrant an allocation under section 482. It has been so held. *Central Cuba Sugar Co.* v. *Commissioner*, 198 F. 2d 214 (2d Cir., 1952), cert., denied, 344 U.S. 874; *Dillard-Waltermire, Inc.,* v. *Campbell*, 255 F. 2d 433 (5th Cir., 1958). See, also, Plumb and Kapp, *Reallocation of Income and Deductions Under Section 482, supra*, at p. 813, and Hewitt, *Section 482 — Reallocation of Income and Deductions Between Related Persons — Up to Date*, 22 N.Y.U. Ann. Inst. on Fed. Taxation 381, 395 (1964). In *Dillard-Waltermire, supra*, the court summarized the matter as follows:

> The appellant undertook to prove absence of a tax motive in order to negative the claim of tax evasion. Even satisfactory proof of a business reason for the transfer of these partially completed contracts to the identical interests freed of any obligation to bear the corporate tax would not be an answer to the Commissioner's claimed right to make the allocation. The statute permits such allocation if the result more clearly reflects the true income of the related businesses. [At 436]

In the light of the foregoing authorities, it is clear that a section 482 allocation was permissible in this case, regardless of Eli Lilly's sound business reasons for its pricing policies. . . .

Finally, Eli Lilly contends that section 482 should not be applied to an intercompany pricing arrangement so as to deny any of the benefits intended to be conferred on Western Hemisphere trade corporations by sections 921–922 of the 1954 Code. Thus far, it appears that no court has been asked to decide this specific question. It has, however, been the subject of extensive commentary by experts in the general area of taxation on doing business abroad. Predictably, divergent viewpoints have resulted. See Baker and Baker, *The Pricing of Goods in International Transactions Between Controlled Taxpayers*, 10 Tax Executive 235 (April 1958); Graves, *Problems in the Allocation of Foreign Income*, 16 Tax Executive 284 (July 1964); Baker and Sarabia, *The Function of Tax Incentives in International Trade*, 26 Tulane L. Rev. 405 (1952); Plumb and Kapp *Reallocation of Income and Deductions Under Section 482, supra;* Hewitt, *Section 482 — Reallocation of Income and Deductions Between Related Persons — Up to Date, supra;* Slowinski, *Tax Planning For Foreign Subsidiary Operations*, 17 N.Y.U. Ann Inst. on Fed. Taxation 331 (1959); Brudno, *The Practical Aspects of Incorporating and Doing Business Abroad*, 14 Univ. of So. Calif. Tax Inst. 345 (1962).

The basic problem is well stated by Plumb and Kapp, *supra*. They say:

> It is in the area of intercompany pricing of products, on an international stage, that Section 482 is destined to play its next and perhaps most significant, role. . . .
>
> The total exemption from United States corporate income taxes of foreign source income of some foreign subsidiaries of United States corporations, and the preferential tax treatment accorded certain domestic corporations engaged in international trade, provide a powerful incentive to tax conscious management to so arrange intercompany price structures as to maximize the earnings of those members of the corporate family which enjoy these benefits, at the expense of the others. . . . The possible variations are infinite.
>
> In Section 482, the Commissioner has a powerful weapon for thwarting the plans of those who would thus minimize the taxes of an affiliated group. Although the authority which Section 482 confers upon the Commissioner is unquestionably adequate to permit him to deal with shifting of this sort, [the authors recognize a contrary view] and its general standard is easy enough to state, the precise application of this provision to any given set of circumstances may present complex problems of accounting, economics, and proof. At 820–1.

I agree with the foregoing view that section 482 is available to the Government even though the resulting reallocation may have an effect on some benefits conferred by another section of the Code. Section 482 (and its predecessor) has been a part of the tax statute for many years. If Congress had intended to make it inapplicable to Western Hemisphere trade corporations, it would have been very simple to have said so at the time the original Western Hemisphere trade corporations provisions were enacted. That Congress did not do so is, of course, very significant. "The silence of Congress is strident." *Commissioner* v. *Beck's Estate,* 129 F. 2d 243, 245 (2d Cir., 1942).

The Third Circuit Court of Appeals has stated the applicable principle in the following language:

> Section 45 [now section 482] is directed to the correction of particular situations in which the strict application of the other provisions of the act will result in a distortion of the income of affiliated organizations. In every case in which the section is applied its application will necessarily result in an apparent conflict with the literal requirements of some other provision of the act. If this were not so Section 45 would be wholly superfluous. We accordingly conclude that the application of Section 45 may not be denied because it appears to run afoul of the literal provisions of Section 112(b)(5) and 113(a)(8) if the Commissioner's action in allocating under the provisions of Section 45 the loss involved in this case was a proper exercise of the discretion conferred upon him by the section. (*National Securities Corp.* v. *Commissioner,* 137 F. 2d 600, 602 (3d Cir., 1943), cert., denied, 320 U.S. 794.)

Accordingly, it is clear that here the Commissioner was authorized to apply the provisions of section 482 despite the resulting impact on some of the benefits conferred by the Western Hemisphere trade corporation provisions of the Code.

For all of the foregoing reasons, it is recommended that the court enter its judgment for defendant and dismiss the plaintiff's petition. . . .

Cooper Corporation

The Cooper Corporation manufactures automatic temperature control systems at its plant in Ohio. The systems are sold for industrial installation. All sales in the United States are handled by company sales engineers, and installation of the systems is supervised by company engineers.

Many systems are custom designed, and in almost every case considerable technical assistance and training is provided by Cooper to its customers. If these services are substantial, Cooper makes a charge for them. Otherwise, all services and installation are included in the price of the system.

Sales in foreign countries are handled almost entirely by foreign representatives. These are completely separate businesses, usually manufacturing similar but noncompeting products. Cooper has no financial interest in any of these businesses. Cooper sells its systems to the foreign representatives, and they in turn resell them and provide all technical services and installation supervision.

Recently Cooper has become dissatisfied with its Canadian representative. Customers have complained of poor service; specifications have not always come through correctly, and Cooper believes its representative is making a large profit that could be Cooper's.

The Cooper management is considering setting up either a branch or a wholly owned subsidiary in Canada to handle all Canadian sales. Sales of the branch or subsidiary are projected at $750,000 for 1968, $850,000 for 1969, and $1 million for 1970. Expenses are projected at $850,000 for 1968, $800,000 for 1969, and $900,000 for 1970. (Sales and expenses are expected to rise but to hold approximately the 1970 percentage relation in years after 1970.) Expenses include the cost of production of the systems sold, plus tariff. If the Canadian operation is run as a subsidiary, the parent might charge it more than cost. All services in Canada would be provided by the branch or subsidiary, and the expenses include these. (Sales comprise 90 per cent sales of systems and 10 per cent sales of services.)

The initial capital investment in the Canadian operation is estimated at $300,000, all of which the Cooper Corporation would provide. Within five years total capital of $600,000 may be required.

The management hopes to reduce costs and to achieve tax savings by having the Canadian operation, if it is set up, handle sales to some European and South American countries. This would involve replacing some foreign distributors and agents by the Canadian organization and interposing a new entity between the parent manufacturer in the United States and the customer. The purpose of the latter would be to divert some of the parent's profits to the Canadian operation, in hope that there would be some tax saving. The parent would sell to the Canadian subsidiary which would in turn sell to customers, or the Canadian branch would act as sales agent for the parent. In either case, some of the profit formerly accruing to the parent would accrue to the Canadian operation. Actual shipment of goods would probably still be direct from the parent to the customer, although services would probably be performed by the Canadian operation.

The company has received the following memorandum from Tax Counsel in Canada. On the basis of this information and your own knowledge of United States tax law, you are to advise whether the proposed Canadian operation should be set up as a branch or a subsidiary.

Memorandum

Operation as a branch

The Canadian operation could be carried on as a branch of Cooper. In this event, Canada would recognize separate accounts kept for the Canadian branch and would impose an income tax only on taxable income attributable to the branch operations. A reasonable allocation of head office and administrative overhead of the U.S. company would be allowed as a deduction in computing the branch income.

To the extent that the branch had profits, it would be subject to the normal corporate rates of tax and to a special tax of 15 per cent of the amount remaining after deducting from taxable income the normal tax and the amounts expended by the branch in new capital investment. This additional or "branch" tax is imposed in lieu of the withholding tax which would be imposed upon dividends of a subsidiary company. But unlike a tax on dividends, it is imposed immediately as the profits are earned. Normal corporate income tax rates are 21 per cent of the first $35,000 taxable income and 50 per cent of the remainder. These rates are increased by 2 per cent on profits earned in Ontario and Quebec because of provincial income taxes.

Losses incurred by the branch could be carried forward for five years against subsequent branch profits.

Operation as a corporation

Alternatively, the Canadian operation could be carried on through the medium of a separate company, which could be incorporated either in Canada or in the United States. It is not easy to judge whether there is any business disadvantage in using a United States corporation. It may be desirable for the Canadian operation to look as "Canadian" as possible, but the fact that a Canadian corporation is foreign-controlled usually becomes apparent fairly quickly.

United States corporation. A separate United States corporation would necessarily carry on its operations in Canada through a branch, and the branch would be taxed as described above. The only reason for using a separate United States corporation seems to lie in the possibility of qualifying this corporation as a Western Hemisphere Trade Corporation, for U.S. tax purposes.

Canadian corporation. A Canadian corporation is subject to income tax at the same rates as a branch, discussed above, except that there is no "branch" tax. Dividends and interest paid to nonresidents are subject to a withholding tax of 15 per cent, although this rate is reduced to 10 per cent if at least 25 per cent of the common shares of the Canadian corporation are owned beneficially by residents of Canada.

Geographical areas qualifying for tax exemption

Consideration might be given to the establishment of a manufacturing plant at some time in one of Canada's areas of "slower growth," some of which are close to metropolitan areas. In particular, the city of Brantford is within fifty miles of Toronto and qualifies as an area for special tax relief. There are other areas throughout Canada.

The special provision afforded in these areas gives a complete exemption from income tax for the first three years of operation, during which time no deductions need be made for depreciation. After the expiration of the three-year period, equipment may be depreciated at 50 per cent a year and buildings at 20 per cent a year (declining balance method).

In order to qualify as a new manufacturing business in one of these areas, it is not necessary that the business be new in Canada. Possibly the procedure which Cooper should consider is to carry on a branch operation in Toronto for a few years until they are satisfied that sufficient volume exists to support the building of a new plant and then at that time consider one of the special areas.

Patent royalties

Although Cooper could not charge patent royalties to a branch, it could charge reasonable royalties to a subsidiary. These would be deductible by the subsidiary for Canadian tax purposes, but there would be a 15 per cent withholding tax applied to them when they were remitted to the United States parent corporation.

Cook Breweries, Inc.

Cook Breweries is a New York corporation, wholly owned by Wettlaufer and Company, Ltd., a Canadian corporation principally engaged in operating various breweries in Canada. Cook Breweries has a net income after tax of about $8 million a year and remits about $5 million dividends to Wettlaufer.

Wettlaufer has recently developed a new beer that possesses unusual taste and texture characteristics. The principal immediate market for this beer is probably the United States, but Wettlaufer expects to exploit the product in several countries. It is not feasible simply to turn over the United States market for the new beer to Cook Breweries, because another New York brewery, Camelot Beverages, Inc., has participated in development of the new beer and must share in the proceeds of its exploitation. The results of the development consist of technical knowledge and trained personnel, which could be made available to any brewery.

Sales of the new beer in the U.S. are expected to begin at close to $3 million and rise to about $30 million, with profits before taxes beginning at about $150,000 and rising to $1.8 million. Sales in Canada are expected to rise from about $1 million to about $10 million, with profits before taxes rising from $50,000 to $600,000.

A preliminary understanding has been reached to the effect that the proceeds of the development are to be shared 75 per cent to Wettlaufer (or Cook) and 25 per cent to Camelot, this sharing to apply to profits earned anywhere — in the United States, Canada, or other countries.

The actual production and sale of the new beer in Canada will almost certainly be handled by Wettlaufer. The same activities in the United States could be handled by Cook, Camelot, a new firm, or any combination of these.

Wettlaufer's tax advisors in Canada have produced the following memorandum. You are retained by Cook Breweries to advise on United States taxes and to produce recommendations based on the United States tax considerations and the memorandum from Wettlaufer's advisors.

Memorandum

Before considering specific alternatives for the new brewery operations, certain basic tax facts should be established. Wettlaufer and Company is subject to Canadian income tax, at a marginal rate of 52 per cent. Dividends from other Canadian corporations are tax-free to Wettlaufer under the Canadian Income Tax Act, and dividends from foreign corporations of which Wettlaufer owns at least 25 per cent of the common stock are also tax-free. Wettlaufer is able to credit against its Canadian income tax any foreign income tax imposed on Wettlaufer directly. But in the case of dividends from foreign corporations, which are tax-free to Wettlaufer, there can be no credit for foreign taxes levied on those dividends.

Any royalty income received by Wettlaufer from Canadian or foreign sources would be taxed as ordinary income. Foreign taxes levied directly on the royalties could be credited by Wettlaufer against its Canadian income tax.

Any dividends, interest, or royalties remitted by Wettlaufer to a foreign corporation would be taxed by Canada at 15 per cent.

Under the terms of the Canada-United States Tax Treaty, a U.S. corporation is not taxable by Canada on its business income unless it has a permanent establishment in Canada, and a Canadian corporation is not taxable by the United States on its business income unless it has a permanent establishment in the United States. In either case, only business income which can properly be attributed to the permanent establishment is taxable by the country in which the permanent establishment is maintained. In the absence of a permanent establishment, neither country may tax the income, from sources in that country, of a corporation of the other country, at more than 15 per cent. This means, for example, that so long as Wettlaufer does not have a permanent establishment in the United States, and it does not have one at the present, any income it derives from the United States will be taxed by the United States at a flat 15 per cent. And the same would apply to any income derived from Canadian sources by Cook Breweries or any other United States corporation with no permanent establishment in Canada.

We see several alternative ways of organizing the new brewery operation:

1. A United states corporation might be set up to be jointly owned by Wettlaufer and Camelot or by Wettlaufer, Cook, and Camelot. This corporation could license Wettlaufer in Canada and either Camelot or Cook or both in the United States, or it could carry on brewery operations itself in the United States. And it could license foreign breweries or set up foreign brewing operations of its own. Any royalties paid under the license by Wettlaufer would be deductible expenses for Canadian tax purposes, but they would be subject to the 15 per cent tax referred to above. Any dividends received by Wettlaufer would be tax-free in Canada but would be subject to a 15 per cent withholding tax in the United States.

2. A Canadian corporation might be substituted for the United States corporation suggested above. A Canadian corporation is subject to an income tax of 23 per cent on the first $35,000 of taxable income and 52 per cent on the balance. Any royalties received from Wettlaufer would constitute ordinary income as would royalties received from the United States. A 15 per cent tax by the United States on royalties received from that country could be offset against Canadian income tax. Dividends and interest remitted to Camelot or Cook would be subject to only 10 per cent withholding tax in Canada, so long as the Canadian corporation were at least 25 per cent Canadian-owned. This requirement would be satisfied if Wettlaufer owned at least 25 per cent of the common stock of the new Canadian corporation. This would probably be the case, since it is our understanding that Wettlaufer and Camelot would contribute their rights to the new beer to whatever entity is chosen, together with technical knowledge and up to $750,000 in capital — 75 per cent from Wettlaufer and 25 per cent from Camelot — and that the new entity would be 75 per cent owned by Wettlaufer and 25 per cent by Camelot. However, some of the 75 per cent ownership, and conceivably all of it, could actually be held by Cook rather than Wettlaufer. If Wettlaufer holds less than 25 per cent, then any dividends remitted by the new Canadian corporation to United States shareholders would be taxed at 15 per cent.

We think there might be an advantage in using a Canadian corporation with a permanent establishment in the United States. That is, the Canadian corporation would set up a branch in the United States to license Camelot or Cook to produce the beer in the United States. United States tax on royalties from Camelot or Cook would be larger we expect in this case than it would be if the Canadian corporation did not have a permanent establishment in the United States. But the U.S. taxes on dividends from Cook breweries to Wettlaufer might be reduced. Our hope would be that Wettlaufer might be able to take advantage of the 85 per cent dividends-received deduction and reduce United States tax on dividends from Cook to an effective 7.2 per cent or less.

Chapter ten

Tax factors in investment companies and personal holding companies

The function of most investment companies is simply to operate a portfolio of securities for the benefit of the investment companies' shareholders. If you face the choice between investing your money directly in a portfolio of securities or investing in the stock of an investment company (which maintains a portfolio), an obvious question is whether there will be any tax difference between the two choices. It should occur to you that unless there are some special tax rules for investment companies, there will be a serious penalty involved in the form of a corporate income tax imposed on the investment company. The penalty could be removed simply by exempting the investment company from income tax, permitting all its income to flow through to its shareholders free of tax so that the shareholders would be taxed as though they had received the income directly.

You should be able to see that exempting the investment company from income taxation is not an entirely satisfactory answer. What if the investment company does not pass its income on to the shareholders, but holds and reinvests it? If the company itself were exempt from tax, then this reinvestment would be tax-free, and the investment company would offer tremendous advantages as a vehicle for investment.

In order to equalize our two original alternatives, then, it might make better sense to exempt the investment company from income tax on the portion of its income that it actually passes on to the shareholders but to tax it on the income it retains.

Some problems, however, still remain. What about long-term capital gains? If the investment company retains these gains and is to be taxed on them, what rate should be applied? The ordinary corporate tax rate on long-term capital gains is 25 per cent, but this is the maximum rate for an individual. And if a shareholder of the investment company has an ordinary tax rate of 30 per cent, then his tax rate on long-term capital gains is only 15 per cent. If the investment company is to pay 25 per cent on its retained long-term capital gains, then clearly our 30 per cent taxpayer would do better, in terms of taxes, to invest his money directly in the stock market and realize his capital gains himself, rather than deal through the investment company.

You should be able to see other problems that will arise in the course of trying to equalize the tax effects for our two methods of investing.

For example, how should interest from tax-exempt municipal bonds be handled? How should the $100 dividend exclusion be handled?

Regulated investment companies

Read sections 851 and 852 of the Code and see how close section 852 comes to equalizing the tax effects of investing directly in the market and in investing through an investment company.

Would it make sense for an investment company governed by section 852 to invest in tax-exempt municipal bonds?

Suppose an investment company receives tax-free dividends from another corporation (dividends which would be tax-free to an individual recipient because the paying corporation does not happen to have any earnings and profits).

Is the benefit of the nontaxability of these dividends passed on to the shareholders of the investment company? Would it be possible for an investment company to compile a portfolio consisting exclusively of government bonds and to encourage people to buy shares in this investment company on the grounds that the first $100 of their dividends from the investment company would be excluded from their income and therefore it makes more sense to buy stock in the investment company than to buy government bonds directly?

It might occur to you that even if the investment company were not given any special tax concessions, the use of an investment company might result in considerable tax saving to an investor in a high tax bracket. If the investor's personal tax rate is greater than 48 per cent, then he might profit from incorporating his portfolio and having the corporate owner of the securities taxed at no more than 48 per cent on its income. If the income can then be reinvested by the corporation, the individual investor will do better than he would by receiving the income personally and reinvesting it. And since a corporation is granted a dividends-received deduction of 85 per cent, which brings the effective corporate tax rate on dividends down to about 7.2 per cent, it is easy to see a tremendous possible advantage in using an investment company as a vehicle for

ordinary stock market investment. Look through section 851 and 852 to
see what the Code does to eliminate or at least greatly reduce this potential advantage. Notice that section 851 begins by excluding a personal
holding company from the "regulated investment companies" which are
entitled to the special tax treatment of section 852. We will come shortly
to personal holding companies.

Section 851 refers to the Investment Company Act of 1940, one of
the statutes administered by the Securities and Exchange Commission. As
a general rule, any company which meets the definition of "investment
company" in the Investment Company Act must be registered with the
SEC if it is to use the mails or any means of interstate commerce. An
"investment company" is a company that holds itself out as being primarily engaged in the business of investing or trading in securities; or is
not primarily in the investing business, but intends to acquire investment
securities having a value exceeding 40 per cent of the company's total
assets.

There are some rather important exclusions from the definition of
investment company which seriously restrict the kind of company that is
given special treatment in section 852 of the Code. If the securities of a
company are beneficially owned by not more than 100 persons and the
company does not make any public offering of its securities, then it is not
considered an investment company. A very closely held company, then,
will not qualify for sections 851 and 852.

> *Can you see any reason for the restrictions imposed by section
> 851(b) in addition to the limitations imposed under section 851(a)?
> What sort of investment company will be given the special tax
> treatment of section 852 and what sort will not?*

It will not generally cost you less in taxes to make use of an investment company to do your investing than to invest directly in a portfolio of
securities. And obviously, if your investment company does not fit the
conditions of section 851, it will not be given the tax treatment specified
in section 852. This is not the final word, however. You will have to
consider the sections applying to so-called personal holding companies.

Personal holding companies

Sections 541–547 deal with personal holding companies. Section
541 tells you why the concept of a personal holding company is important: there is a very serious tax penalty imposed on undistributed personal
holding company income. How serious is the penalty?

> *For an individual in the top tax bracket, which is 70 per cent, is it
> less desirable to have investment income accumulate in a personal
> holding company rather than to receive it directly?*

Section 545 tells you what it is that is subject to the penalty tax—the
undistributed personal holding company income. And section 543 tells
you how to determine personal holding company income, from which the

undistributed portion must be determined. A personal holding company may be a highly desirable device quite apart from tax consequences. That is, a family may find it very convenient to place all of its investments in a single corporation and have the family members simply own shares in this corporation. For one thing, it may be possible for a member of the family to give away or to leave to his heirs his share of the family investments without any need for selling the investments, reducing them to cash, and then dividing up the cash.

If you are going to use a personal holding company, what will you have to do to avoid the penalty tax? On the basis of section 543, what sort of income should your company have in order to escape entirely the classification of personal holding company? And finally, under section 542, how must a company be owned in order to avoid the classification?

A common way to prevent a closely held investment company from being classed as a personal holding company is to invest sufficient of the company's assets in real estate that sections 542(a)(1) and 543(a)(2) exclude the company from the personal holding company classification.

Bearing in mind that the conditions of these sections must be met for a taxable year and that the Internal Revenue Service may successfully dispute items in a tax return long after the return is filed, what precautions must be taken during the taxable year if the owners of a company are depending upon rental income to protect them from the penalty tax on undistributed personal holding company income?

Hillsdale Corporation

A group of three men, unrelated to one another by blood or marriage, has purchased a large tract of land with a house and barns for $70,000. They value the house at $30,000, the barns at $1,000, and the land at $39,000. Their purpose in buying the property was chiefly to build homes on it for themselves. It is unlikely that these homes will be constructed for another ten to fifteen years, and in the meantime the three men expect to use the property for vacation and general recreational purposes. When the time comes to build homes for themselves, they hope to sell building lots on the property to others. Probably at least fifty large lots could be made available for sale.

The three men own the property as tenants in common; that is, each one has an undivided one third interest in the entire property.

The house is rented, and the tenants pay $50 a week in rent. Expenses for utilities, maintenance, and repairs on the house run about $1000 a year and are paid by the three owners. Property taxes on the entire property are about $900. It seems likely that $1000 worth of timber and $1000 worth of hay could be sold from the property each year, at no expense.

When they bought the property, the three men were not primarily interested in a profitable investment. But the land is well located, and it seems likely that its value will rise substantially in ten to fifteen years. Selling building lots at from three to four times their cost is a distinct possibility.

The men have been considering incorporating the property. The advantage of limited liability of a corporation appeals to them, as does the easy transferability of shares of stock. They are concerned, however, at the possibility of income tax penalty if the property were incorporated.

In terms of taxes, what will be the consequences of incorporation, and would you advise for or against it?

Chapter eleven

Real estate investment

The income tax aspect of real estate has made it popular for a long time with high tax bracket investors. For the most part, the tax advantages lie in the fact that a substantial part of the profit from real estate investment can be expected to come from long-term capital gains, while during his holding period the investor can generally take advantage of substantial depreciation deductions against his taxable income. In Chapter three we discussed opportunities for converting ordinary income into capital gains and into investments that generate depreciation deductions and matching capital gains. Historically, much of the attraction in real estate investment has rested on this latter possibility. In 1964, when section 1250 was added to the Code, the opportunity was substantially reduced. The effect of this new provision will be seen in some of the tables to follow.

Depreciation and capital gains

If you can purchase depreciable real estate, write it off against income that is taxed at a high rate, and then sell the real estate for about what you paid for it, you may be able to show a substantial profit due entirely to the difference between the tax saving from the depreciation and the tax paid at a lower rate on the capital gain. Of course, if the property can be sold for more than its original cost, and if there is some income derived from it during the holding period, your rate of return will be that much greater.

For purposes of illustration, we are going to consider an investment of $1 million in a depreciable building with a life for depreciation purposes of twenty years and with a zero expected salvage value. We are making no allowance for investment in nondepreciable property; that is, we are not allowing for any land, for example, to go with the building. We will assume that when the building is sold, it will be sold for its original $1 million cost. This is a fair assumption, if it is a good commercial or residential building and is reasonably well located. We are also going to assume an annual rent (after all expenses except depreciation) of 6 per cent of the original cost of the building, or $60,000. This is before any income tax.

Table 1 shows the rate of return an investor would receive from this building, depending upon whether his income tax rate is 50 per cent or 65 per cent and depending upon when he sells the building. The rates of return shown are after income tax, and depreciation is assumed to be taken for tax purposes on a straight line basis.

Table 1: After-tax rate of return
(Straight line depreciation)

$1,000,000 building, depreciated over 20 years.
Rental income 6% of cost, before depreciation.
Sale is at original cost.

Sale at end of year	After-tax rate of return With tax at 50%	With tax at 65%
1	4.25%	4.10%
2	4.28	4.13
3	4.30	4.16
4	4.33	4.17
5	4.36	4.20

Table 2 shows the results of going to accelerated depreciation. In this case, a 50 per cent income tax rate is assumed, but the after-tax rates of return are shown for four different depreciation methods.

Table 2: After-tax rate of return
(Four depreciation methods)

Sale at end of year	After-tax rate of return when tax rate is 50%			
	Straight line	150% declining balance	Double declining balance	Sum-of-the-years digits
1	4.25%	4.88%	5.50%	5.38%
2	4.28	4.84	5.44	5.38
3	4.30	4.83	5.39	5.39
4	4.33	4.80	5.35	5.39
5	4.36	4.78	5.30	5.39

As you might expect, the rate of return is increased if depreciation is taken by one of the accelerated methods. But notice also for the declining balance methods that the rate of return generally declines as sale of the building is postponed, whereas with straight line depreciation, the longer the building is held the higher the rate of return.

If the investment can be leveraged with borrowed money, of course, the rate of return may be significantly increased. Table 3 shows after-tax returns to an investor for two cases: where one third the purchase price is borrowed and where two thirds the purchase price is borrowed. It is assumed that the loans are at a 5 per cent interest rate and that they call for uniform annual payments including interest and principal amortization.

Table 3: After-tax rate of return
(Leveraged investment)

Tax rate is 50%
Double declining balance depreciation is taken.
Loan is at 5%, with uniform annual payments.

Sale at end of year	After-tax rate of return	
	$\frac{1}{3}$ of investment borrowed	$\frac{2}{3}$ of investment borrowed
1	7.00%	11.50%
2	6.90	11.30
3	6.83	11.09
4	6.74	10.87
5	6.66	10.64

All of the examples so far have assumed that on the sale of the building the difference between the sale price and the depreciated book value is taxed as a long-term capital gain. This was the case until 1964. The introduction that year of section 1250 reduced but did not eliminate the possibility of creating depreciation deductions and matching long-term capital gain. Since section 1250 has no effect in cases where straight line depreciation is used, the figures in Table 1 would not be changed on the basis of section 1250. The figures in Table 2, however, are different since the introduction of the depreciation recapture, and Table 4 shows the effect of section 1250 on the rates of return in Table 2.

Table 4: After-tax rate of return
(Four depreciation methods)

Same as Table 2 except that the effects of section 1250 are accounted for.

Sale at end of year	After-tax rate of return			
	Straight line	150% declining balance	Double declining balance	Sum-of-the-years digits
1	4.25%	4.25%	4.25%	4.25%
2	4.28	4.34	4.42	4.40
3	4.30	4.51	4.72	4.72
4	4.33	4.63	4.97	4.98
5	4.36	4.72	5.15	5.21

As you might expect, the rates of return using the accelerated depreciation methods are somewhat reduced from those shown in Table 2. The rates corresponding to a short holding period are changed, considerably more, however, than the rates corresponding to a long holding period.

One of the results is that the rate of return is now higher the longer the holding period, just the reverse of the relationship shown in Table 2.

The effect of section 1250 on the example shown in Table 3 is demonstrated below, in Table 5.

Table 5: After-tax rate of return
(Leveraged investment)

Same as Table 3, except that the effects of section 1250 are accounted for.

Sale at end of year	After-tax rate of return	
	$\frac{1}{3}$ of investment borrowed	$\frac{2}{3}$ of investment borrowed
1	5.12%	7.74%
2	5.38	8.29
3	5.84	9.18
4	6.19	9.82
5	6.45	10.25

We discussed in Chapter Three the fact that when depreciation recapture was first introduced into the Internal Revenue Code with section 1245, which became effective at the end of 1962, the real estate interests were successful in having real property excluded from this new provision. Table 6 compares rates of return for no depreciation recapture, recapture under section 1245, and recapture under section 1250.

Table 6: After-tax rate of return
(Comparison of recapture provisions)

Tax rate is 50%
Double declining balance depreciation is taken.
Investment is not leveraged.

Sale at end of year	After-tax rate of return		
	No recapture	Recapture under sec. 1245	Recapture under sec. 1250
1	5.50%	3.00%	4.25%
2	5.44	3.07	4.42
3	5.39	3.15	4.72
4	5.35	3.23	4.97
5	5.30	3.29	5.15

In this example the investor is clearly better off under section 1250 than he would have been if section 1245 had been made applicable to real property. However, the table does not take into account that when the new Guidelines were published in 1962 they substantially shortened the permissible depreciable lives of a great many assets but tended to lengthen the depreciable lives of real property (Chapter Eight). This happened because the Treasury had no intention of conferring benefits through the Guidelines on investments which were not subject to depreciation recapture under section 1245. When section 1250 was enacted, no change was made in the Guidelines. Hence, the real estate industry sacrificed a possible shortening of depreciable lives under the Guidelines when it was successful in having real estate excluded from section 1245.

A number of tax gimmicks connected with real estate have to do with the use of mortgages. We will mention only one of these. Suppose you purchase a property actually worth about $100,000 for $1 million, giving $100,000 in cash and a note for $900,000 secured by a mortgage on the property. You provide in the note that in the event you fail to pay it, the seller may have recourse only against the mortgaged property and not against any of your other assets. This is an unusual kind of note, but one that is used fairly frequently in the real estate industry. The $900,000 payment comes due at the end of the useful life of the property, say, at the end of twenty years. Over the twenty-year period, you take depreciation based on the cost of $1 million, which produces considerable tax savings if you are in a high income tax bracket. At the end of the twenty-year period, you simply default on the mortgage and the seller takes his property back. You will, of course, realize capital gain, although there will be no depreciation recapture (why?). But the tax on the capital gain will probably be a small price to pay for the depreciation deductions which you enjoyed over the twenty years.

Section 1038 was added to the Internal Revenue Code in 1964; what effect does it have on the scheme described above?

Real estate as a capital asset

Throughout the discussion above we have assumed that the real estate investment was an investment in a capital asset, producing capital gain at the time of sale. We have already discussed problems in the definition of a capital asset in Chapter Three. You should, however, take a look again at section 1221 and see what the status of real estate is in terms of the definition of a capital asset, and you should refer to Chapter Three for a discussion of sections 1221 and 1231.

Form of ownership

Our discussion so far has assumed real estate investments made by an individual. The same consequences would result, of course, from investments made by a corporation, except that the corporate tax rate would have to be used rather than the individual tax rates we have worked with. Where several individuals invest in a single piece of real estate, some problems arise.

If the individuals purchase the property as tenants in common or form a partnership to hold the property, the tax consequences we have been discussing for the individual will apply. Recall the discussion of the taxation of partners in Chapter Two. But if a substantial number of individuals are to invest in a single piece of real estate, then a tenancy in common or a partnership may present undesirable complications.

In the case of a tenancy in common, all dealings with the property will require the signatures of all the owners. This makes the management of the property somewhat complicated, and the transfer of the interest of one of the owners presents further difficulties. In the case of the partnership, it may be necessary for all the partners to participate in any transaction involving the property. There are further complications connected with the transfer of an interest in the property, and as in the case of the tenancy in common, the investors have difficulty limiting their liability for losses beyond the value of the property.

The obvious answer to all these problems may seem to lie in the corporation. The corporate form offers limited liability, easy transferability of interests of investors, and a centralized management that may rest with a single individual. Unfortunately, the tax consequences of using a corporation may not be attractive. To begin with, a corporation normally involves double taxation; that is, the corporation is going to be taxed on its profit from the real estate in which it invests, and then the shareholders will be taxed either on dividends or on capital gains. We have seen, in the discussion of corporate reorganization, the possibility of liquidating a corporation without a double tax on the sale of its assets; that is, it is possible in most cases to realize capital gain on a corporate asset with a tax either at the corporate or at the shareholder level but not both. However, it may be difficult to classify real estate held by a corporation as other than that "used in the trade or business" of the corporation, especially if ownership of the property was the sole purpose for forming the corporation. Recall the treatment, under section 1231, of real property that is used in a corporation's trade or business, and look at section 341 to see what happens on the liquidation of a corporation that has been set up for the sole purpose of constructing or acquiring an investment in real estate.

It might occur to you that the provisions in the Code governing regulated investment companies (which we discussed in Chapter Ten) might facilitate investment in real estate. However, if you look at section 851, you will see that a company investing primarily in real estate could not qualify.

What about Sub-Chapter S corporations? These corporations, which we referred to in Chapter Two, can elect partnership rather than corporate taxation. Take a look at section 1372 and see whether there is any possibility of using a Sub-Chapter S corporation for real estate investment.

Sections 856, 857, and 858 were added to the Internal Revenue Code in 1960 to provide a vehicle for real estate investment somewhat similar to the regulated investment company. The vehicle must be organized legally, however, not as a corporation but as a trust. Real estate investment trusts were not unknown before 1960, but they were treated for tax purposes as corporations and hence carried all the disadvantages we have referred to above, including double taxation. The Treasury objected to the special tax treatment for real estate investment trusts. The argument was essentially that the special treatment given to regulated investment companies really prevents triple rather than double taxation. The income of the investment company originates in a corporation that is itself subject to tax. If taxes were imposed on this corporation, on the investment company, and on the individual investor, there would be three layers of taxation. Eliminating taxes on the investment company itself restores the customary double taxation, where the industrial corporation is taxed and the individual investor is taxed. In the case of the real estate investment trust, however, the trust itself is not usually investing in another taxable entity. It is generally producing revenue directly from business assets. These arguments suggest that a distinction should be drawn between the real estate investment trust that actually operates a business, and the trust that invests in other real estate operations and derives "passive" investment income from them.

Do you see any such distinction drawn in sections 856, 857, and 858?

At present, the real estate investment trust offers probably the best vehicle for a large number of people investing in a piece of real estate. The investors achieve limited liability and easy transferability of their interests in most cases, and they also achieve a partnership tax status. This does not mean that the corporation is never appropriate as a vehicle for real estate investment. One aspect of corporate taxation that has proved quite beneficial to a number of real estate corporations is the fact that a corporate distribution to a shareholder is taxed as a dividend only if the corporation has "earnings and profits." If the real estate operations, with large depreciation deductions, have led to no "earnings and profits," the tax consequences of distributions to shareholders are not serious.

Installment sales and tax-free exchanges

In Chapter three we discussed the special tax treatment given to sales made for installment payments and the possibility of exchanging one piece of property for another without the realization of gain. Section 453 deals with installment sales, and sub-section (b) deals specifically with sales of real estate. Sections 1031–1036 deal with tax-free exchanges. Section 1031 is the most important.

Leases

As a general rule, the tax differences between leasing and owning property are these: the owner of a piece of property will be able to depreciate it for tax purposes, and if he has financed the purchase by borrowing, he will be able to deduct interest payments in computing taxable income; a lessee of property is not entitled to any depreciation deductions, but all of his rent payments are deductible for tax purposes. The claim is often made that the deductibility of rent makes leasing superior to owning an asset. An analytic comparison of the cost of owning with the cost of leasing, however, involves a great deal more than taxes and is a fairly complicated business. In the case of real estate investment, the tax factor may become unusually important because land is not depreciable.

For example, suppose you are offered a choice between purchasing a building and land (and probably financing a large part of the purchase with a loan) or, on the other hand, purchasing the building outright but renting the land. In the case of the purchase, you end up owning both land and building. But you have made a larger investment since you had to purchase the land. And you are not able to depreciate any of your investment in the land, while any rent payable for the land would have been fully deductible. Obviously, the choice depends upon a number of factors including the size of the investment, the rent demanded, interest rates on borrowed money, the rate of return you can obtain on funds, and your expectation of residual values. In many cases, the lease will be more attractive than ownership.

Manuel D. Mayerson v. Commissioner[1]

Hoyt, Judge: Respondent determined deficiencies of $11,018.48 and $22,312.75 in joint income taxes of petitioners for 1960 and 1961, respectively. Certain issues have been settled between the parties. A preliminary issue is whether the statutory notice of deficiency constitutes a determination which places the burden of proof to show error in the determination upon the petitioners. The principal issue remaining is whether petitioners are entitled to depreciation deductions on a business property located at 8th and Walnut in Cincinnati, Ohio, and, if not, what is the proper amortization period for $10,000 in payments made in connection with the acquisition of that building. A subsidiary issue is whether petitioners erroneously computed the deduction claimed for depreciation with respect to other income property on Forest Avenue. A portion of this depreciation deduction was disallowed.

Findings of fact

Some of the facts have been stipulated and are found accordingly and adopted as our findings.

Petitioners are husband and wife and are residents of Cincinnati, Ohio. Their joint returns for the years involved were filed with the district director of internal revenue, Cincinnati, Ohio. Petitioner, Rhoda Mayerson, is a party herein only by reason of having filed a joint return with her husband, Manuel D. Mayerson, and the latter will hereinafter be referred to as the petitioner.

Petitioner has been a licensed real estate broker for approximately 20 years. In addition to his brokerage activities, he has owned many investments in real estate and has been instrumental in developing several shopping centers and many motel and apartment projects, remodeling older structures when necessary.

[1] 47 T.C. (Tax Court of the United States) 1966.

The property which is the subject of the primary controversy here is located at the northwest corner of 8th and Walnut Streets, Cincinnati, Ohio, and hereinafter will be referred to as the 8th and Walnut Building. Petitioner first became interested in acquiring this commercial property in the latter part of 1959. The building was owned by the Estate of Edith W. Balch and petitioner contacted the coexecutor of the estate, Henry W. Hobson, Jr., a Cincinnati lawyer, to discuss the possible sale of the building. At the outset petitioner was informed that the estate wanted $275,000 cash for the property and that if he was not able to pay cash the price would go up to a top price of $332,000.

The history of the building relative to its net profits over the years was discussed in detail during the sales negotiations. At one time the building had produced a relatively good income but toward the last years of Edith Balch's life and during the period of administration of the Balch Estate the building had not been profitable.

Another concern of petitioner was the existence of 72 outstanding building orders against the building imposed by municipal authorities in order to insure conformance with the Cincinnati Building Code. Petitioner considered these building orders carefully since the exact costs for necessary corrective action could not be precisely ascertained, and they could have involved tens of thousands of dollars.

Petitioner was only interested in the purchase of the 8th and Walnut Building and the Balch Estate was only interested in selling the building. The Balch Estate was not interested in leasing the property to petitioner or obtaining a new manager.

Petitioner was particularly interested in remodeling this older property in order to enhance its profit potential. Several alternative possibilities for the building were discussed, including conversion into a motel or hotel, development into a downtown apartment project or a major garage installation, or attraction of a single user for the entire property.

Petitioner's lack of available funds made it impossible for him to pay cash for the building. Conventional mortgage financing was investigated but it found that such financing was unavailable due to the building's age, condition and the outstanding building orders. After extensive negotiations, representatives of the Balch Estate agreed to convey the title to the building with financing based upon a purchase money note in the face amount of $332,500 secured by a long-term mortgage. If the purchase money obligation was paid off within the first year, or the two succeeding years, the price would be reduced to $275,000 or $298,750, respectively. Thereafter, the price would increase to the face amount of the mortgage note, maximum of $332,500.

A valid warranty deed was executed and the property was conveyed to petitioner on December 31, 1959. The deed was presented to the Hamilton County, Ohio, County Auditor on December 31, 1959, where it was noted for transfer, and the formal registration with the Recorder of Hamilton County, Ohio, was completed on January 5, 1960.

In connection with the transaction, petitioner on the same date executed and delivered to the sellers documents entitled "Mortgage Note" and "Purchase Money Real Estate Mortgage." The document entitled "Mortgage Note" provided as follows:

FOR VALUE RECEIVED, on or before ninety-nine (99) years from date, the undersigned, Manuel D. Mayerson, Trustee, promises to pay to the order of DeWitt W. Balch and Henry W. Hobson, Jr., Co-Executors of the Estate of Edith W. Balch, deceased, their successors or assigns, whose present address is 1232 Federal Reserve Bank Building, Cincinnati 2, Ohio, the principal sum of Three Hundred Thirty-Two Thousand Five Hundred Dollars ($332,500.00), under the conditions contained herein and subject to the limit of liability as provided for herein; Five Thousand Dollars ($5,000.00) of principal shall be payable on December 31, 1959, and Five Thousand Dollars ($5,000.00) of principal shall be payable on January 4, 1960.

There shall be no obligation on the maker to make any further payments of principal at any particular time prior to due date, but he shall have the privilege of making payments, but shall not be obligated to, on account of principal at any interest payment date as hereinafter provided, but any such principal payment shall not be in an amount of less than Twenty-Five Thousand Dollars ($25,000.00).

Interest shall be the sum of Eighteen Thousand Dollars ($18,000.00) per year, payable in monthly installments of Fifteen Hundred Dollars ($1500.00) each on the last day of each month, beginning January 31, 1960. When and if the principal owing on this note shall have been reduced below the sum of Three Hundred Thousand Dollars ($300,000.00), interest on the remaining balance shall be calculated at the rate of 6% per annum on the unpaid principal, and shall be payable in equal monthly installments monthly at the times hereinbefore stated.

It is further agreed that if the two payments aggregating Ten Thousand Dollars ($10,000.00), payable on December 31, 1959 and January 4, 1960, as aforeprovided, and all interest shall have been paid, the principal amount of this note may be fully satisfied at any time after January 5, 1960, and before December 31, 1960, by the payment of Two Hundred Seventy-five Thousand Dollars ($275,000.00), the said Two Hundred Seventy-five Thousand Dollars ($275,000.00) to be reduced by any payments that may have been made in addition to the Ten Thousand Dollars ($10,000.00) paid on December 31, 1959, and January 4, 1960, and upon such payment this note shall be cancelled.

It is further agreed that if the two payments aggregating Ten Thousand Dollars ($10,000.00), payable on December 31, 1959 and January 4, 1960, as aforeprovided, and all interest shall have been paid as herein provided, the principal amount of this note may be fully satisfied at any time after December 31, 1960, and before December 31, 1962, by the payment of Two Hundred Ninety-eight Thousand Seven Hundred and Fifty Dollars ($298,750.00), the said Two Hundred Ninety-eight Thousand Seven Hundred and Fifty

Dollars ($298,750.00) to be reduced by any payments that may have been made in addition to the Ten Thousand Dollars ($10,000.00), paid on December 31, 1959, and January 4, 1960, and upon such payment this note shall be cancelled.

This note is secured by a mortgage of even date herewith on real estate situated in Cincinnati, Ohio.

In the event of default in the payment of any installment of principal or interest on this note when due, or in the event of default in the performance of any of the covenants contained in the mortgage to be performed by the mortgagor, the holder of this note may, at his option, without notice, declare the principal of this note and the interest thereon to be immediately due and payable and may proceed to enforce the collection thereof by suit to foreclose the mortgage, but his sole recourse, except for interest then due, shall be to the mortgaged property and the maker's liability for any other amounts owing hereunder, shall be limited to the loss of the real estate covered by the mortgage and there shall be no personal liability whatever on his part. The holder, by acceptance hereof, waives the right to bring an action or suit for personal judgment hereon, except for accrued interest.

The pertinent provisions of the document entitled "Purchase Money Real Estate Mortgage" provided as follows:

. . . And the said Grantor, for himself and his successors in trust and assigns, does hereby covenant and agree with the said Grantees, their successors and assigns, as follows:

1. To pay the note hereby secured in accordance with its terms, but subject, however, to the limit of liability therein and herein provided, and all other amounts herein agreed to be paid by the Grantor when and as the same shall become due under any covenant or stipulation herein contained, subject, however, to limit of liability herein contained. . . .

In the event of loss, if permitted by Grantees' mortgagee, the proceeds of the foregoing insurance policies shall be applied at the option of the Grantor either to the reduction of the mortgage indebtedness secured hereby or to the repair and restoration of the damage. Should it be applied to such repair and restoration and there be an overage, the overage shall be applied to the reduction of the mortgage indebtedness. It is further agreed, if permitted by Grantees' mortgagee, that if the damage be of such nature as in the opinion of the Grantor shall not warrant the application of the proceeds to the construction of a building similar to that now on the premises, the Grantor may demolish whatever is left of the present structure and either replace it with a different type of structure or none at all, provided, however, that such action shall not be taken without the consent of the Grantees, which consent shall not be unreasonably withheld. If such course is taken, proceeds of insurance shall be used to place the property in proper condition and the balance shall be applied to the reduction of the mortgage indebtedness.

4. To maintain or cause to be maintained the buildings and improvements upon said premises in good condition and to repair, renew and replace the same whenever necessary and not to commit or permit any waste thereon or thereof.

5. To improve the mortgaged property by complying with all building orders outstanding against the property as of the date hereof with due diligence and within a reasonable time and, thereafter, to keep the property free of any building orders by any public or other authority authorized to issue the same by complying therewith with due diligence and within a reasonable time. . . .

7. That upon failure of Grantor to maintain insurance as above stipulated or to deliver said renewal policies as aforesaid or to pay said premiums, the Grantees may effect such insurance and pay the premiums therefor, and upon Grantor's failure to pay any taxes, charges, rates and assessments as above stipulated or if there shall be at any time any prior liens or encumbrances on said premises, Grantees may, without notice to or demand on Grantor pay the amount of any such taxes, charges, rates or assessments or prior liens or encumbrances and redeem the property from any tax sale with any expenses attending the same, including Attorneys' fees. In either of such events, the Grantor agrees to repay to the Grantees, with interest at the rate of six per cent (6%) per annum thereon, upon demand, any amounts so paid by the Grantees, and the same shall be a lien on said premises and be secured by these presents.

8. The Grantor will comply with all laws, ordinances and regulations of all public authorities relating to the Mortgaged Premises and will not remove or demolish any buildings thereon or any of the mortgaged properties situated therein without the consent of the Grantees, which consent shall not be unreasonably withheld; nor shall Grantor sell or convey any part of the premises hereby conveyed without the written consent of Grantees, which shall not be unreasonably withheld. The foregoing limitation of conveyancing shall not be applicable to conveyances to any person for whom the Grantor is holding title and all limitations of liability provided for herein shall have like application to the Grantor and any persons for whom the Grantor holds title.

9. That the Grantor will pay to the Grantees any and all sums, including costs, expenses, reasonable Attorneys' fees, which Grantees may incur or expend in any proceeding to sustain the lien of this mortgage or its priority (except for mortgage hereinafter re-

ferred to) or to defend against the liens or claims of any person or persons asserting priority to this mortgage (except for mortgage hereinafter referred to) or in discharge of any such claim or lien or in connection with any suit at law or in equity to foreclose this instrument or to recover any indebtedness hereby secured or in which it may be necessary or proper to prove the amount thereof or for any extension of title to said premises together with interest on said sums at six per cent (6%) per annum until paid and any amounts so paid by the Grantees shall be a lien on said premises and be secured by these presents. . . .

Notwithstanding anything in this mortgage or in the promissory note contained to the contrary, the sole and only personal liability of the Grantor shall be the obligation to make the two payments on December 31, 1959, and January 4, 1960, aggregating ten thousand dollars ($10,000.00), and the payments to Grantees provided for in Paragraphs 7 and 9 above and the interest provided for in the promissory note, and the Grantees' only recourse in case of any default in any other of Grantor's obligations shall be against the mortgaged property only, and to foreclose the mortgage and in no event and under no circumstances, except as provided in this paragraph, shall a money judgment be taken against Grantor. It is further agreed and understood that Grantor's obligations under Paragraphs 7 and 9 and for interest on said note shall terminate, except as to amounts then due, upon the first to happen of the following: (1) Proceedings being commenced to foreclose this mortgage or to otherwise regain possession of the mortgaged property, or for the application of rents for the benefit of the mortgagees; or (2) upon proffer of a conveyance thereof to the Grantees by the Grantor, except for sums for costs, expenses and reasonable attorneys' fees, which may accrue thereafter by reason of a proceeding described in Paragraph 9. Grantees hereby waive the right to bring or maintain any action or suit for a personal judgment, except as provided in this Paragraph.

Both of the preceding documents will hereinafter be referred to jointly as the purchase money mortgage.

Petitioner paid $5,000 in December of 1959 and $5,000 in January of 1960 as provided for and required by the note. It was understood by the parties that petitioner would find the best use for the property as soon as possible and after finding such use seek conventional financing for the purpose of liquidating the purchase money mortgage. The time for accomplishing the foregoing plan was indefinite, but the parties discussed the possibility of five to ten years or less.

Petitioner held title to the building as trustee. An unrecorded trust agreement named his wife as the beneficiary of the trust. Under Ohio law, such an arrangement is categorized as a dry trust and subsequent purchasers are entitled to consider the trustee as the sole owner of the property.

Following the transfer of title, petitioner contacted architects and had engineering surveys made of the property. Costs of conversion were explored with several independent contractors. Apartment or motel conversions were investigated in detail. Petitioner spoke to hundreds of people in connection with the possible conversion of the building. Installation of new elevators was considered as well as refacing the entire structure.

The outstanding building orders were reduced from 72 to 25 by March 4, 1960, and were further reduced to 6 by December 16, 1964. This was done by petitioner at his expense in order to keep the building open and also to comply with the requirements of the purchase money mortgage. Boilers were purchased by petitioner and installed in the 8th and Walnut Building in January of 1961 at a cost of $13,000.

In addition to repairs required by the building orders and normal maintenance petitioner has made several major improvements. Garage entrances were widened, the building was rewired, the lobbies were reconditioned with the installation of new ceilings and fronts. Several thousands of dollars were spent to create offices on the second floor of the building as part of an experiment to test the potential for renting office space at highly competitive rates. Costs of repairs to the building in the amount of $9,847.67 and $8,931.11 were deducted on petitioner's income tax returns for 1960 and 1961, respectively, and these deductions have not been questioned by respondent or disallowed in the deficiency notices issued for those years.

Following the transfer of title in 1959, petitioner executed leases with tenants and paid utilities, insurance, and real estate tax bills. In late December of 1964, petitioner learned that the owner of a nearby building was contemplating another area for a garage. After discussions with the owner of this building, petitioner convinced him to lease the entire 8th and Walnut Building. By using this lease as collateral, petitioner was for the first time able to get a conventional mortgage loan from a financial institution. After securing this loan, petitioner negotiated with the Balch Estate and in January of 1965 the parties agreed to a settlement to discharge the note and purchase money mortgage by the payment of the flat sum of $200,000. Petitioner made no payment of principal with respect to the purchase money mortgage from the time of the initial $10,000 down payments until the negotiated settlement resulting in payment of $200,000 to discharge this lien.

Petitioner had never dealt with Henry W. Hobson, Jr., the coexecutor of the Balch Estate, prior to the negotiations concerning the 8th and Walnut Building. The two men were not even acquainted with each other prior to these dealings. Neither the Balch Estate nor the trust which succeeded to its interest claimed a deduction for depreciation on the building after December 1959.

A deed from petitioner as trustee would be necessary to transfer legal title to the 8th and Walnut Building to any person or entity. A title insurance company was willing in December of 1964 to issue a title insurance binder in support of such a conveyance in any amount desired.

In the field of mortgage lending, it is a usual practice with respect to income-producing property that mortgagors have their liability limited to the specific security that is covered by the mortgage. It is also a frequent practice in the field of mortgage lending to allow the mortgagee to waive payments of principal on income-producing properties in distress or incentive situations.

Petitioner allocated $200,000 of the alleged purchase price of the 8th and Walnut property to the depreciable building and claimed depreciation during the years in question based upon this amount. By a 30-day letter dated September 26, 1963, petitioner was advised that the Internal Revenue Service was disallowing all depreciation on the 8th and Walnut Building for the following reason:

> The disallowance of depreciation in full on 8th and Walnut was based on the fact that the transaction made by the taxpayer in obtaining the building was a lease and not a purchase. The taxpayer's down payment of $10,000 was determined to be cost of obtaining the lease and amortizable over the life which is 99 years.

The statutory notice of deficiency dated April 9, 1964, contained the following determination for 1960:

> It has been determined that depreciation claimed [in] the amount of $18,025.00 is excessive, and not an allowable deduction in accordance with section 167 of the Internal Revenue Code of 1954. See Exhibit A for computation of the adjustments.
>
> You are hereby allowed amortization on the $10,000.00 cost of obtaining lease on 8th and Walnut Building, in accordance with section 178 of the Internal Revenue Code of 1954. See Exhibit A for computation of the adjustment.

The determinations for 1961 relating to depreciation on the 8th and Walnut Building contained in the same notice of deficiency were identical in all respects except for the amount disallowed. Exhibit A to the notice of deficiency showed that no depreciation attributable to the 8th and Walnut Building was allowable, but allowed an annual deduction of $101.01 as amortization over a period of 99 years for the $10,000 down payment which was classified as the cost of obtaining a 99-year lease. The notice of deficiency did not alter petitioner's claimed interest deductions for the years 1960 and 1961 relative to the purchase money mortgage, and did not provide for or allow any deductions for rental payments under a lease.

The parties have agreed that if it is determined that petitioner is entitled to claim depreciation with respect to the 8th and Walnut Building, then, for the purpose of determining the depreciation deduction the following shall apply:

Allocation of investment in entire property . . . . 60.15 per cent building
39.85 per cent land
Method of depreciation . . . . 150 per cent declining balance
Useful life . . . . 25 years

Opinion

Respondent determined that petitioner's claimed deduction for depreciation of the 8th and Walnut Building was excessive and not allowable under section 167 during the years in question. A depreciation deduction is allowed for property used in a trade or business or held for the production of income. Section 167(g) of the Code provides that the basis for the depreciation deduction is the adjusted basis provided in section 1011 for the purpose of determining the gain on the sale or other disposition of such property. Generally, the adjusted basis for determining gain or loss from the sale of property is the amount paid for such property in cash or other property. Sec. 1.1012–1, Income Tax Regs. Thus, in a situation of outright purchase, the amount paid for the property constitutes the depreciable basis. Moreover, it is well accepted that a purchase money debt obligation for part of the price will be included in basis. This is necessary in order to equate a purchase money mortgage situation with the situation in which the buyer borrows the full amount of the purchase price from a third party and pays the seller in cash. It is clear that the depreciable basis should be the same in both instances.

Respondent's position is essentially that the purchase money mortgage involved in this case was a nullity and that a capital investment in the subject property had not occurred. The $10,000 cash down payment was treated in Exhibit A to the deficiency notice as the cost of obtaining a 99-year lease, thus qualifying for amortization deductions over the term of the lease. This treatment gives rise to the inference that respondent determined that the transaction actually resulted in the creation of a long-term lease. On brief, respondent adds the additional contention that in effect all petitioner acquired was an option to purchase at any time during the alleged lease.

Respondent's position apparently results from his objections to certain features of the purchase money mortgage. Petitioner was not personally liable on the mortgage, and the only recourse available to the mortgagee in case of default was foreclosure against the property; the property was the only security under the mortgage agreement. Respondent argues that when there is no enforceable and binding personal obligation with respect to the purchase price, no debt is created.

The absence of a debt is also indicated by the indefinite amount of the alleged obligation, according to respondent. This is evidently a reference to the fact that petitioner could pay off the mortgage in the first or two succeeding years with an amount stipulated in the purchase money mortgage which was less than the face amount due after the expiration of three years. Thus, the amount due on the mortgage could fluctuate between three different sums depending upon whether payment occurred within the first year, the second or third year, or years thereafter.

Respondent also emphasizes the fact that after two initial payments of $5,000 each, no portion of the principal of the purchase money mortgage was due on or before 99 years from the date of the obligation. Petitioner did have the option, however, to make payments of principal at any time during the term of the mortgage. Petitioner was obligated to pay a fixed sum of $18,000 per year, designated as interest, in monthly installments. If the principal due on the mortgage was reduced below $300,000, then interest was payable at the rate of 6 per cent per year on the unpaid balance.

It is undisputed that petitioner became the owner of legal title to the 8th and Walnut Building. There is no hint of a sham transaction in the transfer of title to the building and respondent makes no contention that the transaction was a sham or rigged to appear to be a sale and mortgage back when it was in fact something else. We are concerned with an arm's-length transaction entered into between knowledgeable strangers for business motives. It is well accepted, however, that depreciation is not predicated upon ownership of property but rather upon an investment in property. *Gladding Dry Goods Co.* 2 B.T.A. 336 (1925). It therefore follows that the benefit of the depreciation deduction should inure to those who would suffer an economic loss caused by wear and exhaustion of the business property. See *Thomas W. Blake, Jr.* 20 T.C. 721 (1953).

Respondent relies upon the preceding cases and general statements in *Weiss* v. *Wiener*, 279 U.S. 333 (1929), to the effect that only a capital investment is depreciable, to support his view that the petitioner did not have a depreciable interest in the 8th and Walnut Building.

We must first decide whether the absence of personal liability with respect to the purchase money mortgage precludes the inclusion of any amount attributable to the mortgage in the depreciable basis of the property. If this is true, depreciation based on the purchase money mortgage should be denied regardless of the existence of a bona fide debt obligation for the mortgage. An analysis of this question must begin with the Supreme Court's landmark decision in *Crane* v. *Commissioner*, 331 U.S. 1 (1947). The *Crane* case involved the question of what the proper basis of inherited property was for the purpose of computing the taxable gain on the sale of the property. The property was received subject to an unassumed mortgage and was sold still so encumbered. The Court held that the basis of the property was the value at the date of death undiminished by the mortgage. The inclusion of the indebtedness in basis was balanced by a similar inclusion of the indebtedness in amount realized upon the ultimate sale of the property to a nonassuming grantee.

The relevance of the *Crane* case, *supra*, to the issue of depreciable basis arises due to section 167(g) which states that the basis for depreciation shall be the same as the basis for gain or loss on a sale or exchange under section 1011. Thus, the *Crane* case, *supra*, constitutes strong authority for the proposition that the basis used for depreciation as well as the computation of gain or loss would include the amount of an unassumed mortgage on the property.

This position was expressly adopted by this Court in *Blackstone Theatre Co.*, 12 T.C. 801, 804 (1949), *acq.* 1949–2 C.B. 1, with the following language:

From *Crane* we can deduce the following applicable principles: (a) the basis for given property includes liens thereon, even though not personally assumed by the taxpayer; and (b) the depreciation allowance should be computed on the full amount of this basis. . . .

The respondent argues that the *Crane* case, *supra*, should not apply in a purchase situation since the basis in that case started with fair market value and not cost, as in the case of a purchase. The reasoning of the *Crane* case, *supra*, however, seems equally applicable to a purchase situation and indeed was so applied in the *Blackstone Theatre Co.* case, *supra*, and *Parker* v. *Delaney*, 186 F. 2d 455 (C.A. 1, 1950). It should also be applied here.

The element of the lack of personal liability has little real significance due to common business practices. As we have indicated in our findings it is not at all unusual in current mortgage financing of income-producing properties to limit liability to the property involved. Taxpayers who are not personally liable for encumbrances on property should be allowed depreciation deductions affording competitive equality with taxpayers who are personally liable for encumbrances or taxpayers who own unencumbered property. The effect of such a policy is to give the taxpayer an advance credit for the amount of the mortgage. This appears to be reasonable since it can be assumed that a capital investment in the amount of the mortgage will eventually occur despite the absence of personal liability. The respondent has not suggested any rationale that would reasonably require a contrary conclusion. The lien created by the purchase money mortgage, like the tax liens in the *Blackstone Theatre* case, should be included in basis for the purpose of computing depreciation. *Blackstone Theatre Co., supra.*

Having determined that the absence of personal liability with respect to a purchase money mortgage does not preclude the inclusion of the mortgage in the depreciable basis of the property, we must decide whether the purchase money mortgage involved in this case should be considered a bona fide debt obligation. Respondent argues that even if the usual purchase money mortgage should be included in depreciable basis, this doctrine would be inapplicable in a situation where the alleged debt instrument does not create any obligation to pay the purchase price.

The bases for respondent's contention that no debt obligation was created are the absence of personal liability on the mortgage and the fact that the principal of the mortgage was not due for 99 years. We have already discussed the relative unimportance of personal liability in modern business transactions. We hold that this does not affect the validity of the mortgage debt. Therefore, if we are to conclude that there was no debt it must be because of the 99-year term for maturity. Although this term does seem unusually long, after viewing the totality of the circumstances and all the evidence of record we have found and hold that a valid debt obligation was created by the purchase money mortgage in question.

Contrary to respondent's asserted position, we do not believe that this transaction was in reality or substance a lease with an option to purchase. The uncontroverted testimony of petitioner and a representative of the Balch Estate was that a sale was intended with an understanding that there would be a conversion to institutional mortgage financing as soon as possible. These witnesses were forthright, impressive and entirely believable. It is clear that the 99-year term was never expected to run its course, but even absent this factor, it should be realized that a definite contractual obligation was created which would have had to be fulfilled by or before a definite date in the future. The sales transaction was normal in every other way, and the actions of the parties to the transaction certainly support our conclusions that a bona fide sale occurred and a valid debt obligation for most of the purchase price was created. Petitioner invested in improvements for the building and undertook the usual duties of a property owner. He worked diligently to find the highest and best use for the property so that he could obtain conventional financing. Within a few years he succeeded and retired the mortgage as the parties understood and hoped.

As we view the evidence before us, we do not have a substance versus form situation here because substance and form coincide. Although it can be argued that the economic realities of the transaction would be the same whether the transaction was characterized as a sale with a purchase money mortgage or a long-term lease with an option to purchase at any time, the evidence is convincing that the parties to the transaction intended a sale and mortgage and the form was consistent with this intent. We therefore hold that the transaction was in substance as well as form an effective sale and purchase money mortgage for income tax purposes.

Respondent's final argument for denial of the depreciation deductions on the 8th and Walnut Building is based on the proposition that even though the purchase money mortgage imposed an obligation on petitioner, the obligation cannot be considered as part of the depreciable basis since the cost of property for the purpose of determining basis for depreciation does not include any amount with respect to obligations which are contingent and indefinite in nature. *Columbus & Greenville Railway Co.*, 42 T.C. 834 (1964); *Albany Car Wheel Co.*, 40 T.C. 831 (1963), affd. per curiam 333 F. 2d 653 (C.A. 2, 1964); *Lloyd H. Redford*, 28 T.C. 773 (1957). An example of the type of contingency referred to in the preceding proposition was present in the *Albany Car Wheel Co.* case. In that case we found that the purchaser-taxpayer's obligation under the purchase agreement to procure a release of the predecessor's liability under a union contract for severance pay was of such a contingent nature that it could not be considered a part of the cost of the assets acquired. Whether it would ever be necessary to satisfy any severance pay obligations was unknown at the time of the sale.

Similarly, in the *Lloyd H. Redford* case, *supra*, the amount of a note was held not to be includable in basis since the note was only payable from profits and it was uncertain whether there would ever be profits.

It was held in the *Columbus & Greenville Railway Co.* case, *supra*, that basis did not include any amount of a mortgage where there was no primary responsibility and no fixed indebtedness for which the taxpayer or its property was liable.

We hold that the doctrine supported by the foregoing cases is inapplicable to the subject purchase money mortgage. Respondent contends that the amount of the obligation was indefinite because of the varying amounts due under the terms of the instrument and the fact that the purchase money mortgage was eventually settled for the negotiated price of $200,000, a substantial reduction from the amount due under the instrument.

There were only two variables in the overall purchase price of the property, and they were specified in dollar amounts. The price depended then upon whether the purchase money mortgage was paid within the first year, the second year, or years thereafter. We would classify such a price reduction for early payment as a bonus discount. The presence of such optional discounts does not make the purchase price indefinite. It merely provided an incentive for very early retirement of the mortgage which did not occur. The cost basis at the time of purchase should be the nondiscount price; the entire principal of the note and mortgage was due unless the discounted sums were paid in the first two years. It was not prepaid so as to provide for the application of the discount provisions and hence no adjustment in basis is required during the years before us. It is evident from the record that if the lien on the property provided by the mortgage were to be discharged at any time prior to its due date, the then fixed amount would necessarily have to be paid. There was nothing contingent or indefinite about the obligation here.

The subsequent settlement of the purchase money mortgage for less than the amount due under the terms of the instrument should not affect the allowable depreciation in taxable years prior to the settlement. In the *Blackstone Theatre Co.* case, *supra*, the taxpayer acquired real estate with outstanding tax liens exceeding $120,000. Although there was no personal liability as to these liens and although the liens were settled five years after the acquisition for $50,000, the depreciable basis for the intervening years was held to include the full $120,000. Here we are concerned with an arm's-length business transaction and there is no logical basis for disregarding the purchase price provided for in the purchase money mortgage.

Since we have decided the depreciation issue involving the 8th and Walnut Building in petitioner's favor, it is unnecessary to decide whether the $10,000 down payment should have been amortized as the cost of obtaining a lease over 25 years, the estimated life of the building, rather than 99 years, the period of the alleged lease. . . .

The Roslyn Apartments

In October 1967, Mrs. Virginia Roslyn received a letter from Mr. David Rogers, a realtor in her city, proposing that she sell an apartment building she owned. (The letter is reproduced below, in Exhibit 1.)

The apartment building was Mrs. Roslyn's sole source of income. Her essential living expenses were not large; she occupied a modest suburban home worth about $17,000 (which she owned free of any mortgage) and drove a car worth about $1,500. Since her husband's death in 1957, however, she had traveled a great deal, spending close to $15,000 a year on cruises, so that her total expenses used up virtually her entire income. (Income data are given in Exhibit 2.)

Mrs. Roslyn was fifty years old and in good health. Her husband had left her the apartment building and her home at his death, together with some life insurance proceeds, most of which had gone to pay estate taxes. She had no children or dependents. Under the provisions of her will, all her property would pass to a younger brother and two older sisters.

The apartment building was located in a residential area that was slowly being taken over by large office buildings. Excellent shopping facilities and convenient public transportation were near at hand. The property had a frontage of fifty feet and a depth of one hundred thirty-five feet. The seven-story building contained forty-two suites. It was constructed of yellow brick with steel sash casement windows, reinforced concrete floors, and fireproof steel framing. An automatic elevator served each floor. There were parking facilities for seventy-five cars in a heated one-story attached garage. The building was well maintained; rentals averaged $170 per month. Normally there was no difficulty renting the apartments, although one ground floor apartment with no view had been vacant from the beginning of January 1967, until the end of August.

Mrs. Roslyn was not particularly interested in the operation of the building—she left this to her lawyer and the building janitor—and she had often considered selling it. It was her only significant asset, except for the house, car, and bank account of about $6,000. (Her lawyer maintained a checking account for the operation of the building with a balance of about $4,000, which belonged, of course, to Mrs. Roslyn.)

At the time of construction, sixteen years earlier, the building had been worth $220,000 and the land $100,000. For estate tax purposes the building had been valued at the time Mrs. Roslyn inherited it at $300,000 and the land at $150,000. Depreciation had been taken for tax purposes on double declining balance (see Table 1 in Exhibit 2). Various items of equipment in the building were depreciable but had been completely written off (the elevator was considered part of the building and was not depreciated separately).

Mrs. Roslyn had received several cash offers of about $550,000 for the land and building. She felt that these offers had been too low and believed she could get $600,000 cash if she tried. She knew that if she kept the building she would soon have to replace both stoves and refrigerators in at least thirty suites, at a total cost of $7500 to $8000.

Out of the proceeds of a sale, Mrs. Roslyn would have to pay off the $80,000 balance outstanding on a mortgage against the building. The mortgage secured a loan that had been made by an insurance company to help finance construction. Mrs. Roslyn had been making principal payments of about $11,000 a year in recent years. She was not sure what she would do with the balance of the proceeds if she should sell. She could obtain a 5 per cent yield on U.S. government bonds or close to 4 per cent on good tax-exempt municipal bonds. Common stocks were another possibility, but the probable rate of return was hard to gauge. The 8 per cent return promised on the mortgage Rogers proposed in his letter was very attractive, and Mrs. Roslyn did not expect that she could earn that much on any other investment, except perhaps common stock.

Mrs. Roslyn's entire income was derived from the building; her only significant personal deductions for tax purposes were her $600 exemption and $1000 in charitable gifts.

Exhibit 1: David T. Rogers

September 30, 1967.

Dear Mrs. Roslyn:

As you know, a client of mine, Mr. Antony Daddario, has been very much interested in your property, the Roslyn Apartments. His investigation of the premises last week with your lawyer convinced him it would be a good investment. Mr. Daddario would like me, on his behalf, to make you a firm offer for its purchase. The price he offers to pay is $555,900, $255,000 in cash and the remaining $300,900 payable over 20 years with interest at 8 per cent, secured by a first mortgage. As you know such a high interest rate is extremely unusual.

Enclosed you will note two documents. The first is my estimate of the operating expenses and net income of the building. The second document shows my suggestions for handling the cash you would receive from the sale so that you would be able to acquire for each of the next 20 years an annual income of $29,980.

I hope you will give serious consideration to Mr. Daddario's offer. Should you or your lawyer wish to see me personally please let me know. Since my client is very anxious to acquire property in the area of your building, should you not wish to sell, I would like to begin negotiations for another building. Therefore, we would appreciate a decision within the next two weeks.

Sincerely yours,

David T. Rogers

DTR:dtl
Enclosures

Enclosure 1. Estimate of income

Rental gross income $89,580.00
      Operating expenses. $30,478.99
      Mortgage payment. . . . . , ... 11,400.00
      Depreciation on building (2% per yr.) 9,000.00

      Land Value $180,000
      Building Value 450,000

Deduct expenses 50,878.99
Present net income $38,701.01*

*Clearly this income level will be maintained only if the building continues to be rented to capacity. If rentals should drop by 20 per cent, income is reduced by $17,916, and net income is then . . . . $20,785.01.

Enclosure 2. Handling of sale proceeds

Cash $255,000.00
Mortgage 300,900.00
Total price $555,900.00

Mortgage amortized over a 20-year period at 8 per cent requires monthly payments to Mrs. Roslyn of $2,527.50 which amounts to $30,330.00 per annum.
    A capital replacement fund (or "sinking fund") would have to be provided out of the mortgage payments if the original amount of the mortgage, $300,900.00, is to be intact at the end of 20 years. A $9100 annual amount, if invested at 5 per cent, will total the original $300,900.00 at the end of 20 years.

Income from mortgage . . . . $ 30,330.00
Deduction for sinking fund 9,100.00
Net income from mortgage . . . . $ 21,230.00

Cash payment of $255,000.00
Deduct existing first mortgage of . . . . −80,000.00
                                         $175,000.00
Invested at 5%, annual income from cash
   proceeds of sale is . . . . $ 8,750.00

Total income
Net income from purchase money mortgage at 8% $21,230.00
Net income from invested cash 8,750.00
Total net income $29,980.00

Exhibit 2: Income statement of the Roslyn Apartments
December 31, 1966

Annual rental gross income $91,980

Expenses
     Municipal taxes $11,405
     Heating 2,632
     Maintenance staff wages 4,000
     Water   460
     Electricity   340
     Insurance   425
     Maintenance 2,800
     Decorating   560
     Supplies..   230
     Management and legal 3,364
     Miscellaneous   288
     Interest on mortgage at 5% 4,285
                                         $30,789

Depreciation on building (see table below) $9,952

                                                  $40,741

Net income before income tax $51,239
Mortgage principal payment $11,400

Table 1: Depreciation on building

Year	Depreciation	Undepreciated balance
1958	$15,000	$285,000
1959	14,250	270,750
1960	13,537	257,213
1961	12,861	244,352
1962	12,217	232,134
1963	11,607	220,528
1964	11,026	209,501
1965	10,475	199,026
1966	9,952	189,075

Chapter twelve

Tax factors in employee
and executive compensation

Tax planning for employee and executive compensation is based essentially on two principles. Because of high personal tax rates, at least on high incomes, there are obvious advantages in finding forms of compensation that avoid these taxes completely, or at least defer the taxes. And because of the corporate income tax, whether or not an item of compensation is deductible to a corporation, is important. From the corporation's point of view, a form of compensation is much more attractive if it is deductible than if it is not; and the sooner the deduction can be taken, the more attractive the compensation is. We will assume that the employer is a corporation. (Noncorporate employers encounter special problems involving the owner-employee.)

The reductions in personal tax rates effective in 1964 and 1965 reduced somewhat the pressure for tax-sheltered compensation schemes. But even under the reduced rates, a corporate executive filing a joint tax return and reporting taxable income of $35,000 is paying tax at a marginal rate of 42 per cent. To give him an extra $5000 after taxes, his employer must raise his salary by more than $9000.

In 1964, the Code was amended to incorporate the effects of "bunched" income. A person whose income rose and fell from year-to-year was at a disadvantage with respect to a person with a steady income, because he paid taxes at very high rates in the good years and averaged a higher rate of tax. Sections 1301–1305 deal with income averaging. The special treatment is available only where taxable income for a year is at least $3000 above 133 per cent of average taxable income for the preceding four years. A student may see a possibility of reducing his taxes during his first year of employment. Section 1303 was intended to limit the use of income averaging to ex-students on their first jobs, while making it available to the person who has simply been unemployed for a while.

Income averaging, of course, only helps the victim of bunched income; it does not bring about any general tax relief on earned income.

As a starting point in a search for tax-sheltered compensation arrangements, we can see if there are forms of compensation that simply do not constitute "income" under the Code and hence are free of income tax.

"Income" v. compensation

We will not be concerned here with a general discussion of the income concept. There are economic definitions of income which differ from taxation definitions, sometimes for good reason and sometimes perhaps not. Here we are concerned only with the definition of income for tax purposes.

The 16th Amendment to the Constitution is not very helpful in defining income, although it is the constitutional basis for the income tax. The 16th Amendment authorizes Congress to collect taxes on "income from whatever source derived." This would seem to give the courts authority to support the taxation of virtually any kind of receipt. But we do not really need to worry much about the breadth of the definition under the 16th Amendment, since the Internal Revenue Code severely restricts the income that is actually to be taxed. There are two reasons for limiting the scope of income in the Code: certain receipts or benefits that might be called income are administratively very difficult to identify, value, and tax; and there may be good policy reasons for not wanting to tax others. Suppose a young farmer from the New Hampshire hills is inducted into the Army and made staff assistant to a Washington-based general. He is given fancy uniforms, a chauffeur-driven car, lavish meals, trips to concerts, the opera, and the like with the general. On the one hand, he has received significant economic benefits and perhaps he should be taxed on them. But on the other hand, suppose he tells you that he hates concerts and opera, gets sick from the rich food, and longs to be out in the field in fatigues with the rest of the "boys." How could we place a value on the so-called benefits which the man has received? And would it make sense to force him to pay taxes out of his cash income on "benefits" which he cannot refuse and does not even value?

If you look at section 61, you will see that gross income is defined to include a wide variety of receipts, including compensation for services. But sections 101–121 describe a number of items which are specifically excluded from gross income, and some of these items are important aspects of compensation.

Gifts are specifically excluded from gross income, but it might seem at first that this provision will be of little importance to a corporation in terms of compensation to executives and employees. However, in some cases it is difficult to distinguish between what is a gift to an employee and what is compensation for services, and certain kinds of payments which most of us regard as compensation have in fact been treated as gifts.

Before investigating how to make use of gifts as a means of compensating employees, we might give some thought to two tax aspects of a gift. First, would the corporation have to pay a gift tax? Section 2501(a) provides an answer to this question. Second, would a gift be deductible to the employer for tax purposes? Section 162 deals with deductions of business expenses, and we will discuss this section in some detail later in this chapter.

Here are two situations that reached the courts on the question of whether a payment was a gift or compensation:

Mr. Duberstein was president of an Ohio iron and metal company and was friendly with Mr. Berman, president of a similar New York corporation. The two would converse by phone occasionally, and Duberstein would give his friend information concerning potential customers for some of Berman's products that were not competitive with Duberstein's. Apparently this information paid off for Berman, and one day Duberstein was surprised by a call from his friend who said that his company had purchased a Cadillac for Duberstein as a gift and that Duberstein should send to New York for it. Duberstein did so (though reluctantly because he already had a Cadillac) and did not report the value of the Cadillac as income because he concluded it was a gift excludable under section 102. The Commissioner disagreed with Duberstein and argued that the car actually was compensation for services rendered. After carrying the case all the way to the U.S. Supreme Court, the Commissioner was upheld.[1]

Mr. Stanton managed the very considerable real estate holdings of Trinity Church in New York City. When he left his job to go into business on his own, the church officers voted him a gratuity of $20,000 "in appreciation of the services rendered. . . ." Stanton treated this as a gift; the Commissioner took issue but this time the Commissioner lost on appeal to the Supreme Court.[2] The two cases were heard and decided together in the Supreme Court where the major issue centered on the proper test to be applied in determining whether or not a statutory "gift" had been made. The Court discussed prior cases that had dealt with the problem. None of these cases had set forth any simple test that could be applied to all sets of facts. They all sought to establish the donor's intention by means of objective evidence, and where "generosity," "admiration," "respect," and "affection" were found, an excludable "gift" would also be found. The mere fact that property was given voluntarily and without value in return, however, had been held not enough to satisfy the statute. In the *Duberstein* and *Stanton* cases, the Commissioner urged the Court to adopt a test to be applied to all cases of this sort—that "gifts should be defined as transfers of property made for personal as distinguished from business reasons."

Notice the implications of such a test. Since a corporation probably has no business making "personal" gifts, the definition might well elimi-

---

[1]*Commissioner* v. *Duberstein*, 363 U.S. 278 (U.S. Supreme Court, 1960.)

[2]*Stanton* v. *U.S.* (same citation as Duberstein; the cases were decided together).

nate gifts by corporations. And if a corporation did make a "gift," it would probably not be deductible under section 162(a). Why?

The Supreme Court rejected the Commissioner's test. It left the question of whether there has been a gift to the trial judge or jury to "be based on the fact-finding tribunal's experience with the mainsprings of human conduct (applied) to the totality of facts of each case."

Gifts to employees can take many forms, of course, from gift certificates to Christmas turkeys to the gratuity Stanton received. In Revenue Ruling 59–58 (1959–1 C.B. 17), the Internal Revenue Service ruled that the value of turkeys, hams, or other merchandise of nominal value need not be treated as taxable income. The Ruling was expressly made not to apply to distributions of cash, gift certificates, or the like, regardless of the amount involved.

Death benefits

Death benefits present problems somewhat like those we found in connection with gifts, and there is a further problem in distinguishing death benefits from gifts.

Suppose Mr. E., vice-president of the C Corporation, dies. Shortly after his death, the board of directors of C meet and unanimously adopt the following resolution: "In recognition of the many years of faithful service which Mr. E. rendered to the C Corporation and to show our affection for his widow, Mrs. E., we hereby resolve that the C Corporation pay to Mrs. E. the sum of $20,000." The money is paid to Mrs. E.

Is she justified in excluding any of it from her income tax return for the year?

Has Mrs. E. received a "gift" which is entirely excludable from her income under section 102, or a "death benefit" which is dealt with in section 101(b)? If section 101(b) applies, how much of the gift is excludable from income?

Prior to 1950, when there was no exclusion for employee death benefits in the Code, the Commissioner took the position that the widow could receive payments as a tax-free gift as long as she rendered no services to the paying corporation. In 1950, however, the Commissioner decided that he had been too lenient and tried to reverse his position by issuing a ruling stating that if the payments were in consideration for the services of the deceased employee, they would constitute taxable income for the widow. Then Congress passed the predecessor of section 101(b), and the Commissioner interpreted this as an approval of his new ruling — that is, he interpreted section 101(b) to be exclusive, preventing the more liberal section 102 "gift" treatment of payments to widows.

The courts failed to agree with the Commissioner. They had already decided several cases in favor of widows, calling payments of this sort "gifts." Since it appeared that the courts had decided this on the basis of their interpretation of the Code and of prior cases and not on the basis of the Commissioner's pre-1950 Ruling, the Commissioner's change of ruling did not serve to change the courts' interpretation. The courts took the position that if the law were to be changed Congress must do it, and they did not interpret section 101(b) as Congressional approval of the Commissioner's ruling. It appeared from the legislative history of section 101(b) that it was intended to liberalize rather than tighten up existing law, as the Commissioner claimed. After losing many cases, the Commissioner admitted that section 101(b) does not apply "to limit to $5000 the exclusion from gross income of an amount paid to a widow of a deceased employee where the payment otherwise qualifies as a gift excludable under section 102(a) of the Code." (Rev. Rul. 62–102, 1962–2 C.B. 37).

The Commissioner still felt that section 101(b) indicates an assumption on the part of Congress that payments to widows *usually* are not gifts, and he would continue to challenge them. Some courts, however, seem very favorably disposed to widows.

We have referred to the importance of a corporation's being able to deduct any payments it makes. In the Revenue Act of 1962, section 274(b) was added to the Code.

How much of the $20,000 death benefit paid to Mrs. E., in the example above, will be deductible by Corporation C?

Would the corporation's claiming a deduction have any effect on the taxes the widow must pay on her $20,000 receipt? That is, in deciding how to treat the $20,000 payment for its own tax purposes, should Corporation C consider whether it may be helping or hurting the widow?

Fringe benefits

Look over sections 104, 105, and 106 which deal with very common fringe benefits. (And section 119 is frequently important to some employees.)

Life insurance is an important benefit that a corporation might provide for its employees. Prior to 1964, the tax treatment of premiums paid by the corporation on a policy insuring the life of an employee (where the proceeds of the policy would go to the employee's estate or his beneficiaries) was covered in Regulations section 1.61–2(d)(2). Congress concluded that the Regulations gave too much freedom to the corporation to provide substantial tax-free benefits to certain employees, and section 79 was added to the Code in 1964.

If a corporation is planning to buy life insurance for its employees, what kind of insurance is best in terms of minimizing taxes?

"Split-dollar" insurance is a gimmick that was popular until the Treasury issued Revenue Ruling 64–328 (1964–2 C.B. 11), and it may still offer some tax advantages. The corporation and an employee jointly purchase a life insurance policy, with the corporation paying the portion of the premium which represents the annual increase in the cash surrender value of the policy and the employee paying the balance. On the death of the employee, the corporation receives the cash surrender value and the employee's estate or beneficiaries receive the rest of the proceeds. As a rule, except in the first year, the employee's portion of the premium is very small compared to the corporation's share, and although the employer's share of the proceeds at death may decrease over time, it will be very high to begin with (almost the full face value of the policy) and will probably always be substantial. In effect, by paying for the cash surrender value portion of the policy, the corporation is financing at no interest charge a large part of the employee's life insurance. The earnings of the insurance company on the premiums paid by the corporation all go to benefit the employee by reducing his premiums; none go to benefit the corporation.

Revenue Ruling 55–713 (1955–2 C.B. 23) established that the employee was not taxed on the corporation's premium payments. The 1964 Ruling revoked the 1955 Ruling and held that the employee is taxable annually on the benefit accruing to him on account of the corporation's payments. This was assumed to be the difference between what he would have had to pay for one year term insurance giving him the same dollar protection and what he actually paid for his "split-dollar" insurance.

> *Before section 79 was enacted, why would "split-dollar" insurance have been more attractive than ordinary group life insurance?*

More complex compensation arrangements

We have talked so far of fringe benefits that generally are tax-free to employees. We turn now to more complicated compensation arrangements where in most cases the employee does not escape tax altogether but may enjoy the benefits of a tax deferral, sometimes to a period when his personal tax rate will have decreased.

We begin this section by considering in a little more detail than we have so far the question of deductibility of payments by the corporate employer. We will also look at deductibility to the employee of certain payments made to him by his employer.

Deductibility

Deductions fall into several groups of sections in the Code. The standard deduction for individuals is found in sections 141–145 and is followed by the deductions for personal exemptions in sections 151–154. Deductions for corporations and for individuals who choose to itemize their deductions are dealt with next in sections 161–182. Deductions allowed only to individuals are covered in sections 211–217, and those allowed only to corporations are dealt with in sections 241–248. The final group of sections deals with items that are not deductible—sections 261–275.

> *If an individual decides to make use of the standard deduction, what other deductions will he be able to take? See the Regulations under section 141.*

Section 162, allowing a deduction from gross income for business expenses, is the key section for our purposes. Notice the requirement of "ordinary and necessary" and "trade or business." For a large publicly owned corporation, there is usually not much doubt whether an expense is deductible under section 162, except for certain expenses that are specifically treated as nondeductible in the Code. For a small, closely held corporation, it is not quite so simple to determine deductibility. Usually the requirement of "necessity" is not challenged by the Internal Revenue Service, even for the small, closely held business. But the "ordinary" requirement has given rise to considerable litigation. As it emerges from the cases, the test seems to be one of "uniqueness," and a unique item of expense cannot be "ordinary." However, an item of expense may be unique in the experience of the particular taxpayer and still be "ordinary," as long as it is not also unique in the experience of the kind of business which the taxpayer carries on.

> *The "trade or business" test caused considerable trouble at one time. Is a person who owns a very large portfolio of securities engaged in the "trade or business" of investing? May he therefore deduct as a section 162 expense the cost of maintaining an office, hiring a secretary, etc., to facilitate his investment program? Since section 212 was added to the Code, the question has not been so serious. If he has a choice, should our wealthy investor seek to deduct his expenses under section 162 or under section 212?*

Employee expenses

The important point to keep in mind in connection with employee expenses is that employees are considered to be engaged in the business of performing services for their employers, and they can incur "ordinary and necessary" expenses in connection with that "business." At least three situations can arise. The employee may simply pay certain business expenses out of his own pocket, with no additional compensation from his employer. In this case, the employee will try to deduct the expenses under section 162. Or it may be that he is exactly reimbursed by his employer for the expense that he has incurred. In this case, the employee will generally not include the reimbursement in his income at all, but the employer will deduct the reimbursement as a business expense. Finally, the employee may be given a sum of money by his employer which is not designed as exact reimbursement of expenses but simply as an extra allowance to cover or help cover the employee's expenses. In this case, the employee will report this compensation as income, but he will also report his actual expenses as deductions.

It is in connection with employee expenses that the greatest problems are likely to arise in terms of whether or not the expenses are truly ordinary and necessary in connection with a business. Travel and entertainment expenses raise obvious problems. Travel expenses are dealt with in Code section 274, added in 1962, and in Regulations sections 1.162–2 and 1.274–4. Entertainment expenses had come under fire from the Internal Revenue Service in the late 1950's, and section 274 was added to the Code by the Revenue Act of 1962. Previous to this, there had been no specific reference in the Code to entertainment expenses. Notice that section 274(b) requires substantiation of travel expenses, entertainment expenses, and business gifts. This eliminates the famous *Cohan* rule which provided that if some deductible expenses were clearly incurred but the exact amounts were not substantiated, a court should allow something rather than disallow the deduction entirely. This had led to deliberate exaggeration of entertainment expenses in the hope that even after deflation of the claim a substantial deduction would be left.

Deferred compensation and postponement of individual income tax — informal plans

So far we have discussed only forms of current compensation. We move now to situations where a corporation proposes to compensate an officer or employee in the future for services performed in the present. This may be due to sudden generosity—the company decides to give an employee a bonus in 1968 for work done in 1966. Or it may be planned—the company agrees with an employee to pay him in whole or in part for his services one year or five years or any number of years after the services have been performed. Two basic questions are posed by any deferred compensation arrangements: when and how can the employer get a deduction, and what are the tax consequences to the employee? A third question might occur to the uninitiated: why would an employee ever want to put off receipt of compensation? The answer, which we will examine in detail, is that he may want to put off receipt until such time that his total income and consequently his tax rate have been reduced (which may well happen after he retires) thus giving him a greater net yield after taxes on the deferred income than he would have realized had he received the income currently.

The tax treatment of the employee is complicated somewhat by the *constructive receipt* doctrine, which is best stated negatively—one cannot avoid being taxed on income simply by refusing to accept it. If you have an unqualified right to receive income, you will be held to have received it for tax purposes under the constructive receipt doctrine. Another rule that causes trouble is the *economic benefit* doctrine. Under this doctrine, anything of value received by a taxpayer as compensation will be taxable when received. A promise to pay money in the future is clearly something of value, and this value may be includible in the income of the employee.

The deductibility of deferred compensation, as far as the employer is concerned, will be determined in part, of course, under section 162, a section we have already discussed. But in a particular case of deferred compensation, section 404 applies as well. Most of section 404 deals with what we might call "formal" deferred compensation schemes such as pension plans, employee annuities, stock bonus and profit sharing trusts, and retirement plans for self-employed individuals. We will discuss some of these later. For the moment, the part of section 404 that concerns us is 404(a)(5). This sub-section deals with what we might call "informal" deferred compensation arrangements. You can see that under section

404(a)(5) the payments in our examples above will be deductible to the employer in the year in which they are made. (It is quite clear that when the compensation is actually paid to the employee, it is nonforfeitable to the employee.)

The situations we have been talking about so far are rather simple because in both our deferred compensation examples, the deferred compensation was not "funded." That is, the employer did not actually set aside the compensation until the time came for it to be paid to the employee. Sometimes the employee may not be willing to take a chance on the employer's ability to pay him when the future date arrives; and the employer may not wish to take a chance on not being able to pay the compensation when it comes due, especially if many employees have deferred compensation arrangements and the payments called for in a future year may be quite substantial. The financial answer to this problem is funding; that is, the employer actually sets aside the funds that will be needed for deferred compensation at the time they are earned, and the deferred compensation arrangement is said to be funded. The funds are usually put into some sort of trust, and the trustee actually pays the compensation over to the employee or officer. In this case the "nonforfeitable" requirement of section 404(a)(5) becomes important. If an employee's right to deferred compensation is "forfeitable," this means that there is a possibility he may lose it. For example, if the employee will get his deferred compensation only if he stays with his employer until he is sixty-five, his rights to the compensation are forfeitable. Consider the case of a funded deferred compensation arrangement for a group of employees where it is provided that if any individual leaves the employer before age sixty-five, he forfeits his right to future payments, but it is also provided that the employer cannot get back any contributions in the case of forfeitures—the fund will merely be split among a smaller number of employees. Here the fund is nonforfeitable as far as the employer and the group are concerned, but it is forfeitable as far as each individual employee is concerned. The courts have said that a case like this does not satisfy the requirements of section 404(a)(5).

From the employer's point of view, then, it is obviously important whether the employee's right to any funded deferred compensation is nonforfeitable. This is the only way in which the employer can deduct currently his contribution to the fund. But what about the tax treatment of an employee where his rights to deferred compensation are nonforfeitable? You may already have guessed the answer from the constructive receipt doctrine, and if you look at section 402(b) you will see an explicit statement in the Code.

> *For tax purposes, would an employee prefer a forfeitable or a non-forfeitable deferred compensation arrangement? For financial, non-tax purposes, which would he probably prefer?*

You should be able to see the dilemma that is posed, at least in tax terms. A possible solution is for the employer to give up a current deduction for his contribution to the deferred compensation fund, waiting for deduction until payments are actually made to the employee, while the employees themselves are not taxed until receipt of their deferred compensation. Would this involve a forfeitable or nonforfeitable plan? Unfortunately, the Regulations take the position that if the employer makes a contribution to a fund and the employee's rights in the fund are forfeitable at that time, the employer cannot take a deduction in that year or in any other year. This rule is stated in Regulations section 1.404(a)-12.

Is this position justified by the language of section 404(a)(5)?

One court held that the Regulation was contrary to the statutes and allowed a deduction to the employer when the trust paid the compensation to an employee.[4] The Commissioner announced his nonacquiescence.

On the whole, funding of informal deferred compensation plans has rather unattractive tax consequences. If funding is called for, it may be best to try to use one of the "formal" arrangements authorized in the Code.

Before we move to "formal" deferred compensation arrangements, we will look a little more closely at unfunded informal arrangements. We raised the issue of employer deductibility in these cases—this is dealt with in section 404(a)(5)—but we did not clear up the question of employee taxability, leaving the doctrines of constructive receipt and economic benefit as obvious obstacles to deferment of income tax for the employee.

Prior to 1960, those who used unfunded deferred compensation schemes had to wrestle somewhat blindly with these two doctrines. Several key court decisions were handed down which helped to clarify the area somewhat. And then in 1960 the Treasury issued its now-famous Ruling 60–31 which has become the bible for those seeking to use unfunded informal deferred compensation arrangements. Revenue Ruling 60–31 (1960–1 C.B. 174) begins by describing several examples of deferred compensation contracts. The first was a contract for the employment of an executive for a period of five years at a stated salary plus another substantial amount for each year worked. The additional amount was to be credited to a bookkeeping reserve account where it would be accumulated and eventually paid in annual installments equal to one-fifth the amount accumulated in the reserve just prior to the first year of payment. Payment would commence only upon the occurrence of certain events:

1) Termination of employment by the corporation
2) Partial retirement (the full-time executive changes to a part-time advisor)
3) Total or partial incapacity

---

[4]*Russel Manufacturing Co.* v. *U.S.*, 175 F. Supp. 159 (U.S. Court of Claims, 1959).

No trust fund was involved in the arrangement; that is, the compensation was entirely unfunded.

Four other examples were described in the Ruling, one involving a profit-sharing arrangement for an executive, another an author's arrangement for deferred royalty payments, another a football player who sought to defer part of a sign-up bonus, and the last a boxer who sought to defer part of his percentage of the gross receipts of a fight. The Treasury then stated the problem to be "whether in each of the situations described the income in question was constructively received in a taxable year prior to the taxable year of actual receipt." Although the economic benefit doctrine as applied to these arrangements is not mentioned specifically in the Ruling, it would seem to be covered where the Ruling states that "a mere promise to pay, not represented by notes or secured in any way, is not regarded as a receipt of income (for a cash accounting method taxpayer)." On the constructive receipt point, the Ruling states that "a taxpayer may not deliberately turn his back upon income and thereby select the year for which he will report it," but adds that "however, the statute cannot be administered by speculating whether the payer would have been willing to agree to an earlier payment." In other words, once the employee has the right to receive compensation, there is no way to defer the tax consequences; but if deferment is agreed to by the employee and his employer before the compensation is earned, the Treasury will not be concerned with whether the employee could have insisted on current payment.

The constructive receipt doctrine cannot be ignored. For example, in the fourth case described in the Ruling, a football player had entered into a standard two-year contract at a specified salary plus a bonus. The player could have received his bonus upon signing the contract, but he suggested instead that the contract be amended to provide that payment of the bonus be made to an escrow agent who would, in turn, pay over the amount to the player in the future. This was done, and the club paid the bonus to the escrow agent who had a binding agreement with the player that the amount was to be paid out to the player only over a five-year period. On these facts the Ruling concluded that the full bonus was taxable to the taxpayer in the year it was unconditionally paid to the escrow agent. Clearly the player could have had the bonus immediately if he had wanted it. It had been paid over to the agent at the player's direction.

A word might be added at this point about "forfeitability clauses" in deferred compensation contracts. These usually take the form of "consultation service" provisions or "no-competition clauses." They provide that the executive will receive his deferred pay only if he holds himself available for consultation or if he agrees not to offer his services to a competitor. Some tax experts recommend that these forfeitability clauses be used despite the implication in Revenue Ruling 60–31 that they are not necessary. These experts feel that once the specified event, such as partial retirement, has occurred and deferred payments have started, there is a possibility of immediate realization of the entire amount for tax purposes under the economic benefit doctrine, if the amount is nonforfeitable. The consultation or no-competition clause, they feel, is good insurance against this result. If a forfeitability clause calls for affirmative services such as consultation, care must be taken to avoid adverse tax effects. When we come to qualified retirement plans, we will see that certain capital gain treatment accorded lump-sum distributions from such plans may be jeopardized if the executive must perform services as an employee after the lump-sum distribution has been made. Some problems may also arise with Social Security benefits. An executive cannot continue to render substantial services after retirement and also claim Social Security. The Social Security Regulations provide that forty-five hours of service or less per month will not be considered substantial services in most cases. A no-competition clause can also, of course, be dangerous for the executive. A business reverse may force him to seek employment with a competitor, but he then forfeits his accrued deferred pay if he has signed a no-competition clause.

Formal deferred compensation plans

When we speak of formal compensation plans, we are referring to compensation arrangements which are described in detail in the Code. These are qualified pension, profit-sharing, stock-bonus plans, and re-stricted stock-option arrangements. Common sense and familiarity with the usual rules of taxation will not enable you to deal with these formal plans; instead, the statute must guide you. In this part of the chapter, we will draw the broad outlines of these plans as set forth in the statute and try to demonstrate the relationship between the several sections of the Code which deal with the plans. To gain an understanding of the details, however, there is no substitute for going to the Code.

Qualified pension, profit-sharing, and stock-bonus plans

Under a typical *pension plan,* predetermined benefits will be paid out of a fund to participating employees upon retirement or death. The fund is made up largely, if not entirely, of employer contributions ac-tuarially determined on the basis of the benefits that will eventually have to be paid out. A *profit-sharing plan* also utilizes a fund to pay benefits, but here the amount of the benefits and the contribution are variable factors. Both depend on the employer's profits. In such a plan, benefits may be paid out, as in a pension plan, on retirement or death and also in the event of lay-offs, sickness, and the like. Finally, *a stock-bonus plan* may provide the same benefits as a profit-sharing plan (pension, lay-off benefits, sick pay); but the employer's contribution need not be depend-ent on profits, and the benefits are distributed in stock of the employer.

Though they are basically different, these statutory plans are tied together by one common theme: they all provide benefits to employees who are no longer working, whose earning ability has been impaired or, in the case of death, to the beneficiaries of the deceased employee who are left without that employee's earning ability. They serve the usual purpose, then, of deferred compensation plans. But for these plans, the Code encourages funding. It allows a current deduction for contributions to the fund. It postpones taxation for the employee participant until payments are actually made to him, which is generally after retirement when lower rates apply, despite the fact the employee's rights in the fund may be nonforfeitable. It provides that the income earned by the fund and any gain realized by the fund will be taxed only upon payout and not as earned. And finally, it provides that certain lump-sum distributions under a plan will be treated as long-term capital gain and taxed at the low capital gains rate.

It should be clear that these tax concessions would be attractive to highly paid executives who stand to gain most from any tax-saving device. But the position of Congress has been that these tax-sheltered schemes can only be justified if they are used primarily for the ordinary worker. Consequently, all through these plans you will see provisions designed to prevent highly paid employees from exploiting these plans for their own benefit. These preventive measures add greatly to the complexity of this area of the Code.

These plans are set up by an employer for the exclusive benefit of his employees or their beneficiaries. If the employer is a corporation, all those who work for the corporation as employees could be participants. This would include top management. If, however, the employer were a sole proprietor or a partnership, the plan could not include the owner or the partners since they are *not* employees. In 1962, the Keogh Act was passed extending some of the benefits of qualified plans to proprietors and partners. The alternative to using the Keogh Act provisions is to incorporate or form an association that will be taxed as a corporation. This may cause problems for the professional man, such as a lawyer, who is faced with legal or ethical obstacles in the way of incorporation. You will see elements of the Keogh Act in the sections we will be discussing, but our consideration will be restricted to corporate employers.

Employee benefits

The key to the taxation of employee benefits under a qualified plan is found in sections 402 and 403 of the Code. An employer may decide to set up a qualified employee trust and make his contributions to the trust, in which case section 402 applies. Or the employer may prefer to buy annuities for his employees pursuant to a qualified annuity plan; in this case, section 403 applies. Both sections refer you to section 72, which governs the taxation of annuities, for the tax treatment of payments actually made to employees. (You might note that the buildup of the trust or annuity values through investment of the employer contributions is tax-free under section 501.) Notice what sections 402 and 403 say about contributions of employers to trust or annuity plans that are *not* qualified under the Code.

> *If amounts contributed by the employer to such nonqualified plans are taxed to the employee when contributed, how is a second tax avoided when the trust or annuity plan pays out to the employee? See Regulations section 1.72–8(a)(1).*

Notice, too, that the exemption for the buildup of the trust or annuity value under section 501 does not apply to a plan that is not qualified. We will not spend any further time on section 501, but this section along with section 503 and sections 511–514 governs tax-exempt organizations, including qualified plans, and restricts the operations of the fund whose income is to be exempt. These sections will be important if a corporation has any idea of using the funds it has set aside in a pension trust for its own purposes.

It is fairly common in funding a pension plan to provide some life insurance protection for employees. The plan might provide for the purchase of a limited amount of ordinary life insurance, limited payment life insurance policies, or endowment policies; or the employer may fund his plan with an insurance company by purchasing retirement income policies from the company. A retirement income policy would typically provide that on the death of the employee, his beneficiary would be paid the accumulated retirement income (cash surrender value of the policy) or the face amount of the policy, whichever is greater. To begin with, the face amount will exceed the accumulated retirement income, but as the employee nears retirement age, the gap will be narrowed. That is, in early years the employee has built up a very small retirement fund but has a large amount of life insurance, whereas when he reached retirement he will have built up a large retirement fund and will have a rather small amount of life insurance in addition to this fund. You should recall from our discussion of life insurance that the purchase of group term life insurance, with limits specified in section 79 of the Code, is not taxable to employees but that the premiums paid for any other kind of life insurance by an employer are taxable as income to the employees. Hence, the portion of each contribution to a qualified plan that is actually used to purchase life insurance is currently taxed to the employee. The amount to be included in his income is the one-year term cost as determined by the insurance company within limits set by the Commissioner of Internal Revenue. See section 72(m)(3).

The employer's deduction

The fundamental difference between pension and annuity plans, on the one hand, and profit-sharing, on the other, results in a basic difference in the deduction provision applicable to the two kinds of arrangement. Briefly, pension plans and annuity plans offer actuarially determinable benefits, and hence the employer's annual deductible contribution is limited to an amount that approximates the cost of the plan or "normal cost," which is the amount needed to fund the pensions that the actuary predicts will come due year by year. If a plan is established after a company has been in existence after some time, and if the plan covers employees who have been with the company for many years and takes this past service into account in the calculation of benefits due, the plan will start with a large pension liability already established. The Code allows the employer to fund these "past service credits" over a ten-year period and to get a deduction for amounts contributed for this funding. This is covered in section 404(a).

By contrast, a profit-sharing plan is premised upon a variable-employer contribution because the contribution will depend on profit. The employer is free to contribute whatever percentage of profits he sees fit, but the Code places a ceiling on the amount of the contribution that will be deductible. The limit is designed to approximate a reasonable contribution for the covered employees.

Notice that carry-overs are provided for excess contribution to pension plans and profit-sharing plans, and in the case of a profit-sharing plan if the employer does not use up his allowable deduction in a given year, he can accumulate the unused amount and use it in a later year, within limits.

Lump-sum distribution

You have already seen that in the case of a qualified plan, an employee is not taxed until payments are actually made to him and that the taxation of these payments is governed by the annuity section of the Code, section 72. Congress foresaw some inequity when a plan makes a very large lump-sum distribution to an employee in a single year. This "bunching" of income may put the employee in, for him, an unusually high tax bracket. The solution to this inequity was section 402(a)(2). This provision is frequently criticized as conferring quite unjustified tax benefits in some cases. The result may certainly be that a lump-sum distribution is taxed at a lower tax rate than would apply to equivalent annuity payments.

The result of the special provision is that considerable care should be given to the choice between taking benefits from a qualified plan in the form of an annuity and taking a lump-sum payment.

Stock options

A stock option is a right to buy stock in a corporation, generally over a period of time and at a pre-determined price. Until 1950 stock options were not given any special tax treatment in the Code. For these options and for options today which do not meet any of the specific requirements of the Code, there were at least four dates on which a taxable event might occur: the date an employee was granted a stock option, the date on which the option became exercisable, the date on which the employee actually exercised the option, and the date on which he sold his stock. The Treasury has generally selected the date of exercise as the appropriate date on which to recognize income. The amount of income would be the difference between the option price and the market value of the stock on the exercise date. This difference is the benefit which the corporation has conferred on its employees through the stock option. And for any option that does not meet the specific requirements of the Code, this difference will probably be taxed as ordinary income. However, in the past it has been successfully argued in court that the purpose of the option was not compensation but simply to give the employee a proprietary interest in the corporation, so that the value of the option should not be treated as income.

The Treasury position was first taken in 1923, and it was in 1937 that the courts drew a clear distinction between situations where the option was used for the purpose of compensation and where the option was intended to increase the proprietary interest of the employee. In this latter situation, on disposition of the stock, any gain over the price the employee paid would be taxed as capital gain. In 1939, the Treasury formally acquiesced in the reasoning of these decisions; but after winning a case in 1945, the Treasury reverted to its original attitude.

In 1950, Congress was persuaded that there was a need to encourage executives to acquire an ownership interest in the corporations they worked for. The concept of the "restricted stock option" was introduced to the Code, with restrictions on its use that were designed to insure that it would be used not for compensation but to bring about this ownership interest. The important conditions on a "restricted stock option" were that the employee could not dispose of the stock sooner than two years after the option was granted or within six months after actually acquiring the shares, that the option price had to be at least 85 per cent of the fair market price at the time the stock option was granted, and that if the option price were 95 per cent of the fair market price at the time of grant, the difference between the option price and selling price would be taxed only at the long-term capital gain rate. As long as an option qualified as a restricted stock option, no tax would be paid until the stock was actually disposed of. In 1954, a few changes in the rules were made, including the imposition of a maximum time limit during which a stock option could be exercised. This was set at ten years.

Options which did not qualify as "restricted stock options" continued to receive the pre-1950 treatment, but in 1956 the United States Supreme Court greatly strengthened the Treasury's hand by concluding that since Congress had chosen to give special treatment to "restricted stock options," it must have intended that for all nonqualifying options ordinary income in the amount of difference between the option price and the market price of the stock on the exercise date would be realized. In 1951, the Treasury promulgated Regulations which apply to nonqualifying as well as qualifying stock options. You can find these in Regulations section 1.421–6(c).

In the late 1950's and early 1960's, stock options came under heavy criticism in and out of Congress. It had become quite clear that whatever the original intent of Congress had been, stock options were being used chiefly as a means of compensating key executives. That the executives were not actually acquiring much of a proprietary interest in their corporation was proved by the fact that in many cases an executive financed the exercise of a stock option by selling stock he had acquired under an earlier option. There was also considerable criticism leveled at the practice of some corporations of reducing option prices when the price of the company's stock declined, so that an executive could make as much money by depressing the price of his company's stock as by increasing it. In 1964, the rules relating to stock options were drastically changed. Two new kinds of stock options were introduced: the "qualified stock option" and the "employee stock purchase plan." "Restricted stock options" will disappear, since the class is limited to options granted before 1964 under the Code's earlier provision.

You will find the "qualified stock option" described in section 422. Contrast the conditions with those in section 424 applying to the old *"restricted stock option," bearing in mind that what Congress had in mind in the 1964 changes was greater assurance that stock options would be used not for compensation but to encourage executives to acquire a proprietary interest in their corporations. Compare specifically the frequency with which an executive could sell stock acquired under an option in order to finance a purchase of more option stock.*

Section 423 governs "employee stock purchase plans." What would you guess was the purpose of Congress in authorizing this new kind of stock option plan, quite different from the "restricted and qualified stock options"?

Notice the rules in section 421 that may result in a disposition of stock disqualifying the acquisition and disposition from the special tax treatment of "qualified stock options." Is the employee worse off as a result of a disqualifying disposition than he would have been if his option had never been qualified in the first place?

We have noted in connection with other forms of compensation the importance of a deduction to the corporate employer. Are any deductions available to corporate employers in connection with stock options?

It seems likely the criticisms of stock options will continue. In 1964, the administration sought to have all special treatment of stock options eliminated from the Code. Congress answered by attempting to enforce the original intention behind the special treatment. Legislative changes have answered the most serious criticism, but stock options remain a highly attractive tax-sheltered form of compensation available to a rather limited group of corporate executives, and these options are bound to be the subject of considerable opposition in the future.

Robinson v. Commissioner[5]

Respondent determined a deficiency in petitioners' income tax for the year 1957, and additions to tax, as follows:

[5]44 T.C. 20 (Tax Court of the United States, 1965).

Additions to tax

Deficiency	Sec. 6654	Sec. 6651 (a)
$313,449.82	I.R.C. 1954	I.R.C. 1954
	$1,043.56	$17,543.33

In amendments to his answer, respondent claims an increased deficiency in the amount of $38,690.23, based upon two amounts which he failed to include as unreported income of petitioners in his determination of the deficiency of $313,449.82, and concedes that petitioners are not liable for the addition to tax of $17,543.33 determined by him under section 6651(a).

The principal question for decision involves the determination of the amount includible in petitioner Ray S. Robinson's 1957 gross income pursuant to contractual arrangements in connection with his participation in the Robinson-Basilio World Middleweight Championship fight. This question turns upon whether Robinson was a member of a joint or partnership in respect of this fight so as to be chargeable with his share of the earnings even though not distributed to him in 1957 and whether he in any event was chargeable by reason of constructive receipt with a greater amount of earnings therefrom than actually reported by him for 1957.

Other questions presented are (1) whether petitioner Robinson received $10,000 in cash in 1957 in connection with opening his training camp for the Basilio fight; (2) whether a $7,600 expenditure for fight tickets was an ordinary and necessary business expense; (3) whether $7,331.91 paid to Ernie Bracca was an ordinary and necessary business expense; (4) whether petitioner paid $2,000 in 1957 for training camp facilities; (5) whether the Commissioner erred in reducing a claimed $4,300 embezzlement loss to the extent of $2,000; and (6) whether petitioners are liable for an addition to tax in the amount of $1,043.56 for underpayment of estimated tax in 1957.

Some of the facts have been stipulated, and, as stipulated, are incorporated herein by reference.

Petitioners, Ray S. Robinson and Edna Mae Robinson, were, during 1957, husband and wife. Their address was 2076 Seventh Avenue, New York, New York. Petitioners filed their joint Federal income tax return for 1957 with the director of internal revenue, New York, New York, on the basis of a calendar year, using the cash receipts and disbursements method of accounting.

Ray S. Robinson (hereinafter sometimes referred to as petitioner) was and is a well-known prize fighter, professionally and publicly known as "Sugar Ray Robinson." During the year 1957, he was the World Middleweight Boxing Champion. He has been a professional prize fighter for more than 20 years; has engaged in approximately 170 professional fights of which 10 or 12 were championship contests; and was the world middleweight champion five times. He has always been a substantial "gate attraction" and has established records for attendance at contests throughout the country.

Professional boxing is a legalized sport which has become a business and which is conducted as a form of public entertainment. All who engage in it, either as boxer participants, managers, or promoters, are, generally speaking, motivated by the desire of profit or monetary gain. Contestants are matched according to weight classes. In each weight class there is at any one time, ordinarily, one recognized world champion. Recognition as a world champion places the individual so recognized in a position to obtain more for his services. Contests in which champions participate have great box office appeal, arouse great public interest, have large audience participation and bring in more revenues from sales of admission tickets, or "gate" and sales of radio and television rights, motion picture rights and closed-circuit telecast admissions, than do non-championship contests.

Promoting professional boxing contests includes the negotiation and execution of contracts with the boxers; the arranging of details necessary to the exhibition of the contest; the selling of tickets of admission; the staging of the contest; the sale of rights to broadcast and to telecast for home television consumption and/or closed circuit theater television consumption; and the sale or distribution of motion pictures. The promotion of a championship bout involves the outlay and/or commitment of substantial sums of money on the part of the promoting corporation.

Professional boxing is conducted in most states under rules and regulations administered by a state governmental authority. In many instances professional boxing is administered under a licensing system by which control and supervision is exercised over the boxers, their managers, promoting corporations, referees, judges, matchmakers, timekeepers, and those in charge of the sale and distribution of admission tickets. In New York, the governing authority is the State Athletic Commission (hereinafter referred to as the Commission) which is a division of the Department of State.

Petitioner during the year 1957 was a professional boxer licensed by, among others, the Commissioner.

International Boxing Club of New York, Inc. (hereinafter referred to as IBC) was, during 1957, a promoting corporation licensed by the Commission. It promoted most of petitioner's professional fights.

At no time was petitioner an officer, director or stockholder of IBC, nor did he ever have a financial interest therein other than claims for moneys due him as a boxer. Petitioner was in no way related to any officer, director or stockholder of IBC.

IBC was during the years 1957 and 1958 a wholly owned subsidiary of Madison Square Garden Corporation (hereinafter referred to as The Garden), a corporation organized and existing under the laws of the State of New York, whose stock was traded on the "over the counter" securities market.

Petitioner was never an officer, director or stockholder of The Garden, and never had a financial interest therein.

James D. Norris during the year 1957 was president of both IBC and The Garden. He and an associate "owned control" of The Garden.

Sometime prior to July 31, 1957, petitioner and IBC conducted negotiations with respect to a proposed title bout to be held at the Yankee Stadium in New York City in September 1957 between petitioner and one

Carmen Basilio. Petitioner at the time was the World Middleweight Champion and Carmen Basilio was the World Welterweight Champion. The contest was to be for the middleweight "crown," with petitioner as the defending champion and Basilio the contender.

As a result of such negotiations, IBC and petitioner agreed to the terms of a contest to be staged on September 23, 1957, between petitioner and Carmen Basilio, or on September 24, 1957, in the event of rain. The terms were evidenced by two instruments executed by the parties and each dated July 31, 1957. One of the instruments was on a standard printed form; the other instrument was in typewritten form.

The rules of the Commission require, among other things, that contracts with boxers be executed on a printed form approved by the Commission and that such contracts be filed with the Commission within 48 hours after execution. Rule B, Subdivisions 1 and 13.

The standard printed form of contract, with blank spaces filled in by typewriter, covered many of the regulatory details with respect to the conduct of the contest and contained provisions to the following effect:

> a. The contest was to be for the middleweight crown between Ray Robinson and Carmen Basilio;
>
> b. The contest was to be held on September 23, 1957 at the Yankee Stadium in Bronx, New York;
>
> c. The match was to be for 15 rounds to a decision; and at a weight not to exceed 160 pounds;
>
> d. IBC agreed to pay after said contest and Ray Robinson agreed to accept, ". . . as in full payment for all his claims and demands for and on account of the performance by him of this contract . . . 45 per cent of the gross receipts derived from the sale of tickets of admission less the Federal and/or State Admission Taxes and compensation for ring officials plus 45 per cent of radio, theater-television, and motion picture receipts, as per agreement presented to the Commission this day;"
>
> e. Details with respect to rules of the contest were contained in the printed body of the contract form including the right of IBC to rescind the contract if Robinson meanwhile entered into another contest and was defeated or did anything calculated to lessen his present value as an attraction.

The instrument in typewritten form was the "agreement" referred to in an insertion in the printed form contract incorporated into the quotation in d, above. That instrument in typewritten form will hereinafter be referred to as the "Deferred Payment Contract." It provided as follows:

AGREEMENT made this 31 day of July 1957 by and between INTERNATIONAL BOXING CLUB OF NEW YORK, INC., a New York corporation having its principal place of business at 304 West 50th Street, New York, New York, (hereinafter called the "Club") and SUGAR RAY ROBINSON of 2076–7 Avenue, Borough of Manhattan, City of New York (hereinafter called "Robinson").

Witnesseth:

WHEREAS Robinson is recognized as the world champion in the middleweight class among professional boxers and the New York State Athletic Commission and National Boxing Association; and

WHEREAS Robinson has requested the Club to promote a boxing match for the middleweight championship of the world between himself and one Carmen Basilio to take place in or about the month of September 1957; and

WHEREAS Robinson insists that the site of the bout be at Yankee Stadium; and

WHEREAS Robinson insists upon receiving forty-five per cent of the gross receipts derived by the Club; and

WHEREAS the promoting of such an outdoor boxing match involves great hazards and financial risk by reason of the uncertainty of the elements and of the very substantial expenses attendant upon such promotion; and

WHEREAS the promoting of such boxing match as Robinson requests might, in view of the financial risk involved, jeopardize the ability of the Club to promote future boxing matches; and

WHEREAS Robinson, in recognition of the substantial financial risks to the Club, is agreeable and willing that this forty-five per cent participation in the proceeds of the match be paid to him, not immediately thereafter, but over a period of years as hereinafter set forth; and

WHEREAS the Club is willing in consideration of Robinson's consent to accept payment over a period of years, to pay the forty-five per cent of the proceeds of the match allocable to him over that which might otherwise be payable; and

WHEREAS the parties will simultaneously with the execution of this Agreement execute a contract on the official form of the New York State Athletic Commission; and

WHEREAS the New York State Athletic Commission has recently approved and adopted the following regulation which provides among other provisions:

> "*Rule* B 15 (14) All compensation to boxers and wrestlers shall be made by check payable to the participating athlete personally who shall sign a receipt for such payment. No payment shall be made to any person or party other than such participating athlete, etc. and

WHEREAS pursuant to such regulation, this Agreement will be submitted to said Commission, for approval, together with the contract hereinabove mentioned.

NOW, THEREFORE, in consideration of their respective undertakings hereinafter contained, the Club and Robinson agree as follows:

> (a) Robinson's participation in the proceeds of the boxing match shall be paid to him as follows:
>
> Forty per cent thereof, as an initial payment, to be made not later than two weeks after the bout takes place;

Twenty per cent thereof during the year 1958 in equal quarter-annual installments, the first of which shall be payable on January 10, 1958;

Twenty per cent thereof during the year 1959 in equal quarter-annual installments, the first of which shall be payable on January 10, 1960;

(b) Robinson, and/or his associates shall have access to the books and records of the Corporation on reasonable notice during business hours for the purpose of ascertaining the correctness of the amounts due him under the provisions of this Agreement.

Except as herein supplemented, the aforesaid New York Athletic Commission form of contract is and shall be in full force and effect.

WHEREVER the term "gross receipts" is mentioned and referred to in this Agreement or in the Agreement on the official form of the New York State Athletic Commission, it shall be defined to mean the following:

"The gross proceeds from the sale of seats of admission to the bout, the sale of theater-television rights, the sale of radio rights, the sale of the motion picture theater rights, and any and all other proceeds received by the Club in connection or in conjunction with the promotion of the bout. The only deductions allowable shall be for State and Federal admission taxes and commission charges for ring officials as set out in the New York State Athletic Commission contract."

In the case of motion pictures the Club may deduct from the gross receipts from motion pictures their actual cost for the actual production of the negative turned over to the theatrical distribution firm, which shall not exceed $30,000 under any circumstances.

The parties agree that neither one shall permit or authorize any firm, individual, or corporation the use or permission to use the film for any package deal or free television usage. The proceeds from any authorized usage of the film at a later date for television or otherwise shall become part of the gross receipts.

In conjunction with the sale of the ancillary rights it is agreed that no sale shall be actually consummated without the written consent of Robinson or his duly authorized representative which consent shall not be arbitrarily withheld. In addition the Club agrees to place a clause in all agreements for the sale of ancillary rights providing that Robinson can inspect the books at reasonable times and on proper notice of the purchaser to make true and correct accountings with respect to such sale. A copy of each such agreement will be furnished to Robinson by the purchaser.

IN WITNESS WHEREOF this Agreement has been duly executed the day and year first above written.

INTERNATIONAL BOXING CLUB OF NEW YORK, INC.

By /s/ JAMES D. NORRIS
/s/ Ray S. Robinson

In order to induce Ray Robinson to execute and in consideration of his execution of the foregoing Agreement, MADISON SQUARE GARDEN CORPORATION hereby undertakes and agrees to cause the INTERNATIONAL BOXING CLUB OF NEW YORK, INC., a wholly owned subsidiary to perform, comply with and adhere to all the conditions in the said Agreement and expressly guarantees payment to Ray Robinson of any and all the sums therein set out.

MADISON SQUARE GARDEN CORPORATION

By /s/ EDWARD S. IRISH
Vice President

In order to induce Ray Robinson to execute and in consideration of his execution of the foregoing Agreement, JAMES D. NORRIS personally undertakes and agrees to the guaranty of performance by the INTERNATIONAL BOXING CLUB OF NEW YORK, INC. and the MADISON SQUARE GARDEN CORPORATION.

/s/ JAMES D. NORRIS
James D. Norris

On July 31, 1957, a meeting of the Commission was held which was attended by petitioner and Basilio, their representatives, and representatives of IBC. At that meeting the two contracts with petitioner were filed with the Commission as required by law. When the Commission was asked by petitioner's attorney during the course of the meeting to approve the contract in typewritten form, its chairman made the following statement:

> We have neither the jurisdiction nor power to approve or disapprove what may be a legal method of payment. I will say this, however, Ray Robinson, the boxer, and the promoting club, the International Boxing Club of New York, Inc., has submitted to the Commission today simultaneously with the official form of club contract of the Commission, a contract between the parties aforementioned setting forth the method of payment to be made to the boxer, Ray Robinson. The Commission has taken notice of this contract concerning the method of payment in accordance with Rule "B", Contracts, Subdivision 14 of the Commission's rules and regulations. The Commission, however, does not approve or disapprove of this contract because it has no power to do so. The question of whether payment can be made as set forth in this agreement is for the federal government to decide. This may present a question for the Internal Revenue Bureau as to the legality of this method of payment and a question of interpretation with respect to payment for taxable fiscal years. It is plain to see that it is a matter for the Internal Revenue Bureau to decide and not this Commission. This is to be filed with the other papers.

On the same date, July 31, 1957, a contract was entered into between IBC and Basilio wherein the parties agreed that Basilio would receive 20 per cent of the gross receipts derived from the sale of tickets of admission plus 20 per cent of radio, theater-TV and motion picture receipts.

During the negotiations which preceded the preparation and signing of the contracts between IBC and petitioner and Basilio, James D. Norris, who was at that time the president of IBC and The Garden, originally proposed to give 25 per cent of the gross receipts to Basilio and 40 per cent to petitioner. Petitioner, however, insisted that he be given 45 per cent of the gross receipts. Norris considered the petitioner to be the more important of the two contestants and told Basilio that, in view of petitioner's insistence on 45 per cent, he would have to accept 20 per cent if the fight were to be staged at all. Subsequently, Basilio accepted 20 per cent. Sixty-five per cent of the gross proceeds was an unusually high amount for IBC to pay to two participants in a championship fight, but a match between these two contestants had an unusually high box office appeal.

During the year 1957, and prior to the execution of the deferred payment contract on July 31, 1957, petitioner had realized gross earnings of approximately $200,000 from two championship boxing contests with Gene Fullmer.

There is no requirement by the Commission that payment to the boxer participants be made immediately after the fight. IBC had in the past executed deferred payment agreements with two other fighters, Rocky Marciano and Carmen Basilio. This, however, was not the customary method of payment. It was the usual practice of IBC and other promoters to pay fighters "soon" after the fight in order to preserve their reputation with the fighters. It made little difference to IBC whether the contract entered into with petitioner provided for immediate or deferred payment of his share of the gross receipts. It did not propose or want the deferred payment provisions and would have been willing to contract on terms providing for payment immediately after the fight. The inclusion in the contract of the deferred payment provisions did not result in petitioner's receiving a greater percentage of the receipts than he would have received if the contract had provided for payment immediately after the fight.

On August 19, 1957 IBC entered into a contract with Theatre Network Television, Inc. (hereinafter referred to as TNT) for the sale to TNT of the right to telecast the fight over closed circuit theatre television. Shortly thereafter a dispute arose between IBC and petitioner with respect to such sale by IBC. As a result of such dispute, the Commission conducted public hearings on August 26 and 29, 1957. The dispute was resolved on August 29, 1957 by a memorandum of agreement dated August 29, 1957 between TNT and Teleprompter Corporation (hereinafter referred to as Teleprompter), and by an amendment on August 29, 1957 of the August 19, 1957 contract entered into between IBC and TNT with respect to the sale of the closed circuit television rights. The memorandum of agreement and the modification of the IBC-TNT contract contained certain provisions that may be summarized as follows:

    a. TNT licensed the rights in four cities to Teleprompter;

    b. Teleprompter agreed to pay TNT $5,000.00;

    c. TNT guaranteed that Robinson's 45 per cent share of IBC's receipts from theater television would equal or exceed $255,000.00, and that Basilio's 20 per cent share of such receipts would equal or exceed $110,000.00;

    d. TNT and IBC agreed on a sharing of the minimum amounts to the boxers;

    e. IBC agreed to turn over one-half of its share of net receipts from the sale of motion picture rights to TNT.

At the hearing conducted by the Commission on August 29, 1957, the president of TNT stated that it was offering petitioner a guarantee of $255,000 out of closed circuit television receipts, and Robinson stated that the offer was "agreeable" to him.

The Robinson-Basilio fight was such an attractive promotion that IBC anticipated a large gate and in selecting the site for the fight considered only an outdoor ball park, rather than an indoor arena such as Madison Square Garden. The most favorable months for staging an outdoor fight are June and September. IBC chose September because that month is by tradition the best month for a major fight and the 23rd of that month, a Monday, because the beginning of a week is a more favorable time to stage a fight than the end of a week. After considering such factors as the availability of Yankee Stadium and the Polo Grounds in terms of baseball schedules, the degree of control that could be exercised over persons attending the fight at each of those parks, and its ability to use Madison Square Garden personnel at Yankee Stadium, but not at the Polo Grounds, IBC selected Yankee Stadium as the site for the fight.

If a major outdoor prizefight, such as the Robinson-Basilio fight, were cancelled a day before it was scheduled, the loss to the promoter might be as high as $50,000 to $75,000. If there were a postponement of 24 hours because of bad weather, there would be a limited amount of refunding for tickets. If there were a postponement for two days or longer, then refunding by the promoter would be substantial. There was no more risk to IBC in promoting the Robinson-Basilio fight than in promoting any other championship match held outdoors.

The contest for the middleweight championship between petitioner and Basilio was held at the Yankee Stadium on the night of September 23, 1957, at which time Basilio gained the middleweight championship.

On the night of the fight, after petitioner entered the ring and during the first round of the contest, IBC was served by respondent with a "Notice of Levy" in the amount of $514,310.72, with respect to unpaid income taxes of petitioner for the years 1955, 1956, and 1957. Of the foregoing amount, $497,435.29 was assessed under the provisions of Section 6851 of the Internal Revenue Code of 1954, representing income

taxes for the period January 1 to September 23, 1957, estimated by respondent to be due by petitioner. This amount included respondent's
estimate of the income tax which would be due on petitioner's total share
of the proceeds from the Robinson-Basilio fight on September 23, 1957.

The "Notice of Levy" read, in part, as follows:

> You are further notified that demand has been made upon the
> taxpayer for the amount set forth herein, and that such amount is
> still due, owing, and unpaid from this taxpayer, and that the lien
> provided for by Section 6321, Internal Revenue Code of 1954, now
> exists upon all property or rights to property belonging to the afore-
> said taxpayer. Accordingly, you are further notified that all property,
> rights to property, moneys, credits, and bank deposits now in your
> possession and belonging to this taxpayer (or with respect to which
> you are obligated) and all sums of money or other obligations owing
> from you to this taxpayer are hereby levied upon and seized for
> satisfaction of the aforesaid tax, together with all additions provided
> by law, and demand is hereby made upon you for the amount nec-
> essary to satisfy the liability set forth herein, or for such lesser sum
> as you may be indebted to him, to be applied as a payment on his
> tax liability.

At no time during 1957 did respondent know exactly how much was
owed by petitioner for income taxes for the year 1957.

The "Notice of Levy" was served under the provisions of Section
6331 of the Internal Revenue Code of 1954, respondent having made a
jeopardy assessment after he estimated the amount of taxes which would
be due from petitioner by cutting short petitioner's taxable year on September 23, 1957.

Petitioner's share of the proceeds from the Robinson-Basilio fight
(including broadcasting and theatre-TV rights but exclusive of motion
picture rights) totalled $483,666.71. His share of the proceeds realized
from the sale of the motion picture rights in 1957 amounted to $32,516.74
and during the period January 1, 1958 through March 31, 1959 amounted
to $11,302.07. Thus, the total amount to which petitioner became entitled
as a result of the Robinson-Basilio fight was $527,485.52, exclusive of an
item of $10,000, hereinafter described, which he received in cash to open
his training camp.

Petitioner's unpaid share of the proceeds of the fight held on September 23, 1957 was commingled by IBC with its own funds and was not
segregated by IBC nor was there any written escrow, trust or other arrangement for the benefit of petitioner. The obligation of IBC to petitioner for
his share of the proceeds of the fight was not evidenced by any note executed by IBC in petitioner's favor. The amount due from IBC to petitioner
appeared on its books as a liability, and as payments were made in respect
thereof they were charged against this liability account.

Prior to the September 23, 1957 fight petitioner had received the
following from IBC which were charged against his share of the proceeds
of the fight:

Advances by check

6/18/57	$ 7,500
7/31/57	2,500
7/19/57	10,000
8/23/57	5,000
	$25,000
190 fight tickets at $40 each	7,600
	$32,600

After the levy of September 23, 1957, the only manner in which petitioner could obtain any of the moneys due him under the July 31, 1957 contracts was by consent of respondent to their release from the effects of the levy.

During the year 1957 conferences were had by petitioner with representatives of respondent for the release of petitioner's share of the proceeds from the effects of the levy. Such conferences continued through 1957, and into 1958. The conferences held in 1957 resulted in the consent by respondent to the release of $107,000 in order to permit petitioner to pay expenses incurred by him in connection with the Robinson-Basilio fight. That amount was in fact thus paid out on November 13, 1957.

During 1958, 1959 and 1960 the following payments were made by IBC to the Internal Revenue Service in behalf of petitioner:

March 19, 1958	$17,349.85
April 11, 1958	42,416.85
	$ 59,766.70
June 4, 1959	$183,385.47
January 11, 1960	$24,183.33
April 11, 1960	24,183.33
July 8, 1960	24,183.33
October 4, 1960	24,183.36
	$ 96,733.35

As a result of a claim against petitioner by Associated Booking Corporation, and an action brought by it to secure payment of its claim from IBC, following which the United States was interpleaded, a settlement was arrived at whereby petitioner and the United States consented to the payment by IBC of $40,000 to Associated Booking Corporation and $8,000 for counsel fees for petitioner's attorney, out of petitioner's share of the proceeds of the fight due from IBC. Such consent was evidenced by a stipulation of settlement executed June 3, 1959, which further provided for the subsequent payments to the Internal Revenue Service set forth in the preceding paragraph, and contained the statement that "The within settlement and payments made hereunder are not to be construed as an admission by the Government that the installment payments made under the agreement of July 31, 1957, are taxable in 1958–1960 instead of in 1957."

In summary, IBC paid out to petitioner or in his behalf, in respect of its total obligation of $527,485.52, the following:

Date	Description	Amount
1957 (prior to fight)	Advances and fight tickets	$ 32,600.00
1957 (after fight)	Amount released from levy to pay expenses incurred in connection with fight	107,000.00
1958	Internal Revenue Service	59,766.70
1959	Internal Revenue Service	183,385.47
1959	Settlement of Associated Booking Corp.'s claim against petitioner.	48,000.00
1960	Internal Revenue Service	96,733.35
Total	. . . .	$527,485.52

Petitioner reported in joint Federal income tax returns which he and his wife filed for the years 1957 to 1960, inclusive, the following amounts from the Robinson-Basilio fight:

Year	Amount
1957	$139,600.00
1958 (Amended)	59,766.70
1959	231,384.81
1960	96,733.35

In determining the deficiency herein for 1957 the Commissioner charged petitioner with his entire $483,666.71 share of the proceeds of the Robinson-Basilio fight, exclusive of motion picture rights; and by Amendments to Answer he claimed an increased deficiency as a result in part of including the $32,516.74 realized in 1957 from the sale of motion picture rights.

The books and records of IBC disclose that IBC realized a net profit of $50,897.33 from the Robinson-Basilio fight and that Chicago Stadium Corporation, a co-promoter, realized $16,029.74. All receipts were paid directly to IBC and all expenses of IBC were paid by IBC.

The contracts entered into by IBC and petitioner in connection with the Robinson-Basilio fight were contracts for personal services and did not create a joint venture.

At some time prior to the Robinson-Basilio fight, when James D. Norris was negotiating with petitioner in respect of the fight, Norris gave $10,000 in cash to or in behalf of petitioner to open his training camp. Norris was subsequently reimbursed for this amount by IBC. The books and records of IBC list under the expenses of the Robinson-Basilio fight an item of $10,000 described as "Training camp expenses — Ray Robinson." This $10,000 item is in addition to all other amounts paid or due to petitioner, as shown in IBC's books and records, and is not included among the other amounts found above as having been paid to or in behalf of petitioner. This $10,000 item represents additional income to petitioner in 1957 and was not reported by him for that year; it was charged to petitioner by the Commissioner in his Amendments to Answer claiming an increased deficiency attributable in part to this item.

IBC customarily gives each contestant a number of free or complimentary tickets to the fight in which he participates for members of his staff, individuals associated with him in training camp, and friends. The number of complimentary tickets issued must be approved by the Commission.

Admission to a fight without a ticket of admission may be gained only by the principals, managers and seconds involved in the fight.

In 1957 petitioner purchased from IBC 190 tickets to the Robinson-Basilio fight at $40 per ticket and his account with IBC was charged for $7,600. Petitioner gave these tickets to members of his family, friends and persons employed at his training camp.

In their 1957 return petitioners claimed a deduction of $7,600 for "Tickets given away for publicity purposes for Basilio Fight." This deduction was disallowed by the respondent. Fight tickets in the amount of $2,000 represent an ordinary and necessary business expense. The remainder was a nondeductible personal expense.

Ernie Bracca was one of petitioner's managers in 1957. The services of a manager normally involve participation in negotiations for a fight, arrangement of training facilities and preparation for the fight.

During 1957 petitioner paid, in addition to other payments, $7,331.91 to Ernie Bracca and petitioners claimed a deduction for that payment in their 1957 return. The claimed deduction was disallowed by the respondent on the ground that it did not constitute an ordinary and necessary business expense. No evidence was presented to show that the $7,331.91 payment was for Bracca's services as a manager; nor was any evidence presented relating to the nature of this payment.

Petitioner trained for the Robinson-Basilio fight at Long Pond Inn, Greenwood, New York. He had been using such facilities as a training camp periodically since 1940. He trained at Long Pond Inn from the early part of August to the latter part of September 1957 and it was used by his staff, his cook and training partners during this period. He paid $250 a week for eight weeks for the use of Long Pond Inn as training quarters, and the total amount expended by him for such rental in 1957 was $2,000.

In petitioners' return for 1957, they claimed a deduction of $2,000 for "Long Pond Inn Training Quarters." This deduction was disallowed by the respondent on the ground that no evidence had been submitted in substantiation thereof.

Sometime during 1957 petitioner gave his secretary, Gloria Pollard, some money to deposit in his bank account. The money was not deposited by her. Petitioner could not find her and never saw her again. He reported the matter to the police. He did not recover, by insurance or otherwise, any part of his loss. In their 1957 return, petitioners claimed a loss from embezzlement in the amount of $4,300. Respondent disallowed the claimed loss to the extent of $2,000 for lack of substantiation.

On April 21, 1958, petitioners filed their joint return for the year 1957. The tax shown to be due on that return, $37,416.85, was paid on the day the return was filed. Petitioners did not make any payment of estimated income tax for the year 1957.

RAUM, Judge:

1. Taxation of Robinson's share of proceeds of fight.

Petitioner's share of the proceeds of his fight with Basilio on September 23, 1957, was $483,666.71, exclusive of motion picture rights, and, by the end of 1957, his share in the proceeds of the sale of the motion picture rights amounted to $32,516.74. As a result of the events described in our findings, he received or there was paid out in his behalf during 1957 in respect of that fight a total of $139,600, which he reported in his 1957 return. The Commissioner's original determination of deficiency for 1957 charged him with omitting $344,066.71 (the difference between $483,666.71 and $139,600) "of the proceeds earned by you in the Robinson-Basilio fight."[6] And in an amended pleading the Commissioner claimed an additional deficiency attributable in part to Robinson's $32,516.74 share of the motion picture proceeds for 1957.

The problem relating to the taxation of petitioner's earnings from the Basilio fight in 1957 arises solely by reason of the fact that he used the cash basis. If he were on an accrual basis the amounts charged to him by the Commissioner might well be includable in his 1957 income. But he was not on an accrual basis, and the question before us is whether the amounts that he had not in fact received in 1957 or that were not in fact paid out in his behalf in 1957 may nevertheless be treated as income to him in that year on a theory of constructive receipt or otherwise. The question is thus not *whether* the amounts in issue are taxable to petitioner, but *when* they are to be included in gross income. At the trial the Government's position appeared to rest mainly upon constructive receipt, but in its brief it states as its "primary contention" that the Robinson-Basilio fight was a "joint venture" in which petitioner was a participant, and that he is therefore taxable on his full distributive share, whether or not it was in fact distributed to him in that year. It argues alternatively that the deferred payment contract was a sham, that it did not represent a binding arrangement between IBC and petitioner, that IBC would have paid petitioner in full immediately after the fight despite the deferred compensation contract, and that petitioner is therefore chargeable with the full amount. It makes other alternative contentions that even if the deferred payment contract is valid, petitioner should have reported greater amounts than the $139,600 appearing on his return, and that the service of notice of levy on IBC did not prevent petitioner's realization of income in 1957 in accordance with his contractual arrangements. We reject all of these contentions.

(a) Joint venture.

Section 7701(a)(2) of the 1954 Code provides that the "term 'partnership' includes a . . . joint venture, or other unincorporated organization, through or by means of which any business, financial operation, or venture is carried on . . . ; and the term 'partner' includes a member in

---

[6]The Commissioner also added $190 in respect of "camp admissions," but this latter item has been conceded by petitioner on brief.

such a . . . joint venture, or organization." And of course, if there is a joint venture, the members, like partners, are chargeable with their respective distributive shares of the income of the joint venture, regardless of whether such income is in fact distributed to them.

A joint venture has been defined in general terms to be a "special combination of two or more persons where, in some specific venture, a profit is jointly sought without any actual partnership or corporate designation" and "an association of persons to carry out a single business enterprise for profit." *Beck Chemical Equipment Corporation*, 27 T. C. 840, 848–849; *Estate of L. O. Koen*, 14 T. C. 1406, 1409; *Chase S. Osborn*, 22 B. T. A. 935, 945. Whether a business undertaking entered into by two or more persons constitutes a joint venture depends largely on the terms of their contract and their actions in carrying out its provisions.

As was noted in *Hubert M. Luna*, 42 T. C. 1067, 1077, "[w]hether parties have formed a joint venture is a question of fact to be determined by reference to the same principles that govern the question of whether persons have formed a partnership which is to be accorded recognition for tax purposes. . . . Therefore, while all circumstances are to be considered, the essential question is whether the parties intended to, and did in fact, join together for the present conduct of an undertaking or enterprise." And the Court further pointed out that the "following factors, none of which is conclusive, bear on the issue . . . (pp. 1077–1078):

> The agreement of the parties and their conduct in executing its terms; the contributions, if any, which each party has made to the venture; the parties' control over income and capital and the right of each to make withdrawals; whether each party was a principal and co-proprietor, sharing a mutual proprietary interest in the net profits and having an obligation to share losses, or whether one party was the agent or employee of the other, receiving for his services contingent compensation in the form of a percentage of income; whether business was conducted in the joint names of the parties; whether the parties filed Federal partnership returns or otherwise represented to respondent or to persons with whom they dealt that they were joint venturers; whether separate books of account were maintained for the venture; and whether the parties exercised mutual control over and assumed mutual responsibilities for the enterprise.

See also *Lucia Chase Ewing*, 20 T. C. 216, 231–232, affirmed on another issue, 213 F. 2d 438 (C. A. 2); *J. Roland Brady*, 25 T. C. 682, 688; *Wm. J. Lemp Brewing Co.*, 18 T. C. 586, 597; *Schermerhorn Oil Corporation*, 46 B. T. A. 151, 158; *Steinbeck v. Gerosa*, 175 N.Y.S. 2d 1, 13, 4 N.Y. 2d 302, 317. It is not "enough that two parties have agreed to act in concert to achieve some stated economic objective." *Mitler v. Friedeberg*, 222 N.Y.S. 2d 480, 485. And an agreement to share in the gross receipts of a specific venture merely as a basis of compensation may be a contract of employment rather than a joint venture. *Sloane v. United Feature Syndicate, Inc.*, 238 N.Y.S. 91, 94; *La Driere v. Martin*, 56 N.Y.S. 2d 436, 437. *Cf. United*

States v. *Johansson,* an unreported case (S. D. Fla. 1961, 8 A. F. T. R. 2d 6001, 6005–6006, 6007, affirmed 336 F. 2d 809 (C. A. 5).

The venture with which we are here concerned involved the promotion of a middleweight championship bout between petitioner and Basilio. The promoter of that venture was IBC. It entered into separate contracts with petitioner and Basilio under the terms of which each fighter became entitled for his services to a specified portion of the gross receipts from ticket sales, radio broadcasting, theater television, and the sale of motion picture rights. There is no evidence of any agreement of any kind entered into between petitioner and Basilio. Nothing was said in the contracts entered into by IBC with petitioner and Basilio about any joint venture, the sharing of any profits that might be realized or losses that might be sustained, or participation by petitioner and Basilio in the control or management of the venture. Contrary to the Government's contention, the portions of the contract giving Robinson access to the books of IBC and those requiring his consent in connection with the sale of the ancillary rights hardly provide for participation in management in the light of all the circumstances involved. These provisions were clearly intended merely for his own protection, to assure him that he would receive the maximum compensation for his services.

The contracts before us provided for personal services by petitioner; they did not, and never were intended to, create a joint venture between IBC and petitioner. Cases cited by respondent in which various elements in combination were held to constitute a joint venture on the particular facts involved, not present here, are distinguishable.

(b) Constructive receipt.

The Commissioner makes the alternative contention that petitioner constructively received his full share of the proceeds of the Robinson-Basilio fight in 1957, and not in 1957, 1958, 1959 and 1960. He urges that the deferred payment contract was a sham; that it was not, before and after its execution, intended by the parties thereto to be binding as to the manner in which petitioner was to be paid; that IBC was willing at any time after the fight in 1957 to make payment in full; and that petitioner's receipt of his share of the proceeds of the fight in 1957 was not, therefore, subject to substantial limitations or restrictions so as to prevent its inclusion in petitioner's 1957 income under the doctrine of constructive receipt.

It is important to note that the Government does not base its constructive receipt argument upon the fact that IBC was willing to enter into a contract on July 31, 1957 to make payment in full to petitioner immediately after the September 23, 1957 fight. Indeed the Government refers to Example (3) in *Rev. Rul.* 60–31, 1960–1 C. B. 174, implying that a bona fide contract providing for deferred payments would be given effect notwithstanding that the obligor might have been willing to contract to make such payments at an earlier time. And that *Revenue Ruling* called attention (p. 180) to the withdrawal of the Commissioner's non-acquiescence in *James F. Oates,* 18 T. C. 570, affirmed 207 F. 2d 711 (C. A. 7), followed by the substitution of an acquiescence, 1960–1 C. B. 5. *Cf.*

Howard Veit, 8 T. C. 809; *Kay Kimbell*, 41 B. T. A. 940; *J. D. Amend*, 13 T. C. 178; *James Gould Cozzens*, 19 T. C. 663. The essence of the Government's argument here is that the contract was a sham and that the parties never intended to be governed by it. We do not agree.

To be sure, there are a number of misleading statements in the "Whereas" clauses, falsely suggesting that the provisions for deferred payment were included for the benefit and at the request of IBC. But those whereas clauses were plainly intended as window dressing merely to support and answer to the Government's possible position that constructive receipt might be predicated upon IBC's original pre-July 31 willingness to contract to make payment in full immediately after the fight. We are fully satisfied that once the contract was executed, it was looked upon by both parties as defining their legal rights, and that there was never any collateral understanding, tacit or otherwise, that the parties would not be bound by its terms.

The Government relies upon certain testimony of IBC's president that IBC would have paid petitioner immediately after the fight if he had insisted on it. We heard that testimony and are convinced that the witness meant merely that IBC would have been willing to contract to make immediate payment, not that it would have ignored its stated rights once a different contract had been executed.

We find that the contract was not a sham, and that the inclusion of petitioner's full share of the proceeds of the fight in his 1957 income may not be predicated upon the ground that the contract did not in fact represent a binding arrangement between petitioner and IBC.

(c) Constructive receipt — further alternatives.

The Government contends that even if it is wrong as to the sham character of the July 31, 1957 agreement, petitioner became entitled in 1957 under that very agreement to more than the $139,600 reported and is chargeable under the doctrine of constructive receipt with at least the amount payable to him in 1957 under the agreement.[7] We hold otherwise.

Petitioner in fact received or there was paid out in his behalf a maximum of $139,600 in 1957. Although he was entitled to more in 1957 under the contract, that was all that he got at that time. And he cannot be charged, even under the doctrine of constructive receipt, with having received anything more in 1957.

The proceeds of the fight were not placed in escrow or trust, or set

---

[7]The Government makes alternative contentions as to the amount payable in 1957 under the contract. (i) Since petitioner was entitled under the contract to receive 40 percent of the proceeds of the fight in 1957, the amount payable in 1957 was therefore at least 40 percent of $483,666.71 ($193,466.68), plus 40 per cent of $32,516.74 ($13,006.70), or a total of $206,473.38. (ii) Alternatively, the Government argues that under the contract as supplemented by the subsequent $255,000 guarantee in respect of closed circuit theater television, petitioner became entitled in 1957 to receive $255,000 plus his contractual 40 percent of the remainder of the fight proceeds. We think that this latter alternative is incorrect in any event, because the $255,000 guarantee did not modify the July 31, 1957 contract as to the time of payment, and under that contract petitioner became entitled to only 40 per cent of the proceeds in 1957. However, it is a matter of no moment here as to which computation is accepted, in view of our holding that petitioner is not chargeable with more than $139,600 for 1957 in respect of his compensation for participating in the Basilio fight.

aside in any special fund, or segregated in any way by IBC for petitioner's benefit. They were comingled with all of IBC's other assets, and petitioner was but an unsecured creditor of IBC. Had IBC meanwhile been declared bankrupt, petitioner's claim against its assets would have rested on no firmer ground than those of other credits similarly situated.

To be sure, IBC probably would have been willing to pay over to petitioner the full amount due him in 1957, but the fact is that as a result of the notice of levy, it withheld payment beyond the amount permitted by the Commissioner. In the circumstances, there are not here present the conditions justifying the application of the doctrine of constructive receipt. To be sharply distinguished are such cases as those where payment had in fact been made to the taxpayer, *cf. Kerr* v. *Bowers*, 66 F. 2d 419 (C. A. 2), certiorari denied, 291 U.S. 663, or those in which a special fund had been set aside for his benefit, *cf. Dwight* v. *Ward*, 20 T. C. 332, affirmed 224 F. 2d 547 (C. A. 9).

2. $10,000 cash payment.

We have found as a fact upon the evidence that IBC paid $10,000 in cash to petitioner or in his behalf to open his training camp. This amount represents additional income to petitioner, and should have been reported by him.

3. Miscellaneous deductions.

(a) Fight tickets.

Petitioner purchased 190 tickets for the Basilio fight at $40 each, or a total of $7,600, which he distributed among various persons. The Commissioner disapproved a deduction in that amount. We think that some of those tickets, such as those distributed to sparring partners or training camp employees, may fairly be classified as reasonably connected with petitioner's trade or business as a professional boxer. On the other hand, it seems clear to us that to the extent that tickets were given to members of his family or personal friends, the expenditure therefor was personal and not deductible. It is not possible on the meagre evidence before us to make any scientifically accurate determination as to what portion of the total represents a deductible business expense. Accordingly, relying upon *Cohan* v. *Commissioner*, 39 F. 2d 540, 544 (C. A. 2), we have found that $2,000 of the amount involved constitutes an ordinary and necessary business expense.

(b) Payment of $7,331.91 to Ernie Bracca.

The Commissioner disallowed a deduction in the amount of $7,331.91 paid to one of petitioner's managers, Ernie Bracca. The fact that such payment was made was not disputed. However, the record is utterly devoid of any evidence showing the nature of this payment. If the payment were for Bracca's services as a manager it would obviously be deductible; on the other hand, it could have been for any one of a variety of purposes unrelated to petitioner's trade or business that would have rendered it nondeductible. The burden of proof was upon petitioner, and it has not been carried. The Commissioner must be sustained as to this item.

(c) Long Pond Inn expenses.

Petitioner contends that he expended $2,000 for use of facilities at Long Pond Inn for training purposes in connection with the Basilio fight. Although the evidence is thin we have found that he spent $250 a week for eight weeks for this purpose. Accordingly, the Commissioner's disallowance of a deduction in the total amount of $2,000 in this respect must be disapproved.

(d) Theft loss.

Petitioner claimed a theft loss in the amount of $4,300. The Commissioner disallowed $2,000 thereof for lack of substantiation. The burden was upon petitioner, and we cannot find on this record that the Commissioner erred. Although we are satisfied that there was an embezzlement we cannot say on the evidence before us that the amount involved was any greater than that allowed by the Commissioner.

4. Estimated tax penalty.

Petitioners did not make any payment of estimated tax for the year 1957. The joint return filed by them for the year 1957 showed a tax due in the amount of $37,416.85 which was paid on April 21, 1958, when the return was filed. In these circumstances, respondent's determination that they were liable for an addition to tax in the amount of $1,043.56 under Section 6654 of the 1954 Code for underpayment of their estimated tax for 1957 must be, and is, sustained. *Estate of Barney Ruben*, 33 T. C. 1071.

Decision will be entered under Rule 50.

Revenue Ruling 64-328 [8]

Where an insurance policy is purchased on the life of an employee under a so-called "split-dollar" arrangement in which the employer provides the funds to pay the portions of the premiums equal to the increases in the cash surrender value of the policy and the employee is to pay the balance, if any, of the premiums, and in which, from the proceeds of the policy payable at the employee's death, the employer will receive an amount

---

[8]1964–2 Cumulative Bulletin, p. 11.

generally equal to the cash surrender value of the policy and the employee's beneficiary will receive the balance, the employee must include in his income the value of the insurance protection in excess of the portions, if any, of premiums provided by him. *Held also:* The proceeds of the policy payable upon the death of the employee are subject to section 101(a) of the Code.

Revenue Ruling 55–713, C. B. 1955–2, 23, revoked.

Advice has been requested regarding the tax effects of a so-called "split-dollar" arrangement between an employer, Y corporation, and its employee, B.

Under the "split-dollar" arrangement, the employer and employee join in purchasing an insurance contract, in which there is a substantial investment element, on the life of the employee. The employer provides the funds to pay part of the annual premium to the extent of the increase in the cash surrender value each year, and the employee pays the balance of the annual premium. The employer is entitled to receive, out of the proceeds of the policy, an amount equal to the cash surrender value, or at least a sufficient part thereof to equal the funds it has provided for premium payments. The employee has the right to name the beneficiary of the balance of any proceeds payable by reason of his death. In practical effect, although the employee must pay a substantial part of the first premium, after the first year his share of the premium decreases rapidly, and in some cases it even becomes zero after a relatively few years. He thus obtains valuable insurance protection (decreasing each year, but still substantial for a long time) with a relatively small outlay for premiums in the early years, and at little or no cost to him in later years.

Two major types of "split-dollar" arrangements are considered: the endorsement system and the collateral assignment system. In the endorsement system, the employer owns the policy and is responsible for the payment of the annual premiums. The employee is then required to reimburse the employer for his share, if any, of the premiums. Under the collateral assignment system, the employee in form owns the policy and pays the entire premium thereon. The employer in form makes annual loans, without interest (or below the fair rate of interest), to the employee of amounts equal to the yearly increases in the cash surrender value, but not exceeding the annual premiums. The employee executes an assignment of his policy to the employer as collateral security for the loans. The loans are generally payable at the termination of employment or the death of the employee.

A similar problem, involving the endorsement system, was considered in Revenue Ruling 55–713, C. B. 1955–2, 23, wherein it was stated that, in substance, the arrangement is in all essential respects the same as if the employer had made annual loans without interest to the employee, of an amount equal to the annual increases in the cash surrender value of the policies. That ruling concluded that the mere making available of money without interest does not result in taxable income to the payee or a deduction to the payer.

The proper tax treatment of such life insurance arrangements between employers and employees has been reconsidered in the light of the statements in the House and Senate Committee Reports pertaining to the Revenue Act of 1964 that legislation to provide the proper tax treatment of "split-dollar" life insurance arrangements had been deferred because it was believed that "the issues involved in this problem, and the proper solution, including the possibility of administrative action, are in need of further study by the Treasury Department." H. Rept. 749, 88th Congress, 62 (1963); S. Rept. 830, 88th Congress, 78 (1964). The problem has been given such further study, and the conclusion has been reached that Revenue Ruling 55–713 incorrectly analyzed the substance of the "split-dollar" arrangement in stating that the substance of the arrangement is in all essential respects the same as if the employer incorporation makes annual loans without interest to the employee.

Even if the arrangement is cast under the collateral assignment system, it should not be treated in substance as involving a loan from employer to employee, since generally the employee is not expected to repay the funds provided by the employer except out of the proceeds of the policy or from funds available to the employee by reason of the surrender or loan value of the policy. Instead, the substance is, whether the endorsement or collateral assignment system is used, that the employer provides the funds representing the investment element in the life insurance contract, which would, in arm's length dealings, entitle it to the earnings accruing to that element. The effect of the arrangement for the sharing of the cost of annual life insurance premiums, however, is that the earnings on the investment element in the contract are applied to provide current life insurance protection to the employee from year to year, without cost to the employee, to the extent that the earnings are sufficient to do so.

The following table illustrates the practical working of the arrangement in the case of an "accelerated ten payment life policy" issued on the life of an employee aged 45, in the face amount of $100,000. (The figures in the first six columns were taken or derived from an actual policy contained in a case before the Internal Revenue Service.)

The cost of insurance per $1,000 shown in column (7) is taken from the table contained in Revenue Ruling 55–747, C. B. 1955–2, 228, at page 229. This table reflects one-year term costs based upon Table 38, U.S. Life and Actuarial Tables, and $2\frac{1}{2}$ per cent interest.

It is implicit in the illustration, that in each year the "split-dollar" arrangement is in effect, the employer allows the annual earnings on the investment element in the policy to provide for the employee, to the extent that they are sufficient to do so, the cost of the current life insurance protection which the employee should bear were the parties to divide the annual premium costs in accordance with their respective interests in the policy, in an arm's length manner where neither party is attempting to confer a benefit upon the other. Taking the third year of the accelerated payment life policy set out in the illustration as an example, the employer pays the annual premium to the extent of the increase in the cash value, $7,690.00. The employee is obligated to pay only $209.50,

Table 1: Accelerated 10 payment life policy

Policy year (1)	Cash value per $100,000 (2)	Gross premiums (3)	Amount provided by employer, Y (4)	Amount paid by employee, B (5)	Proceeds payable to employee B's beneficiary (6)	Cost of insurance per $1,000 (7)	Value of insurance to employee, B (6)×(7)[1] (8)	Value provided by employer, Y (S)−(5) (9)
1	$7,291.00	$7,899.50	$7,291.00	$608.50	$92,709.00	$6.30	$584.07	0
2	14,775.00	7,899.50	7,484.00	415.50	85,225.00	6.78	577.83	$162.33
3	22,465.00	7,899.50	7,690.00	209.50	77,535.00	7.32	567.56	358.06
4	30,375.00	7,899.50	7,899.50	0	69,625.00	7.89	549.34	549.34
5	35,791.00	5,268.50	5,268.50	0	64,209.00	8.53	547.70	547.70
6	41,356.00	5,268.50	5,268.50	0	58,644.00	9.22	540.70	540.70
7	47,080.00	5,268.50	5,268.50	0	52,920.00	9.97	527.61	527.61
8	52,977.00	5,268.50	5,268.50	0	47,023.00	10.79	507.38	507.38
9	59,062.00	5,268.50	5,268.50	0	40,938.00	11.69	478.57	478.57
10	65,356.00	5,268.50	5,268.50	0	34,644.00	12.67	438.94	438.94
11	66,385.00	0	0	0	33,615.00	13.74	461.87	461.87
15	70,462.00	0	0	0	29,538.00	20.73	612.32	612.32
20	75,373.00	0	0	0	24,627.00	31.51	776.00	776.00

[1]The figures in column (8) represent the figures in column (6) multiplied by the corresponding figures in column (7) and divided by $1,000.

although he receives current insurance protection in the $567.56. The employer confers the benefit of the difference between these amounts ($358.06) by in effect allowing earnings on the investment element to be applied in payment of the cost of the employee's current insurance protection. If the parties were to divide the annual premium in accordance with their respective interests in the policy the employer would pay $7,331.94, and the employee would pay $567.56. Even after the 10 year premium paying period, earnings on the investment element in the contract are used to provide the cost of the employee's insurance protection.

In the typical "split-dollar" arrangement, then, the purpose is, and the effect is, to provide an economic benefit to the employee represented by the amount of the annual premium cost that he should bear and of which he is relieved. It is well settled that the providing of life insurance results in an economic benefit to the insured. See, for example, *Burnet* v. *Frederick B. Wells,* 289 U.S. 670 (1933) Ct. D. 688, C. B. XII-1, 261. An employee who receives an economic benefit under an arrangement with his employer generally must include in his gross income the value of the benefit received. *Commissioner* v. *John H. Smith,* 324 U.S. 177 (1945), Ct. D. 1633, C. B. 1945, 49; *Commissioner* v. *Philip J. LoBue,* 351 U.S. 243 (1956), Ct. D. 1798, C. B. 1956–2, 967. In a situation such as this, in which the economic benefit to the employee is a continuing annual benefit so long as the "split-dollar" arrangement is kept in force, the amount to be included annually is the annual value of the benefit received by the employee under the arrangement, which is held to be an amount equal to the one-year term cost of the declining life insurance protection to which the employee is entitled from year to year, less the portion, if any, provided by the employee. The cost of life insurance protection per $1,000, as shown in the table contained in Revenue Ruling 55–747, *supra,* may be used to compute the one-year term cost.

It is further held that the employer is not entitled to any deduction for its share of the annual premiums since it "is directly or indirectly a beneficiary under such policy" within the meaning of section 264(a)(1) of the Code. G. C. M. 7997, C. B. IX-1, 210, *Wyoming National Bank of Wilkes-Barre* v. *Commissioner,* B. T. A. Memo. Op. Dkt. 50012 (January 27, 1933). *Cf. Omaha Elevator Company* v. *Commissioner,* 6 B. T. A. 817 (1927).

It is further held that the provisions of section 101(a) apply to the proceeds of the policy payable upon the death of B, both as to the portion received by Y corporation and as to the portion received by the designated beneficiary of B.

The same income tax results obtain if the transaction is cast in some other form resulting in a similar benefit to the employee.

In view of the foregoing, Revenue Ruling 55–713 is revoked. The revocation is effective as to policies purchased under "split-dollar" arrangements or utilized to establish such arrangements after November 13, 1964.

Pension Fund of the Laborers' District Council of Western Pennsylvania

The District council pension fund is a little unusual in that it provides pensions for employees of several companies. The fund takes the form of a trust set up by the District Council, representing the construction laborers, and the Master Builders' Association of Western Pennsylvania, representing the employers. As you might expect, a single collective bargaining agreement applies to the union and all the employers, and the pension fund was set up under that agreement.

The following are excerpts from the terms of the pension trust agreement:

Article 1: Definitions

Section 3. Employer *means:*

(d) An Employer who employs Employees represented in collective bargaining by the Council, by a Local which is a member of the Council or by the International Union; or

(e) An Employer who is a member of an Association or an independent Employer, who . . . becomes a party to this Agreement . . .

Section 4. Employee *means:*

(a) An Employee of an Employer as above defined who, from time to time during the term of this Agreement, shall be represented by the Council, a Local affiliated with the Council, or the International Union . . .

Section 10. Break in service *means:*

(a) Failure of an Employee to work for a minimum total of 300 hours for which contributions are made on his behalf in each year of any consecutive two year period; or

(b) Payment in cash of an Employee's Vested Interest. In the event of such a Break in Service, all prior service credits to which said Employee would be entitled under this Plan shall not be credited, and shall be lost. Provided, however, that for the purpose of this Plan, the 300 hour requirement for each year shall be proportionately reduced during any year when the Employee is absent for any of the following reasons:

(a) Service in the Armed Forces of the United States in time of war or other national emergency, provided he shall not have re-enlisted;

(b) Lockouts or duly authorized strikes;

(c) Employment by an Employer hereunder in another capacity;

(d) Sick leave, approved by the Trustees . . .

Article II: Crediting of service

Section 1. Past service.

An Employee who is employed by an Employer as herein defined, and who was a member on June 27, 1956, of a Local Union affiliated with the Council on that date, shall be credited with past service (called "Credited Past Service") from the time he was last initiated into a Local Union affiliated with the Council prior to June 27, 1956. Transferees from Locals not affiliated with the Council will be credited upon entrance into the Plan with service from the date of the transfer only . . . Employees who are not members of the Council or any Local affiliated with the Council shall be credited with Credited Past Service from the first day of their last period of continuous employment by the Council or an Employer as herein defined . . . .

Section 2. Credited future service.

An Employee shall be credited with a number of years of future service (called "Credited Future Service") based on his service after June 27, 1956, or after a subsequent Break in Service and prior to the date of his retirement or termination of employment, as the case may be, equal to the lesser of:

(a) The number of complete years and complete quarters elapsed to the date of his retirement or termination of employment, whichever is applicable; or

(b) The number of years (taken to the next lower quarter) determined by dividing the number of hours for which contributions were made on his behalf by 1,000.

Article III: Eligibility for pension benefits

Section 1. Normal retirement.

On and after July 1, 1958, an Employee who has reached the age of sixty-five (65) with at least one (1) year of Credited Future Service, whose employment is terminated or who elects to retire, shall be eligible for the retirement benefits provided for in Article IV hereof.

Section 2. Early retirement.

On and after July 1, 1958, an Employee who has reached the age of fifty-five (55) with at least one (1) year of Credited Future Service may retire at his option and shall be eligible for early retirement benefits as provided in Article IV hereof.

Article IV: Retirement and death benefits

Section 1. The Retirement benefits, which are not guaranteed by the Employers nor the Trustees, shall be as follows:

(a) Normal Retirement—On and after August 11, 1965, the normal retirement benefit of an Employee eligible for retirement and who applies therefor shall be an amount equal to $3.15 per month multiplied by the sum of the Employee's years of Credited Past Service, if any, plus 2.4% of the total amount contributed for him after his most recent Break in Service, if any.

(b) Early Retirement—The early retirement benefit of an Employee eligible for early retirement and who applies therefor shall be an amount determined as in paragraph (a) of this Section 1 but reduced by one-half (1/2) of one per cent (1%) multiplied by the number of months between his retirement and age sixty-five (65).

Section 2. On and after August 11, 1965, upon the death of a Retired Employee who has been in the industry and has been credited with a total of five (5) past and future credit service units, the designated beneficiary of such Retired Employee or any other person legally entitled thereto, shall be paid the sum of Five Hundred ($500) Dollars.

Article V: Commencement and duration of benefits

Section 1. Retirement benefits shall be payable to an Employee who is eligible therefor and has filed an application therefor as of the first day of the month after such Employee becomes eligible . . .

Section 2. Retirement benefits shall be suspended during any period in which the Employee returns to active service with an Employer . . . .

Section 3. In lieu of any pension benefits provided in Article IV hereof, each eligible Employee upon retirement shall have the right to take a reduced monthly pension payable as aforesaid for the remainder of his life with the provision that if he dies before the monthly benefits paid to him have exhausted his Vested Interest (as defined in Article IV hereof), the balance of such Vested Interest shall be paid to his named beneficiaries or heirs-at-law. The amount of the reduced pension shall be computed on actuarial formulas applicable to the individual case.

Section 5. Any Retirement Benefit to be paid to an eligible Employee under the provisions of Sections 1, 2, or 3 of this Article V which amounts to less than $10.00 per month may be paid quarterly, semi-annually, or in a lump sum equal to the actuarial equivalent thereof in lieu of payment for life, as the Board of Trustees in their sole option shall determine.

Article VI: Vested interest on termination of employment

Section 1. The amount contributed for the benefit of any Employee shall vest in such Employee in accordance with the following schedule:

Years of credited future service	% of contributions vested on termination
0-2	0
3	25
4	31
5	37
6	43
7	50
8	56
9	62
10	68
11	75
12	81
13	87
14	93
15 and over	100

Section 2. Termination of Employment shall be deemed to have occurred when there is a Break in Service as herein defined.

Section 3. The amount of Vested interest, as provided above, standing to an Employee's credit shall be paid to the Employee on termination of employment other than by reason of death or retirement in the form of deferred pension payable at age sixty-five (65) or in a reduced pension payable at ages between fifty-five (55) and sixty-five (65) or in such other manner, including the payment thereof in cash, as the Trustees in their sole discretion shall determine.

Section 4. In the event of the death of an Employee prior to his retirement, the amount of Vested Interest standing to his credit shall be paid in a reasonable time to the beneficiary or beneficiaries said Employee shall have designated on a form approved by the Trustees. If any Employee shall fail to designate a beneficiary, the Trustees shall be empowered to designate a beneficiary or beneficiaries on his behalf, but only among the following in the order named: the (1) spouse, (2) children, (3) parents, (4) brothers and sisters, nephews and nieces, and (5) estate of the Employee.

Article VII: Payments to trust fund

Section 1. Effective June 27, 1956, and continuing through May 31,

1957, each Employer shall pay monthly into the Trust Fund on or before the 15th day of the following month, the sum of Five Cents (5¢) per hour worked by the Employees of such Employer.

Section 2. Beginning June 1, 1957, and continuing through May 31, 1958, each Employer shall pay as aforesaid into the Trust Fund the sum of Ten Cents (10¢) per hour worked by the Employees of such Employer.

Section 3. For a period of five (5) years beginning June 1, 1957, there shall be no increase in the amount of the Employer's contribution over the amount provided for in Section 2 of this Article.

Section 5. The entire obligation of the Employer hereunder shall be limited to the payment of such moneys as provided herein. No other financial contribution or payment shall be required of the Employer for any reason.

Section 6. In any case in which Sections 1 and 2 hereof are not applicable, the applicable collective bargaining agreement shall prevail.

Article XI: Administration of the fund

Section 1. The Pension Fund shall be administered by a Board of Trustees, half of whom shall be designated as Employer Trustees and half of whom shall be designated as Employee Trustees. One (1) of such Trustees shall be appointed Chairman of the Fund and one (1) of such Trustees shall be appointed Secretary-Treasurer of the Fund, it being provided, however, that at all times one (1) of these officers shall be an Employer representative and one (1) of these officers shall be an Employee representative. The respective offices shall be filled by Employee and Employer Trustees alternately on an annual basis.

Section 4. N. S. Stirone, Milton Piper and Frank Costello are hereby designated as Employee Trustees and Sherman T. Rock, William C. Bowden and Pasquale Navarro are hereby designated as Employer Trustees . . .

Article XIII: Approval by internal revenue service

Section 1. This Agreement and Declaration of Trust shall be submitted to the Internal Revenue Service for approval for such tax purposes. The parties agree that the Trustees may make such amendments to this Agreement and Declaration of Trust as may be necessary to obtain such approval.

1. What do you suppose is meant by the "approval" of the Internal Revenue Service, specified in Article XIII, Section 1?

2. The trust agreement shows some careless drafting. What retirement benefits are actually prescribed, and what benefits were intended?

3. What may an employee or anyone else receive from the trust under the following circumstances, and what will the tax treatment be in each case?
a) The employee dies before retirement
b) He quits his job and goes to another employer
c) He becomes disabled and cannot work
d) He retires
e) He dies after retirement

4. When are the employers entitled to a deduction for contributions to the pension fund?

Chapter thirteen

Estate and gift taxes

Although it may not be obvious to you at this point why a discussion of estate and gift taxes is included in this book, they do have implications for a number of the topics we have already discussed. The handling of personal investments requires an appreciation of the impact of estate and gift taxes and possibilities for minimizing those taxes. Decisions relating to the form of ownership of investments, the distribution of ownership within a family group, the realization or postponement of capital gains, and the method of transfer from older to younger generations are all affected by estate and gift tax considerations. These considerations become particularly important where ownership of a business is largely concentrated in the hands of an individual or a family group. The business may be a proprietorship, a partnership, or a corporation, but no matter what its legal form, plans for meeting estate or gift tax payments without liquidation or sale of the business are important. Finally, there are implications for corporate compensation policies in the estate and gift tax law. The planning of both pension benefits and life insurance benefits for employees involves consideration of estate and sometimes gift taxes.

There are two kinds of taxes generally imposed in a transfer of property at someone's death: estate taxes and inheritance taxes. The federal government imposes only an estate tax; many of the states impose inheritance taxes. An estate tax is imposed on the estate of a deceased person. The rate of tax is independent of who receives the estate, except that there may be certain exclusions and exemptions for charitable bequests and bequests to a surviving spouse. An inheritance tax, on the other hand, is imposed upon what a beneficiary receives from an estate.

Inheritance tax rates are generally a function of the relation of the beneficiary to the deceased. Amounts received by a surviving spouse or by a child of the deceased person are likely to be taxed at lower rates than amounts received by parents or brothers or sisters, which in turn are likely to be taxed at lower rates than amounts received by persons not related to the deceased. It has been argued that a federal inheritance tax would be preferable to the estate tax, and this reasoning seems to have impressed most of the states.

Gross estate

Sections 2031–2044 of the Internal Revenue Code deal with the gross estate. Sections 2031 and 2033 should be read together, as they describe in general terms what goes into a gross estate.

Sections 2035, 2037, and 2043 are all concerned with the nature of the transfer of property at death. Section 2037 deals with cases where the transfer of property is not made in a will but for some other reason takes place at a person's death. Section 2035 deals with gifts made by a person who expects to die soon, for the purpose of avoiding estate tax. And section 2043 deals with transfers that are not entirely bequests and yet not entirely paid for either.

Section 2040 deals with the special problems that arise where property is held in a joint tenancy or a tenancy by the entirety (which is a joint tenancy between a husband and wife). Most married couples use joint bank accounts and if they own a home, hold it as joint tenants. The most important characteristic of a joint tenancy is the automatic right of survivorship. If two people own property as joint tenants and one of them dies, the other automatically is entitled to the entire property, regardless of any will made by the person who died. For this reason, joint tenancies are popular with married couples. Whether or not the husband or wife has a will, the survivor will automatically inherit their home. And the fact that the will need not mention the home may keep the home out of the estate of the deceased person, for probate purposes. This can reduce the cost of probating the estate and frequently reduce state taxes.

Section 2039 relates to pension benefits. Where a retired person receives a pension in the form of an annuity—usually monthly payments—he generally has the option when he retires of taking an annuity for the balance of his own life or taking a joint and survivor annuity, to be paid until both he and his wife have died. The joint and survivor annuity arrangement is by far the more popular. The question arises, of course, whether the retired person, at his death, leaves anything to his widow. That is, must his estate include the value of the annuity payments she will receive for the rest of her life? Section 2039 answers this question.

Section 2042 deals with the proceeds of life insurance. Usually, under group life insurance protection provided by an employer for employees, the proceeds of the life insurance are paid to the employee's estate when he dies.

Is this a sensible arrangement, considering section 2042? How can you arrange insurance on your own life so that the proceeds will not be included in your estate and made subject to estate taxes?

Taxable estate

Sections 2051–2056 of the Code deal with calculation of the taxable estate. As you would expect, expenses of the estate and charitable contributions are deductible and not subject to tax. Sections 2053 and 2055 cover these deductions.

The two most important deductions are the $60,000 exemption under section 2052 and the marital deduction under section 2056. The former simply means that an estate of less than $60,000, after expenses and charitable gifts, is not subject to tax at all. The second is a little more complicated. The origin of the marital deduction lies in community property laws. Until 1942, beneficiaries of persons who died residents of community property states enjoyed a significant estate tax advantage. A widow could generally claim that half the property acquired by her husband during his life belonged to her and therefore was not a part of his estate and not subject to estate taxes. The husband could, of course, use the same argument with respect to property left by his deceased wife. To correct the inequity between residents of community property states and residents of other states, Congress in 1942 amended the Code to eliminate the advantage enjoyed in community property states. Then in 1948 when joint income tax returns were introduced, Congress restored the earlier advantage but made it available to everyone. Notice how section 2056 accomplishes the same thing as was accomplished before 1942 by community property.

The marital deduction is enormously important in tax planning because of the very large reduction it can bring about in an estate tax. Consequently it becomes very important to know exactly what kinds of bequests to a surviving spouse will qualify for the marital deduction. This is an extraordinarily complicated aspect of estate taxation. We will refer to just one aspect of it later in the chapter.

Considering sections 2052 and 2056 together, how large an estate can a person leave completely free of federal estate tax?

The estate tax

Section 2001 defines the progressive estate tax rates. Section 2011 establishes the credit for state death taxes. Since this credit is subtracted from the federal estate tax, it is clear that up to a certain extent a death tax imposed by a state does not actually cost the estate of a deceased person anything. It simply diverts taxes from the federal government to a state government. Hence, every state imposes death taxes that will at least amount to the credit authorized under section 2011.

Section 2013 deals with the problem that arises where one person dies leaving property to another person who dies soon after. Avoiding the heavy burden of successive estate taxes once presented difficult problems in estate planning, but section 2013 makes this planning considerably easier.

Installment payments

Section 6166 was added to the Code by the Technical Amendments Act of 1958. It met the argument that the federal estate tax caused serious hardship where the owner of a business attempted to keep the business within his family after his death. What frequently happened was that in order to pay estate taxes, it was necessary either to liquidate or to sell the business. This was unfortunate for the family, and it had consequences for the entire economy that were felt to be undesirable.

Gift tax

Clearly, if the estate tax is going to be effective at all, there must be something to prevent a person from disposing of all his property, or substantially all of it, before his death, tax-free. We have already seen that certain gifts made by a person before his death may be included in his estate as gifts in contemplation of death, under section 2035. But as you can see from that section, it has very limited application to gifts generally.

A gift tax is not an essential corollary to an estate tax. For example, in the United Kingdom, where estate tax rates are extremely high, there is no gift tax. The rule with respect to gifts in contemplation of death is rather more strict, however. In the United Kingdom any gift made within five years of death is treated as made in contemplation of death, regardless of the motive of the donor. And gifts made more than five years before death may be treated as gifts in contemplation of death, depending upon the circumstances. But gifts that are not in contemplation of death are completely tax-free. This has made possible the transmission of some very large English estates through several generations with no tax whatever.

Section 2502 of the Code taxes gifts at rates that are three quarters of the corresponding estate tax rate. But note that section 2503 applies the tax to the *net* gift. In the case of the estate tax, the tax is figured on the taxable estate, from which the taxes have not yet been deducted. That is, the estate tax is not on the net estate that passes to beneficiaries but on the net estate plus estate taxes. Compared with the estate tax, then, the gift tax is a little lower than it at first appears.

Notice that the gift tax is a progressive tax, and that in determining your rate bracket, you must take into account not just the gifts made in a single year but all of the gifts made since June 6, 1932. This means that as the years go on, if you make gifts continually, you work yourself into higher and higher gift tax brackets.

There are two important exclusions from the gift tax: one is described in section 2503(b) and the other in section 2521. And as you might expect, there is a provision analogous to the marital deduction for the estate tax. Sections 2513 and 2523 deal with gifts made by one spouse with the consent of the other, and by one spouse to the other.

In the case of a married couple with four children, how much can the father give his children free of gift tax?

Section 2517 relates to benefits under a pension plan. We discussed the choice that an employee can generally make when he retires between a pension annuity payable until his death and a pension annuity paid as long as either he or his wife is alive.

Why might this choice involve gift taxes, and what does section 2517 accomplish?

Basis

In any particular case where you are trying to decide whether it is better for a person to give away property during his lifetime or to leave it in his estate, some thought should be given to the basis rules in sections 1014 and 1015 of the Code.

Section 1014 has been the subject of a good deal of criticism. In 1964, the administration proposed legislation to impose a capital gains tax on an estate; a tax would have been imposed as though the event of death constituted sale of the assets in the estate at their fair market value with consequent realization of gains. The proposal never became law, however, and section 1014 stands as an exception to the general rule that the basis of an asset can be increased only as the result of a transaction giving rise to taxable gains. Section 1015, on the other hand, describes the consequences you ought to expect from a transaction in which no gain or loss is realized for tax purposes.

Uses of trusts and life estates

Tax aspects of inter-vivos trusts are extremely complicated. An inter-vivos trust is one set up by a living person during his lifetime. We are not going to be concerned with this kind of trust. A testamentary trust, on the other hand, is a trust established by someone at his death, usually in a will. The purpose of a testamentary trust is generally to give someone the benefit of assets in an estate for a limited period of time.

There are many reasons which have nothing to do with taxes for the establishment of a testamentary trust. For example, a person with very young children may wish to provide in his will that on the event of his death, property will be held in trust for the children with the income from the trust, and perhaps the principal under certain circumstances, to be used for the benefit of the children. But there are tax reasons as well for wanting to establish a trust. For example, a father might leave his entire estate to be placed in trust at his death, with his son drawing the income of the trust for life, with the income next going to a grandson for life, and with a great-grandson finally receiving the principal of the trust on his twenty-first birthday. There are legal limits to the life of such a trust. The most common rule is that the trust must terminate within "lives in being plus 21 years." In the example above, as long as the son and grandson are alive at the testator's death, the trust may last up to twenty-one years after the death of the survivor of the two. This makes it possible for the trust to pay its income to the son or the grandson until both are dead, and then to pay income to a great-grandson, terminating on his twenty-first birthday.

In terms of estate taxes, what has been accomplished in the example above is that a single estate tax was paid on the testator's death, but no estate taxes were paid on the son's death or on the grandson's death, since the ending of a life estate in a trust is simply not a taxable transfer.

It might occur to you that an obvious arrangement for a man to make in his will would consist of a trust distributing income to his widow for her life and then distributing its principal to his children. But take a look again at section 2056 to see what happens to the marital deduction in this case.

> *Bearing in mind the value of the marital deduction and the advantage of the trust, can you think of a simple strategy to minimize estate taxes for a man who wants to be sure that his widow will be taken care of for life, and to pass his property to his children?*

U.S. v. Rhode Island Hospital Trust Co.[1]

Before Aldrich, *Chief Judge;* Coffin, *Circuit Judge;* and Caffrey, *District Judge.*

Opinion of the court

Coffin, Circuit Judge: This appeal presents the question whether the proceeds of a life insurance policy on decedent's life are properly includable in the gross estate of the decedent by reason of the alleged possession at his death of "any of the incidents of ownership, exercisable either alone or in conjunction with any other person," under section 2042 of the Internal Revenue Code of 1954, 26 U.S.C. § 2042.[2]

The Commissioner of Internal Revenue having included the proceeds of an insurance policy on the life of Holton W. Horton (decedent) in his gross estate and the sum of $14,185.85 in federal estate taxes and $1,004. 67 in interest having been paid, the plaintiffs, co-executors under his will, made timely claim for refund and brought this action for recovery under 28 U.S.C. § 1346 (a), alleging that such sums were erroneously assessed. The matter was submitted to the district court upon an agreed

---

[1] 355 F. 2d 7 (United States Court of Appeals, 1st Circuit, 1966).

[2] The relevant part of the taxing statute, section 2042, is as follows: "The value of the gross estate shall include the value of all property— "(2) Receivable by other beneficiaries.—To the extent of the amount receivable by all other beneficiaries as insurance under policies on the life of the decedent with respect to which the decedent possessed at his death any of the incidents of ownership, exercisable either alone or in conjunction with any other person. . . ."

statement of facts and depositions. The district court found for the plaintiffs, D.R.I., 1965, 241 F. Supp. 586, and the government appeals.

The facts, undisputed, are of two kinds: "intent facts"—those relating to the conduct and understanding of the insured and his father, who was the instigator, premium payer, and primary beneficiary of the policy; and the "policy facts"—those revealed by the insurance contract itself.

Decedent's father, Charles A. Horton, was a textile executive, a prominent businessman in his community, and according to the testimony, "a man with strong convictions and vigorous action." Charles and his wife, Louise, had two sons, decedent and A. Trowbridge Horton. In 1924, when decedent was 18 and Trowbridge 19, their father purchased an insurance policy on the life of each boy from Massachusetts Mutual Life Insurance Company. The policies were identical, each having the face amount of $50,000, the proceeds being payable to Charles and Louise, equally, or to the survivor.

Charles Horton's purpose was to assure that funds would be available for his wife, should he and either son die. Charles kept the policies in his safe deposit box and paid all premiums throughout his life. Under the policies, however, the right to change beneficiaries had been reserved to the sons. In January, 1952, the boys' mother, Louise, died. In March, 1952, Charles told each of his sons to go to the insurance company's office and sign a change of beneficiary form. The amendment executed by decedent named his father as primary beneficiary, with decedent's wife, brother, and the executors of administrators of the last survivor being the successive beneficiaries. After this amendment, decedent continued to retain the right to make further changes, but none was made. Decedent died on April 1, 1958, survived by his wife and father. His father died on October 2, 1961.

The father, Charles, regarded the policies as belonging to him, saying at one point that it would be "out of the question" for the sons to claim them. Decedent's brother never discussed the policies with his father, never asked for a loan based on the policies, obediently signed the change of beneficiary form at his father's request, and considered the policy on his life as the property of his father. Decedent's widow recalled only that decedent had once told her that his father had a policy on himself and his brother but that "in no way did it mean anything to us or would it ever. It was completely his." She added that her husband, the decedent, had wanted more insurance of his own, but was not able to obtain it.

Coming to what we call "policy facts," a careful reading of the policy, captioned "Ordinary Life Policy—Convertible," reveals the following rights, privileges, or powers accorded to the decedent.

—Right to change beneficiary. In the application, an unrestricted change of beneficiary provision was elected by striking out two alternative and more limited provisions.[3] The policy itself indicated reservation

---

[3] It is noted that with regard to the unrestricted option (Option A), the policy application contains the following words: "If a [sic] is chosen the policy may become part of the estate in case of bankruptcy."

of "the right successively to change the beneficiary" by the insertion of typewritten dashes where, otherwise, the word "not" would have been inserted.

—Assignment. No assignment would be recognized until the original assignment, a duplicate, or a certified copy was filed with the company. The company did not assume responsibility for the validity of an assignment.

—Dividends. The insured had the option to have dividends paid in cash, used to reduce premiums, used to purchase paid-up additions, or accumulate subject to withdrawal on demand.

—Loans. On condition that the unlimited right to change the beneficiary was reserved, as in this case, the company would "loan on the signature of the insured alone."

—Survival. Should no beneficiary survive the insured, the proceeds were payable to his executors and administrators.

—Alteration. The policy could be altered only on the written request of the insured and of "other parties in interest."

—Discharge of company's obligations. The company would not be responsible for the conduct of any trustee or for the determination of the identity or rights of beneficiaries. Payment at the direction of a trustee or in good faith to a beneficiary would discharge the company of its contractual obligations. Beneficiaries were advised by the policy that they need hire no firm or person to collect the amount payable under the policy, but that they would save time and expense by writing to the company directly.

—Voting. Decedent, by virtue of the policy, was a member of the Massachusetts Mutual Life Insurance Company and entitled to vote.

The plaintiffs contend that the district court properly held that decedent possessed no incidents of ownership in the policy; that the term "incidents of ownership" refers to the rights of insured or his estate to the economic benefits of the policy; that the question of possession of such incidents is one of fact; that such possession depends upon all relevant facts and circumstances, including the intention of the parties; and that these facts and circumstances clearly establish that decedent's father was the real owner of the policy, while decedent was merely the nominal owner, having no real economic interest in it.

The government asserts that, as a matter of law, the facts bring this case squarely within the reach of section 2042, as applied by the cases, notwithstanding the evidence as to the intentions and extra-policy circumstances of the parties, and the lack of economic benefit to decedent.

At the outset we are confronted with the issue of the nature of this review. It is undoubtedly true that the question of possession of incidents of ownership of a life insurance policy is one of fact, the plaintiff having the burden of proving nonpossession of all. *Piggott, Estate of* v. *Commissioner*, 6 Cir., 1965, 340 F. 2d 829; *Fried* v. *Granger*, W.D. Pa., 1952, 105 F. Supp. 564, *affirmed*, 3 Cir., 1953, 202 F. 2d 150; *Hall* v. *Wheeler*, D.Me., 1959, 174 F. Supp. 418; *Collino, Estate of* v. *Commissioner*, 1956, 25 T.C. 1026. But where all of the evidentiary facts appear, we are faced with a question of law not of fact. Were we to proceed otherwise, cases presenting identical or closely similar facts in this technical and complex field could be decided oppositely, to the disadvantage of equitable tax administration.

Taking the subsidiary facts as presented to the district court, we differ with its conclusion that "the decedent's father was actually the real owner of the various incidents of ownership in said policy." But in differing we recognize that early holdings and occasional dicta, early and late, have invited litigation. This is the kind of case where the government enters, appearing to seek its pound of flesh on the basis of petty technicality, while the taxpayer's decedent generally appears as a person who had very little to do with the insurance policy which is causing so much trouble to his estate. If such hard cases have not made bad law, they have at least made bad dicta. Although the Supreme Court has recently (indeed, since the principal hearing of this case before the district court) spoken strongly and succinctly on this issue in *Commissioner* v. *Estate of Noel*, 1965, 380 U.S. 678, of which more will be said, we think it appropriate to set forth the considerations of fact, law, and policy which have persuaded us.

To begin, the statute which bears on this case has a reason for being, is part of a general rationale and tax law pattern, and is deliberately precise. Before the Revenue Act of 1942, the tax criterion governing cases in this area was "policies taken out" by the decedent on his own life. Section 302(g), Revenue Act of 1926, ch. 27, 44 Stat. 9. This led to difficult problems of interpretation, which the courts resolved by creating two criteria: "payment of premiums" and possession of "incidents of ownership." The Revenue Act of 1942, ch. 619, 56 Stat. 798, section 404, eliminated the "policies taken out" language, and sanctified the judicial gloss, with Congress, in its committee reports, including an illustrative list of the kinds of rights included under "incidents of ownership." These included decedent's right to change beneficiaries, to borrow, to assign, to revoke an assignment, and to surrender or cancel. H. Rep. No. 2333, 77th Cong., 2d Sess., p. 164, 1942–2 *Cum. Bull.* 372, 491.[4]

In acting this way, Congress was, we think, trying to introduce some certitude in a landscape of shifting sands. In the provision which was the predecessor of section 2042, it was not trying to tax the *extent* of the interest of the decedent. That it knew how to do this is evident, for example, from a reading of section 2033 of the Internal Revenue Code of 1954, 26 U.S.C. § 2033, which includes in the gross estate of the decedent "the value of all property . . . to the extent of the interest therein . . ." What it was attempting to reach in section 2042 and some other sections was the *power* to dispose of property, the same power that the Supreme Court recognized as a basis for exercise of the tax instrument in *Chase National Bank* v. *United States*, 1929, 278 U.S. 327. Power can be and is exercised by one possessed of less than complete legal and equitable title. The very phrase "incidents of ownership" connotes something partial, minor, or even fractional in its scope. It speaks more of possibility than of probability.

---

[4]Subsequently, the Revenue Act of 1954 eliminated the premium payment test, leaving possession of "any incidents of ownership" as the sole criterion. 26 U.S.C. § 2042. Sen. Rep. No. 1622, 83d Cong., 2d Sess., p. 472 et seq.

Plaintiffs seize on section 20.2042–1(c)(2) of the Treasury Regulations on Estate Tax, which says ". . . the term 'incidents of ownership' is not limited in its meaning to ownership of the policy in the technical legal sense. Generally speaking, the term has reference to the right of the insured or his estate to the economic benefits of the policy." Plaintiffs urge that there must be "a real control over the economic benefits." To this there are two answers. First, it is clear that the reference to ownership in the "technical legal sense" is not abandoned and supplanted by reference to "economic benefits." Second, the regulation goes on to list illustrative powers referred to by Congress in its reports. All of these are powers which may or may not enrich decedent's estate, but which can affect the transfer of the policy proceeds.

Viewed against this background, what power did decedent possess? This is the relevant question—not how did he feel or act. Did he have a capacity to do something to affect the disposition of the policy if he had wanted to? Without gaining possession of the policy itself, he could have borrowed on the policy. He could have changed the method of using dividends. He could have assigned the policy. He could have revoked the assignment. He could vote. Should he have gained possession of the policy by trick (as by filing an affidavit that the policy was lost), force, or chance, he could have changed the beneficiary, and made the change of record irrevocable. See *Alfama* v. *Rose*, 1949, 323 Mass. 643. Other such possibilities might be imagined. We cite these only to evidence the existence of some power in decedent to affect the disposition of the policy proceeds. In addition, he always possessed a negative power. His signature was necessary to a change in beneficiary, to a surrender for cash value, to an alteration in the policy, to a change in dividend options. Even with this most limited power, he would be exercising an incident of ownership "in conjunction with" another person. *Commissioner* v. *Karagheusian, Estate of,* 2 Cir., 1956, 233 F. 2d 197; *Godfrey* v. *Smyth* 9 Cir., 1950, 180 F. 2d 220; *Hall* v. *Wheeler*, D. Me., 1959, 174 F. Supp. 418.

The existence of such powers in the decedent is to be distinguished from such rights as may have existed in decedent's father or duties owed the father by decedent. It is, therefore, no answer that decedent's father might have proceeded against him at law or in equity. The company made it clear in the contract that it bore no responsibility for the validity of an assignment, that it could pay a beneficiary without recourse, and that it was under no obligation to see to the carrying out of any trust. It even made clear that a beneficiary need only write to the home office to receive payment. Should a third party—for example, an innocent creditor who had given valuable consideration to decedent—receive the proceeds of the policy, the proceeds of a loan on the policy, or the cash value, it could not be said that the transaction between decedent and such third person would in all such cases be nugatory. For decedent had some powers— which could, if exercised alone or in conjunction with another, affect the disposition of some or all of the proceeds of the policy.

Nor is it a compelling argument that decedent lacked physical possession of the policy. *Commissioner* v. *Estate of Noel,* 1965, 380 U.S. 678; *Piggott, Estate of* v. *Commissioner,* 6 Cir., 1965, 340 F. 2d 829; *Godfrey* v. *Smyth*, 9 Cir., 1950, 180 F. 2d 220; *Hall* v. *Wheeler*, D. Me.,

1959, 174 F. Supp. 418. Moreover, as we have noted, some rights could be exercised without physical possession of the policy.

The cases arising from similar facts over nearly a quarter of a century give little support, in their holdings, to plaintiffs. Even *Doerken, Estate of* v. *Commissioner,* 1942, 46 B.T.A. 809, heavily relied upon by plaintiffs, turned on the issue whether or not decedent (as opposed to a corporation in which he had a one-fourth interest) had "taken out" the policy on decedent's life. It was not a decision that decedent possessed no incidents of ownership. Decisions in subsequent cases have, on the evidence presented, almost uniformly held the "policy facts" (reservation of rights in the policy) impregnable to attack from the "intent facts." *Piggott, Estate of* v. *Commissioner,* 6 Cir., 1965, 340 F. 2d 829; *Hall* v. *Wheeler,* D. Me., 1959, 174 F. Supp. 418; *Fried* v. *Granger,* W. D. Pa., 1952, 105 F. Supp. 564, *affirmed,* 3 Cir., 1953, 202 F. 2d 150; *Collino, Estate of* v. *Commissioner,* 1956, 25 T.C. 1026; *McCoy, Estate of* v. *Commissioner,* 1961, 20 T.C.M. 224.

Morrow, Estate of v. *Commissioner,* 1953, 19 T.C. 1068, was cited by plaintiffs as a case holding that even though the decedent designated a beneficiary who actually received one-half the proceeds of the policy, the policy proceeds were not includable in decedent's estate. This is a misreading of the facts. In *Morrow,* decedent's employer had purchased the policy and retained all rights, including the right to change beneficiaries. However, it had, as part of its employee insurance plan, undertaken to pay one-half of the proceeds to decedent's family, and had asked decedent to designate a member or members of his immediate family. The court held that such persons were not beneficiaries under the policy, that the employer was the only beneficiary, that its contract obligation, if any, was to pay a sum equal to half the policy proceeds to such persons, and that this was not a contract of insurance and thus not within the thrust of the predecessor to section 2042.[5]

Finally, and most recently, the Supreme Court, in *Commissioner* v. *Estate of Noel,* 1965, 380 U.S. 678, dealt with a factual situation at least as favorable to the decedent's estate as that in this case. In *Noel,* two airline flight insurance policies were purchased on decedent's life, the two premiums of $2.50 each being supplied by decedent's wife. Decedent was quoted as having instructed the sales clerk to "give them to my wife. They are hers. I no longer have anything to do with them." The contracts reserved to the decedent the rights of assignment and change of beneficiary. Several hours later decedent died when his plane crashed. Three alternative arguments were made to support the conclusion that decedent had reserved no incident of ownership in the policies: (1) that decedent's wife purchased the policies and therefore owned them; (2)

---

[5]The reservation of a right in the insured to change the beneficiary was found to be of no significance and the policy proceeds were held not includable in his estate in *Lamade* v. *Brownell,* M.D. Pa., 1965, 245 F. Supp. 691. However, in that case, unlike the one before us, there existed an absolute assignment of the policy, the assignees of the policy were recognized by the insurer as the owners of the policy and could act independently of the insured, and had the insured attempted to change the beneficiary such attempt would have been ignored by the insurer.

that, even if decedent had owned them, he had given them to her; and (3) that even if he had reserved contractual powers, such powers were illusory, being impossible to exercise between take-off and crash.

The court rejected the first contention by saying that the policies themselves rebut the wife's claim of complete ownership with an irrevocable right to remain the beneficiary. As to the second, it held that the power to assign the policies remained in the decedent at the time of his death since the alleged assignment had not been endorsed on the policies as was required.

The third point, that of illusory power to exercise the retained legal rights, was answered in the following language, 380 U.S. at 684:

> "We hold that estate tax liability for policies with respect to which the decedent possessed at his death any of the incidents of ownership depends on a general, legal power to exercise ownership, without regard to the owner's ability to exercise it at a particular moment."

To the principal of heavy predominance of the "policy facts" over the "intent facts" there must be added the caveat that, where the insurance contract itself does not reflect the instructions of the parties, as where an agent, on his own initiative, inserts a reservation of right to change a beneficiary contrary to the intentions which had been expressed to him, no incidents of ownership are thereby created. *National Metropolitan Bank* v. *United States*, Ct. Cl., 1950, 87 F. Supp. 773; *Schongalla* v. *Hickey*, 2 Cir. 1945, 149 F. 2d 687. The case before us presents no such issue, for the right in decedent to change beneficiaries was recognized on the one occasion when it was exercised and this right continued thereafter.

While decisions against the estate of a passive but power-possessing decedent may often conflict with the honest intentions and understanding of premium-paying beneficiaries and insureds, the alternative of abandoning the insistence on the governing nature of the contract, in most cases, is less desirable. The drawing of a useful line would be impossible; there would be a much wider range of varying decisions on similar facts; and there would be an invitation to unprincipled estate manipulation. As government counsel has pointed out, there could always be a formally executed side agreement under which the insured clearly surrenders to the beneficiary all his rights to the policy, such agreement to be brought to light only in the event of the decedent's dying before the beneficiary.

In any event, the statute has been on the books since the Revenue Act of 1942. This is only one of a number of cases applying it in the face of considerable external evidence of intent. Charles Horton, who caused the policy to be taken out, saw fit to vest decedent with rights in the policy and to allow such rights to continue for thirty-four years. Charles was a successful businessman and with as much incentive, opportunity, and capacity to be aware of the laws of the land as most people. It is difficult to speculate what purpose he thought was being served by his son's retention of rights in the policy. Had he wished to deprive his son of all incidents of ownership in the policy, this result could easily have been accomplished. But the step was not taken. We find that the decedent died, possessing at least an incident of ownership in the policy on his life.

Judgment will be entered vacating the judgment of the district court and ordering judgment for the defendant.

Estate of Walter Perry

Walter Perry is the general manager of the New Hampshire division of a large national manufacturing company. The division was originally a company owned by Perry, which he had established many years ago on an investment of $25,000. Five years ago he traded all the stock in the company for a large block of stock in the national manufacturing concern. The trade was a tax-free exchange, and the stock Mr. Perry received (for which there is a readily ascertainable market) was worth about $3.5 million. Today the stock is worth $4 million, and Perry is concerned about what he should do with it.

Perry is fifty-five years old. His current income consists of a $65,000 salary and dividends of about $48,000, of which $45,000 is attributable to his block of stock in the company for which he works. He expects to retire at sixty-five. His best guess is that his salary will be $75,000 by the time he retires, and on this assumption his pension, which will be fully taxable to him, will be $35,000 a year. He will receive this pension until his death, and if he should die before his wife, she will receive two-thirds of his pension for the rest of her life.

Perry's assets consist of the $4 million block of stock already mentioned, about $75,000 worth of other securities, New Hampshire real estate (which he owns jointly with his wife) worth $40,000, and life insurance payable to his estate (on which he has paid all the premiums and over which he has complete control) of $100,000.

Perry's wife Helen is fifty-two years old. She has no income or property of her own, except for the half interest in her husband's real estate. She contributed no funds to the purchase of the real estate; it was paid for entirely out of her husband's earnings.

The Perrys have two children. Their son Arthur is thirty-one years old. He is an employee of the federal government, and his salary is about $13,500. He was recently married and as yet has no children. He owns a home and has a few investments but no substantial property. Their daughter, Susan Perry Rawlins, is twenty-seven years old and married to a doctor. They have two children. Her husband earns about $19,000 a year; he owns a home, a car, a few securities, and has a modest bank account. But like his brother-in-law, he has no substantial property.

Perry has never given any of his stock to his wife or children. Until a few years ago, he hoped that his son would take over the family business, and he expected to leave substantially all the stock in his business to the son. When it became evident that Arthur had no interest in the business and never would have, Perry decided to merge his company into a larger corporation. The merger was completed five years ago, and Perry received the stock described above. He agreed at the time of the merger not to dispose of any of this stock for a period of five years. He is now free to do what he likes with the stock, and it is clear that he is the last member of his family who will be associated with the management of the company. He is anxious to handle the stock in a way that will bring the greatest financial benefit to his family.

Currently, Perry and his wife are giving about $10,000 a year to charity and are spending almost all of their after-tax income. They of course file joint income tax returns, and apart from charitable deductions and the deduction for state income taxes, they report only about $4000 in (nonbusiness) deductible expenses in computing taxable income. Perry believes they could live comfortably on about $40,000 a year after taxes (and after charitable contributions), but he wants to be sure of at least that much. He expects that by the time he retires, the dividends on his stock will have about doubled.

Perry is considering the possibility of selling some of his stock outright. He could invest the proceeds in municipal or state bonds, on which the interest is exempt from federal income tax. Currently he could obtain about $2\frac{3}{4}$ per cent on municipal bonds. He is also considering the advisability of making a gift of some of his stock to his wife or to his children. He is concerned that his wife be adequately provided for, for the rest of her life, but he intends that ultimately all of his assets, except for a charitable gift discussed below, will be divided equally between his children.

For some years, Perry has intended to leave $500,000 to the college he attended. He is wondering whether it would be better, in the interest of reducing taxes, to make a series of annual gifts totaling $500,000.

As a tax consultant, advise Perry of the consequences of the alternatives he is considering. Prepare calculations for the following specific possibilities:

(1) Perry sells all his stock and invests the proceeds, less taxes, in municipal bonds (of which a quarter are New Hampshire bonds) yielding $2\frac{3}{4}$ per cent. On his death, he leaves $500,000 to his college and the rest of his property to his widow. Five years later, she dies and leaves everything to the children.

(2) Perry does not dispose of any of his property before his death. On his death, he leaves $500,000 to his college and everything else

*to his widow. At the time of his death, the value of the stock is $6
million. Five years later, Mrs. Perry dies and leaves everything to
the children. At the time of her death, the value of the stock has
risen another 10 per cent.*

*(3) Perry gives some stock to his children, keeping enough to pro-
vide the dividend income he and his wife need to give them $40,000
a year after taxes, charitable gifts, and deductible expenses but
selling enough to pay gift taxes. In addition to his regular charitable gifts of $10,000 a year, he gives $10,000 a year in stock for
fifteen years to his college. At the end of fifteen years he dies, leaving $350,000 in stock to the college. He leaves the real estate to his
wife, together with enough stock to bring her total income after
taxes, $10,000 of charitable gifts, and $4,000 of other deductions, to
$25,000. The balance of the stock he leaves to their children. Mrs.
Perry dies five years after her husband and leaves everything to the
children. At his death, the value of the stock has increased by 50 per
cent, and on her death, it has increased by another 10 per cent.*

*Compare what the children will have after their mother's death in
(1), (2), and (3). Should the Perrys make better use of the estate tax
marital deduction in (3)?*

Additional data

The value of Mrs. Perry's interest in her husband's pension will *not*
be included in his estate, under section 2039 of the Internal Revenue
Code.

Perry has never used any of the "specific exemption" for gift tax,
under section 2521 of the Code, nor has his wife.

The expenses of a funeral and estate administration will probably
be about $25,000.

Mr. and Mrs. Perry are residents of New Hampshire. New Hampshire has no general income tax but does impose a tax of 4¼ per cent on
interest and dividends received by residents. The tax is on gross receipts;
no deductions are allowed, but there is a $600 personal exemption. Joint
returns are not permitted; each recipient of dividends and interest is
entitled to his $600 exemption and is taxed on the excess. Interest on U.S.
government obligations, interest on obligations of New Hampshire or any
of its municipalities, and interest paid by banks in New Hampshire are
exempt from this tax.

New Hampshire has no gift tax, but the state does impose both an
inheritance tax and an estate tax.

Inheritance tax

86:6 *Taxable Property and Tax Rate.* All property within the juris-
diction of the state, real or personal, and any interest therein, belonging to domiciliaries of the state, and all real estate within the
state, or any interest therein, belonging to persons who are not domiciliaries of the state, which shall pass by will, or by the laws regu-

lating interstate succession, or by deed, grant, bargain, sale or gift, made in contemplation of death, or made or intended to take effect in possession or enjoyment at or after the death of the grantor or donor, to any person, absolutely or in trust, except to or for the use of the husband, wife, father, mother, or lineal descendant, or for the care of cemetery lots, or to a city or town in this state for public municipal purposes or to or for the use of educational, religious, cemetery, or other institutions, societies or associations of public charity in any state, other than this state, territory or country the laws of which, at the time of the death of the decedent, either (1) do not impose a transfer tax or death tax of any kind or (2) grant an exemption similar to that hereby provided to the domiciliaries of such state, territory or country in favor of property passing to charities in this state, shall be subject to a tax of eight and one-half per cent of its value, for the use of the state. For the purposes of this section all adopted children in the decedent's line of succession shall be treated as natural children in determining "lineal descendant."

Estate tax

87:1 *Tax Imposed.* In addition to the taxes imposed by chapter 86 an estate tax is hereby imposed upon the transfer of all estates which are subject to an estate tax under the provisions of the United States internal revenue code and amendments thereto where the decedent at the time of his death was domiciled in this state. The amount of said New Hampshire estate tax shall be equal to the extent, if any, of the excess of the credit allowable under said United States internal revenue code over the aggregate amount of all estate, inheritance, transfer, legacy and succession taxes paid to any state or territory or in the District of Columbia in respect to any property in the estate of said decedent. Provided that such estate tax hereby imposed shall in no case exceed the extent to which its payment will effect a saving or diminution in the amount of the United States estate tax payable by or out of the estate of the decedent had this chapter not been enacted. The tax hereby imposed shall be for the use of the state. Furthermore an estate tax is hereby imposed upon the transfer of real property and tangible personal property in this state of every person who at the time of his death was a resident of the United States but not domiciled in this state, and upon the transfer of all property, real and personal, within this state of every person who at the time of his death was not a resident of the United States, the amount of which shall be a sum equal to such proportion of the amount by which the credit allowable under the applicable United States revenue act for estate, transfer, legacy, succession and inheritance taxes actually paid to several states exceeds the amount actually paid for such taxes exclusive of estate, transfer, legacy, succession and inheritance taxes, as the value of the property in this state bears to the value of the entire estate subject to an estate tax under the provisions of the United States internal revenue code.

Index

Index to Code Sections

Regulations Sections